CITIES OF AMERICA

CITIES OF AMERICA

by

GEORGE SESSIONS PERRY

Essay Index Reprint Series

BOOKS FOR LIBRARIES PRESS
FREEPORT, NEW YORK

INTERNATIONAL STANDARD BOOK NUMBER:
0-8369-1840-1

LIBRARY OF CONGRESS CATALOG CARD NUMBER:
70-128286

PRINTED IN THE UNITED STATES OF AMERICA

☆ ☆

Acknowledgments

THE AUTHOR thanks the editors of *The Saturday Evening Post* for permission to reprint these articles, all of which originally appeared in that magazine.

In writing this book I have received generous and much appreciated assistance from Judge Elijah Adlow, James F. Albright, Jack Alexander, Gus Backman, Malcolm W. Bingay, Alice Dixon Bond, Cassie and John Mason Brown, James P. Connolly, William Cooke, Isabel Currier, Leland W. Cutler, Crate Dalton, Stanton Delaplane, Dorothy Cameron Disney, Edward N. Doan, C. L. Douglas, Morris Edwards, Jake Ehrlich, Richard Ellegood, A. E. Ellsworth, Larry Fanning, Ray Felton, John Ferran, H. Findlay French, Clayton Fritchey, Helen C. Frost, Douglas K. Fuller, Robert Fuoss, Joe Gilmore, Eugene Goossens, Major General Ulysses S. Grant III, Edith Haggard, Philip Hamburger, Virginia and Jim Hamilton, Lucille Young Hays, Ben Hibbs, Boyce House, Al Hughes, Charlie Hughes, Jean T. Hulburd, Joseph Henry Jackson, Tarleton Jenkins, Harnett Kane, Ed Kessler, Tom Knight, E. Leo Koester, Jim Larson, Preston Leavitt, Edwin N. Lewis, John Frederick Lewis, Jr., Dorothy Wright Liebes, Dan London, Louis Lundborg, Marihelen MacDuff, Milton MacKaye, Frank Malone, Stanley Marcus, John Marsh, Pete Martin, Holland McCombs, John H. McGinnis, Mary McGrory, Elizabeth Ann McMurray, Lee G. Miller, Marjorie Mills, Margaret Mitchell, W. E. Mullins, Boswell Newton, J. C. Nichols, Warren Ogden, Norma Patterson, Dick Pearce, Salvatore Pinto, Eleanor Pollock, William Poole, P. J. Rinderle, Roy Roberts and other members of the Kansas City *Star* staff, John William Rogers, Florence and Frank Rosengren, Lyle Saxon, Clem Schramm, Harrison Smith, Martin Sommers, Claude Stanush, Hal Steed, Adela Rogers St. Johns,

Frank M. Stoll, Jack Stratton, Charles P. Taft, Robert Tallant, Lon Tinkle, Guy Toombes, John Wallace, Green Peyton Wertenbaker, John W. Wilds, Maurice L. Wilson, Ruth Winant, and David Wittels.

Contents

1 : *New Orleans*

IN SOME ways gaudy old New Orleans very much resembles an alluring, party-loving woman who is neither as virtuous as she might be nor as young as she looks, who has a come-hither eye, an engaging trace of accent in her speech, and a weakness for the pleasures both of the table and the couch—a *femme fatale* who has known great ecstasy and tragedy, but still laughs and loves excitement, and who, after each bout of sinning, does duly confess and perhaps partially repent.

One of its most fundamental and important attributes is that life in New Orleans is practically never boring. Almost every day is a fête day. Bright-colored balloons are hawked on Canal Street the year round, and at the drop of a hat, New Orleans has a parade, with, of course, the most elaborate ones coming during the Carnival season, which reaches its climax on Mardi Gras. Yet no day is more thoroughly enjoyed than All Saints' Day, when all New Orleans loads itself down with chrysanthemums and goes to the cemeteries to picnic and gossip and decorate the graves of its dead.

It is a town whose fascinating and dramatic past can be read in the torture devices to be seen in its museums and in the dainty silver filigree jewelry which once adorned its Creole belles but is now to be found, and by tourists pawed over, in the Royal Street antique shops. It has every natural blessing of the tropics, incredibly luxuriant foliage and flowers. Its shiny magnolias and massive old live-oak trees, festooned with Spanish moss, are spectacularly beautiful. It is a town where an architect, a gourmet or a roué is in hog heaven.

But that's only half the story.

New Orleans is also venal and corrupt, and its own people, the electorate, have been a willing party to its ravishment and debauchery.

1

Its French Quarter has festered with dives as vicious and sinister as any in Marseille or on Rotterdam's Schiedamschedyke. It's ridden by powerful superstitions, and you can still buy Voodoo paraphernalia at the drugstore. Racketeering and shakedowns have long been regarded as work-a-day chores that nobody gets excited about. The city has been physically dirty, and was apparently indifferent to its filth. So far as government is concerned, it has for years been harder to find a moral qualm in New Orleans than in almost any other American city. Social responsibility in New Orleans, generally speaking, has long meant serving good Sazerac cocktails and delicious *pompano en papillote*.

But you can't take complicated New Orleans in one bite. It was a long time getting to be the way it is, and to understand it, you've got to start at the first.

Polyglot New Orleans is the result of many ingredients delicately combined and slowly simmered for centuries. It speaks French, Spanish, Italian, German, Portuguese—and English, sometimes with a neo-Brooklyn accent, "ersters" for "oysters," etc., which experts guess was introduced by the inhabitants of New Orleans' Irish Channel. The city's life and growth are indeed so intricate that the only two all-pervading qualities are composed, to borrow from Tom Wolfe, of time and the river.

The city is the alluvial product of these two tireless streams. The soft rich earth upon which New Orleans is built, and into which, according to Harnett Kane, it is slowly sinking, was brought by the river to this spot that was once occupied by the sea. And because the Mississippi was plainly to become the great femoral artery of American commerce and travel, a party of French explorers, by a stratagem, deflected the British from the present site of New Orleans in the year 1699, and subsequently built a city there which the homesick Frenchmen called "La Nouvelle Orléans."

Soon New Orleans was being surrounded by a network of plantations, all built by slave power. And the city's people were fast shaking down into sharply defined social levels, with the more elevated of these avidly preserving the traditions of the court of France.

Then in 1763, after France had taken the count in the Seven

Years' War, the proprietorship of New Orleans passed, somewhat circuitously, to Spain. Eventually, these two nationalities, the French and the Spaniards, fell busily to breeding that special New Orleans race: the Creoles, in whom these two cultures and languages would become so subtly fused.

In 1788 wooden New Orleans was razed by fire, and that part of the city now known as the French Quarter, though its architecture is predominantly Spanish, began to be built. Then, fifteen years later, the United States made the Louisiana Purchase, and New Orleans, nearly a century old, cultured and exquisite, was sold to the Yankee barbarians of the North.

Orleanians were outraged and bitter. They snubbed the crude, ham-handed, red-necked Americans, who ultimately found it necessary to build their own community across the city moat, which was later to be called Canal Street. The Americans thought the Creoles decadent. These Creoles, according to Lyle Saxon's brilliant biography of the city, *Fabulous New Orleans,* "were a people given to merrymaking and laughter. . . . They lived luxuriously. And they seemed careless of the morrow.

"Now with the . . . snobbishness on the part of the Creole and intolerance on the part of the puritanical Americans, there was immediate discord.

"But . . . one thing took the American unawares. . . . Louisiana is a fertile land where a living is easily made. It is warm nine months in the year. And there seems to be a certain insidious chemical substance in the atmosphere which tends to destroy puritanism."

Finally the more relentless Americans became richer and were, for that reason, tempting matrimonial catches. Scarcely a dozen years after the Louisiana Purchase, American and Creole, fighting together under Andrew Jackson, defeated their common enemy, Great Britain, on the fields of Chalmette. And the Golden Age of New Orleans had begun.

The first steamboat, the *Orleans,* had come down the river from Pittsburgh in 1812. Life along the levee became more and more busy and exciting. Soon steamboats were several deep at the wharves, waiting for room to come in and unload. New Orleans became the third largest and the wealthiest city in the nation. The Mardi Gras Carnival attained incredible proportions of extravagance and fantasy. The opera and the theater flourished. The city's social life was dazzling, and its gambling spectacular. There were bear-and-bull fights, and frequent duels either behind the Cathedral, Dumas style, or under the Dueling Oaks in what is now City Park.

Many a young Creole gentleman looked forward to no social event with keener interest than that with which he anticipated a Quadroon Ball.

There were hundreds of mulatto, quadroon or octaroon girls, many of them startlingly pretty, but since there was a law against intermarriage between the races, the system of *placée* became an accepted part of the social structure. It worked something like this: These "free women of color" made the approximate equivalent of a debut at a Quadroon Ball, in dresses as elaborate as any seen in the horseshoe of the French Opera House. Their mothers had raised them as carefully, given them as good educations, as the children of planters and rich merchants, and had taught them social grace and poise. The only male attendants at the Quadroon Balls were wealthy young white men. When one of these blades took a fancy to a quadroon girl, arrangements were made with her mother. The young lady was set up in a domicile of her own, with an allowance adequate for her needs. And though some of these liaisons lasted until death parted their principals, they were usually terminated when a young Creole married.

Further to console its senses, New Orleans was developing a cuisine all its own that often superseded the best of France and Spain. The delicate sauces of the French were combined with the fiery seasonings of the Spanish to produce such dishes as gumbo and jambalaya and crawfish bisque. The early Alciatores established Antoine's in 1840, and were warming up to create oysters Rockefeller. The more flamboyant French dishes such as *café brûlot* and fowl *flambée* had been carried over from the city's French heritage.

Orleanians ate, drank, and made merry, knowing that tomorrow they might very well die in one or another of the plagues of cholera and yellow fever which now and again swept through the swampy, rat-and-mosquito-ridden city. But despite these plagues and the ever-present menace of the encircling, rambunctious river, New Orleans reached its peak of lavishness in the three decades between 1830 and 1860.

Then the greatest disaster of all befell this city which had grown rich off cotton and sugar cane and slaves: home-town-boy General Pierre Gustave Toutant Beauregard ordered his men to crack down on Fort Sumter. The Civil War was on, and had to be fought to its slow, bloody, agonizing end.

Mr. Lincoln freed the slaves, and there was no longer anyone to work the plantations. The railroads, with appalling swiftness, de-nuded the river of its freight traffic. New Orleans was humbled and crumbled. Between the Civil War and World War I, it remained pretty much on the ropes. The re-inauguration of barge traffic on the river in the early part of this century gave her some measure of relief, as did the importation of disease-resistant sugar cane from Java, which saved Louisiana's failing sugar industry. Too, there was the discovery, in this period, of oil in Southern Louisiana. But it was the forty-cent cotton of World War I that brought really flush times back to New Orleans.

However, the year 1919 also brought tragedy to New Orleans. According to the *Times-Picayune* of December 4:

The French Opera House burned early this morning. . . . Gone is all the glory which marked the building for more than half a century. . . .

Children . . . learned their first lessons in art and music while watching the singers upon the brilliantly lighted stage. Later, the girls as debutantes received homage as they sat in the horseshoe, surrounded by flowers, admiring and admired, loving and beloved. Still later, as matrons, they joined gay parties, listening to the . . . same dear, cherished operas. . . . They watched their daughters and sons growing to love light and color and music as they had done, in the old Opera House.

. . . The opera is hallowed in their hearts; it belongs to them by right of years of possession. For in New Orleans, and in New Orleans alone, is the opera so personal, so completely ours.

. . . There is a pall over the city; eyes are filled with tears. . . .

The heart of the old French Quarter has stopped beating.

New Orleans went into mourning, and still hopes, even now, through its Opera House Association, to rebuild it.

Today's New Orleans, which claims to be the largest industrial city in the South, is a prosperous, jam-packed city of some 600,000 souls. Relatively speaking, this prosperity is also enjoyed by its 200,000 Negroes, even though large numbers of them live in slums on unpaved loblollies called streets.

The Number One man in New Orleans' Negro circles—great Negro musicians in this birthplace of jazz are too numerous to name—is smart, able Albert W. Dent, now president of Dillard University, who made New Orleans' fine Negro hospital, Flint-Goodridge, a going concern, just as he did its penny-a-day hospital insurance.

Being disfranchised in local elections, New Orleans Negroes have not, since Reconstruction days, been a factor in the city's cancerous politics, which for generations have been corrupt enough to make your hair stand on end.

New Orleans city and parish (county) governments are one and the same, which, to start with, means that usually the governor of Louisiana has got his big nose in the city's business.

During Huey Long's reign he shut down on New Orleans' normally substantial revenues from the state until he starved it into forcing the resignation of its own elected city government, so that Huey could put in his own man, millionaire politician Robert S. Maestri. Huey then had Maestri's term of office extended so that the people would not too soon have a chance to vote him out. Huey also had the city government of New Orleans reorganized in such a way that Maestri became virtually a dictator. The power of the Commission Council was reduced to that, more or less, of office boys, and Maestri could hire and fire important department heads, such as fire and police chiefs, at will.

When, five years later, New Orleans finally got a chance to vote Maestri out, the city was faced with a delicate problem. New Orleans is a glad-time town that loves the sight of a fleet filly, a spinning roulette wheel, a straight flush or a natural seven on the face of the dice. Too, tourists are big business in New Orleans, and Orleanians believe tourists like a high and libidinous old time such as could be had in a town as wide open as the one Maestri was running. Some 30,000 citizens were getting something out of the city machine, which Maestri had taken over, along with the town itself. About 35,000 persons were getting an income out of one or another form of vice, gambling, prostitution, etc. Many a poor man had got a basket of groceries, and many a rich one, who might have fought the machine, was disinclined to have his tax assessment blow up in his face. Moreover, Maestri had a talking point in that he had pulled New Orleans out of the bankruptcy into which his pal Huey had helped plunge it. New Orleans gave Maestri another chance.

In late January of 'Forty-six, New Orleans voted again. Running against Maestri, on a good-government ticket, was thirty-four-year-old Colonel de Lesseps Morrison, with a record that was not only hound-tooth clean, but full of substantial accomplishments. He set out to destroy the machine and the city's one-man government.

New Orleans newspapers, the *Times-Picayune*, the *States*, and the *Item*, came out for Morrison with all guns blazing. Morrison was, nevertheless, in the anomalous position of being a white-knight reform candidate in a town that had rather be drawn and quartered than reformed. Throughout the campaign, he danced on a needle point, having to denounce the corruption of the machine out of one side of his mouth while, out of the other, he had to assure the city he meant to "clean up" not "close up" the town.

Yet Maestri had troubles too. The war had caught him short of equipment and men, and the streets and garbage collection had gone to pot. In greeting distinguished guests, "dese-dem-and-dose" Maestri had always been a flop. Significantly, not only in New Orleans but all over the land, protest was the dominant mood of the times.

But, since the city machine, the Old Regulars, had for so many years been able to dominate elections, many a Morrison worker was haunted by doubt, and the gamblers, even on Election Day, would lay four to one that Maestri would win.

The next day all papers carried joyful banners screaming that

Morrison, the underdog, had come from behind to win. The New Orleans *States*, in a voice that quivered with emotion, declared:

For the first time since Huey Long's heyday the city is free. FREE!
Do you understand what that means?
New Orleans can hold its head up.
The dawn is here for the city!

This same morning after the election, Jack McCarthy, Morrison's campaign manager, took me to Morrison's hideaway in a downtown hotel. Morrison and his wife had gotten away from his delirious supporters at three in the morning. We were met at the door by Mrs. Morrison, young, pretty, in a daze of surprise over her husband's victory; in, also, a nightgown, a hastily-donned fur coat and one stocking. With unruffled, intuitive poise and graciousness, she took us in to her husband, who was still in bed, wearing an army undershirt, and talking, with conviction, over the phone. They looked nice. It seemed enviable someway to be young, the mayor of New Orleans, full of beans, triumph, and a kind of determined righteousness—with one giant slain and an eagerness to mow down the rest.

Morrison hung up the phone and said, in reply to questions, he was not only going to restore majority rule in the Commission Council to New Orleans' city government and run out of town a couple of big-time Eastern crooks who had earlier worn the footprints of La Guardia on their pants, but that he was going to make an all-out try to license gambling in New Orleans and use the proceeds to replace certain tax reductions he had promised the people. By this device, he was he said, determined to blot out pay-offs to the police.

The road to the attainment of these goals means breaking the will of many a no-holds-barred fighter. It's going to be rough, and he knows it. For that matter, there will be great difficulty in maintaining a coherent point of view among the diverse elements that backed him. But, for inspiration, he has the example of his friend, Louisiana's great former Governor Sam Jones, who took the remains of the Long machine apart. And though New Orleans' political historians regard any fundamental deviation from the city's venerable political crookedness as preposterous, Morrison is in the saddle and is ready to ride, as the champion of clean government—or, perhaps, the phrase is clean Southern government. I asked him what plans he had for improving the lot of New Orleans' huge Negro population. I regret to say, he changed the subject.

New Orleans' great problems have not been limited to the political arena. She has, from the first, had one engineering problem that was staggering: drainage. The drainage level of dish-shaped New Orleans lies below sea level, river level, and that of its huge aquatic backyard, Lake Pontchartrain. Moreover, the climate, with its annual rainfall of approximately five feet, would be too wet for Noah. In one peak year, the cost of equipment and of pumping the drainage water up and out of town cost the city 20 per cent of its total expenditures.

Many of its streets were built with open drainage canals in the middle. Subsequently these canals, though still functioning, have been covered over, and this covering beautifully planted with grasses and palms, azaleas, oleanders and camellias. It is difficult to think of an American city with more beautiful roadways, and, on upper St. Charles Avenue, the old town houses of the sugar planters are as lovely and stately, as nourishing to the imagination, as any in the nation.

The only hill in all New Orleans is in Audubon Park. This little hummock was built by the PWA so that New Orleans' children could have a hill to charge up and down. In this park, incidentally, is the site where the process for the granulation of sugar was discovered, and along one edge of it lives doughty old Elizabeth Meriwether Gilmer—Dorothy Dix to you and me. New Orleans' City Park, cow-ranch big, spreads out over a flat sixteen hundred acres.

The New Orleans innkeepers such as Roy Bartlett, of the top-notch Roosevelt Hotel, are now plotting and planning to steal the National Motor Boat Championship Races from Detroit, in order to drag in tourists during the dog days. It was this same group which helped successfully to promote the Midwinter Sports Carnival, built around the Sugar Bowl football game, to fill in the gap between the beginning of the racing season at Thanksgiving and Carnival time in the spring. These events, plus the Spring Fiesta and other assorted celebrations, will give New Orleans a year-round succession of tourist attractions.

But New Orleans hotel men's biggest plan is to get Rockefeller—the man, not the oyster—to subsidize the restoration of the French Quarter as he did Williamsburg, Virginia.

These men realize that the French Quarter, as is, is dirty and shabby and be-clip-jointed. But the atmosphere, the old houses with their fascinating histories, the wrought-iron grill-work lacing the sky, are still there. They want to have its pristine loveliness restored, and Mr. Rockefeller appears to be interested.

Everybody in New Orleans is interested in the colorful old city-owned French Market, famed for its sunrise coffee, for such delicacies as strawberries, fish, oysters and shrimp, barrels of iced frogs' legs and bayou catfish, all of which New Orleans' environs so richly afford.

Again, crabs pour into New Orleans by the millions, as do baby green turtles. These fish and shellfish are worth some $15,000,000 a year. From Louisiana's forests of pine and nigh-expended swamp-grown cypresses comes in excess of $45,000,000 worth of lumber a year. From her marshlands trappers bring millions of fur-bearing animal pelts, chiefly muskrat, amounting to more than $7,000,000 annually, or a fourth of the nation's production. Louisiana's biggest farm crop is cotton and cotton seed, which in 1944 brought in nearly $80,000,000. Rice, which loves lots of water to grow in, ranks second, with a value of about $40,000,000. Corn and sugar cane pretty much tie for third place, with a value of $26,000,000 each.

By 1944, Louisiana had climbed to third place among the states in the production of oil. Her fields were relatively new and reserves good. Also very much to the point was the fact that since the turn of the century, Louisiana, then containing a million and a third people, had now grown to contain two and a third millions. And a fourth of all Louisianians live in the Crescent City.

But New Orleans' greatest and most enduring resource, the one that will be there when the oil is gone and the lumber cut, is her great, virtually unique port. Not only has she direct contact with Kobe and Liverpool and Rangoon by going down the river, and barge communications with Detroit and Chicago and Memphis and St. Louis by going up the river, but she can also send her barge traffic over an inland protected waterway around the eastern perimeter of the na-

tion from the mouth of the Rio Grande to the northeastern population centers. Her pride is her eleven and a half miles of steel-shed-
covered water front which, along with her inner harbor on the industrial canal, will accommodate about a hundred ships at a time. The
river-front wharves, unlike New York's, which are slotted with
berths, run smoothly along the levee, so that ships coming up the
river may slide alongside and tie up without ever turning broadside
to the current, which varies from a knot and a half at low water to
five knots at high.

New Orleans' widely strung out port is connected by the city's
117-mile-long Public Belt railway, which is in politics, but the port is
out and on a nonprofit, but business basis. Incidentally, the law which
took the port out of politics was written by young de Lesseps Morrison when he was in the Louisiana legislature. Present port authorities
like to point out that while the Long regime had 3,200 people on the
pay roll to handle 13,000,000 tons of freight, the present politically
snow-white dock board handled 24,000,000 tons in 1940 with only
700 employees. These same port authorities proudly claim that seventy cents of every dollar New Orleans earns results directly or in-
directly from the port. Without the port, for example, New Orleans
could not very well have had the great Higgins plant, which built
crucial thousands of landing craft and PT boats and cargo vessels
during World War II.

About two thirds of the port's business is export trade. The rest
comes ambling down the Mississippi, which today carries more tonnage than in steamboat days. Automobiles come from Detroit, but
the main flow of traffic is Midwest grain and flour, about two thirds
of all the Midwest's export surplus. Barges pull up to one side of the
grain elevators and have their cargoes sucked out at the same time
that other metal tubes are pouring grain into blue-water bottoms.
When the barges start back upstream, they are more often than not
loaded with green coffee, since they are not peart enough to get fast-
ripening bananas to their destinations in time.

Orleanians no longer must tear out for the high ground every
time the river starts to rise. These days, it is necessary only to
open the Bonnet Carré spillway a short distance up the river and

dump the surplus into commodius Lake Pontchartrain. But since all river ports suffer from a tendency to develop shifting sand bars where the river meets the sea, and since the Mississippi in particular is such a big-time cutup, New Orleans is now dedicated to the huge job of cutting a new sixty-mile, deep-water opening to the sea—one which will be free from the river's lumbering tizzies.

New Orleans also plans a foreign-trade mart and a foreign-trade zone, to occupy a part of its world's largest cotton warehouse. Much of the warehouse isn't needed any more since these days most of the Mississippi Valley cotton is used domestically, and only western cotton is exported, and then principally through the port of New Orleans' arch-competitor, Houston.

New Orleans' huge Moisant Airport has taken over from the old New Orleans, *née* Shushan, Airport, which previously carried the main load, and which, like most latter-day New Orleans developments, including the enlarged 3,000-bed Charity Hospital, grew to the accompaniment of raucous scandals and busy little excursions to the penitentiary.

One of New Orleans' newest and most interesting clubs is the handsomely furnished, nine-story International House, where foreign customers may be luxuriously housed and put into a receptive mood. For foreign buyers, like tourists, enjoy a good plate of vittles at Antoine's, Arnaud's, Galatoire's, Kolb's or La Louisiane. They like to sip liquid jade at either of the Old Original Absinthe Houses or develop a piratical mood at Café Lafitte, to savor a Ramos gin fizz in the city of its birth, to ogle the girlie shows in the French Quarter, to gamble and frequent the haunts where romance is for hire. And nowhere are these pleasures more easily available than in the American Shanghai near the mouth of the great river.

To look at New Orleans coldly and analytically, is to have slipped up, a little meanly, on the blind side of a town that wants you not to moralize, but to enjoy yourself. Where it gets you is that it's a kind of municipal prodigal child, and, like most people, a sinner. Between New Orleans and the average human being, understanding comes easy. Most of the people who live there adore it and just plain wouldn't live anywhere else.

And it was not entirely true, up until a short while ago, that the heart of old New Orleans had stopped beating. There was still a living spark that sometimes glistened in the night. It was in a room in the old St. Charles Hotel where, until his death, Lyle Saxon maintained a salon, and where most of the interesting natives, as well as a large part of the distinguished visitors to New Orleans, gathered.

You were met at the door by shiny, milk-chocolate, pearly-toothed Joe Gilmore, Lyle's man, and led into a high-ceilinged room in which the most striking piece of furniture was a high old four-poster bed with a scarlet sunburst tester.

Here you met an elegant, charming gentleman of the Old South, and one of its greatest raconteurs, Creole, not by birth, but by sympathy and inclination. The introductions to the other guests were each apt little essays in biography.

When the phone rang, Joe Gilmore handled the call. If Lyle was not well, Joe said, "Saxon speaking." Perhaps it was an out-of-town visitor asking the way to Lyle's room. Joe, still ostensibly in the role of Saxon, would inquire, "Well, where is you at now?" Then, having given adequate directions, he began brewing coffee for the guests, Creole coffee thick enough, almost, to putty windows. It was Joe who, when Dorothy Parker left Lyle's room, turned around and remarked with approving surprise, "Well, she certainly never said nothing unpleasant to *us!*"

Out of the conversation and recollections here, the old New Orleans came quickly and easily into being. The old French Opera House came back to life again with its myriad candles reflected in the jewels on the Paris gowns. The surrounding plantation houses were not ruins, but the scenes of all-night balls with whole steamboats full of guests from the city. One felt the sinister power of the Voodoo queen, Marie Laveau. The faded fans in the Royal Street shops were bright again in the hands of the decorous young ladies at the Quadroon Balls. Creole ladies and gentlemen graciously received old friends in the quiet, flower-laden courtyards on Esplanade Avenue. At dawn on Sunday morning the old French Market was again a lively gumbo ya-ya, which is to say, everybody talking at once: chattering vendors, nuns and housewives bargaining intently for a pound of catfish heads for soup, dentists publicly pulling teeth to the accompaniment of brass bands to drown out their victims' yells.

On the river, phantom showboats announced their arrival with calliopes bravely tooting "Waiting for the *Robert E. Lee.*"

That was Saxon's New Orleans. And though much of it in its material form is gone, it will always be as much a part of New Orleans as the red beans and rice, the dirt swept under the rug, the river itself. For the rigors of her advancing years have, at least thus far, been unable to blight that thing which, at the sight of an invitation, a costume and a mask, makes her old heart leap, her eyes light up, and her voice wholly unable to suppress a gay tune—which just possibly might allude to the land of cotton and that old times there are not forgotten.

2: New York

NEW YORK, to the rest of America, is a stupendously rich, glamorously theatrical, noisy, over-excited, idea-ridden, un-American, brutally expensive, rolling torrent of man-swarm. That, and, of course, a skyline.

To a New Yorker it's just home, and his own personal piece of it is a neighborhood of a couple of thousand people. The rest of New York's 7,690,000 people, its hundreds of square miles of vertically extruding real estate, and those thousands of sights and sins and smells and sensations not directly involved in the New Yorker's life, simply do not live in his mind as experience, but, except when his attention is directed to them, as echo.

New York might be compared to a broad lake, through a part of which runs a current, a stream of outland Americans, some en route to and from Europe, more coming to market and pausing to have a good, if slightly bewildering, time. Since New York's metropolitan area is the nation's biggest manufacturing center, it naturally has many wares to sell. But when the marketplace closes for the day, the visitor sees before him an exciting, endlessly manifold city and he goes cavorting over it.

Most of New York's well-publicized skylarking, incidentally, is done by the pilgrims from Main Street, vast numbers of whom hit town with a bead drawn on its fleshpots. When the day's work is done, the New Yorker, if for the moment he is in that sublime position of having no out-of-town friends to entertain, usually heads for that little interior community, the village in which he lives.

For example, when I am in New York, I live in a small midtown apartment. Passing trucks and busses, kids frolicking or fighting in the street, make it noisy, and New York's dirty air makes it a hard place to keep clean. But it is, nevertheless, a residence in a small town. I know the people who run the shops, and they know me. I could live the rest of my life without going more than a block away for such living requirements or services as are sold in stores or performed by dentists, doctors, lawyers, etc.

Many aspects of New York life are reflected in our little neighborhood. The grocery is run by an Italian family, which is part of the city's million people of that particular origin. This family is very lively and its members love to yell back and forth across the store at each other as they sell their preserved eggplants and other rich and wonderful Italian fare. The cop on the corner is, of course, one of the town's 500,000 Irish—although not all New York cops are Irish—and the laundryman is one of its 1,000,000 Russians. Elsewhere in our neighborhood are representatives of New York's 500,000 Germans, 400,000 Poles, 300,000 Austrians. The heart of most New York neighborhoods is the delicatessen, since New Yorkers are often without the time, energy, inclination or facilities for cooking dinner after a day's work. It is here that the person with one room, a hot plate and a coffeepot, may stop in the evening, buy two slices of bacon, one egg, a few slices of bread. Having no refrigerator, he must buy only what can be used for his next meal. Our delicatessen is run by Mr. Morris Schwartz, one of New York's two million Jews. He is an extremely nice man, and I suspect the most popular one in the neighborhood. Our maid is a Negro. She lives with 500,000 other Negroes in Harlem, is penalized for her color by Harlem's landlords, but is, like so many of New York's Negroes, considerably above the ability-level of most Southern Negroes.

Inland Americans sometimes point out that the masses of New York, particularly those on Manhattan Island, cannot fiercely love this land since so few of them own any of it. Yet each of my neighbors has a vested interest in the town and the nation. They may not own their own homes in this city of apartment-dwellers, but many of them do own their businesses. And of New York's 100,000 stores, most of them are much more like Mr. Schwartz's than like Macy's. The savings of the city workers who own neither land nor businesses are invested in America through bank deposits, insurance policies, stocks and bonds.

The biggest immigrant group in the city is the one composed of the fugitives from America's small towns, who, incidentally, find when they get there that the town is interested only in what they can do; that their family tree, so far as New York is concerned, can be an old sweet-potato vine. If they are pretentious, New York will never stop hacking away at those pretensions. Yet it is compassionate to the genuine eccentric—especially on Broadway, Columbus Circle, Union Square, and in Greenwich Village.

But if life in New York is, in actuality, different from the way it appears to the rest of the world, the New York myth is nevertheless a thing of vital and fundamental importance to the growth and spirit and healthy metabolism of the city. It is the prime reason for the fact New York does a bigger tourist business in the winter than Miami, and a bigger one than Atlantic City in the summer, when New York's steamy air is almost unbearable. It is this myth that so irresistibly attracts the venturers of small-town America, the same myth that in the past lured to itself the chance-taking, chance-making immigrants from the slums and ghettos of Europe and Asia, keeping alive the constant influx of the young, the shrewd, the vital, the daring. The myth has the complementary effect of expelling the inept, the disillusioned and the unfortunate, since there isn't room for everybody.

The strands, design, and pigmentation of the New York myth come from the subjective interweaving in the minds of the beholders of such world-famed sights as the Brooklyn Bridge; the Third Avenue bars and antique shops; Rockefeller Center and the Bowery flophouses; the Metropolitan Opera House and Nedick's orange drink stands; café society, which goes, primarily, not to eat but to be seen; the loping old elevated trains; the packed, thundering subways; the bands; the parades; the ten-dollar-a-ticket "Cause" banquets, for, when touched, New York's Runyanesque heart is meltingly generous; the crimson, shrieking fire engines roaring down automatically opening lanes of heavy traffic; that inhabited javelin, the 102-story Empire State Building; the stone lions in front of the Library; and the appalling statistics that veritably poleax the imagination. New York spends

$2,000,000 a day keeping the city manicured, governed, a going concern. A passenger train arrives every fifty seconds, twenty-four hours a day. Even before war destruction was visited upon Europe's capitals, New York had more telephones than London, Paris, Berlin, Rome and Brussels put together. Two hundred and fifty or so billions of dollars clear its banks in a year, dollars that go not only to the tax collector and the publican, but to the aspirant hoofer from Keokuk, the confidence man from Tallahassee, indeed to whoever captures the imagination of the depositors of that wealth, sells them a sufficiently exciting, sufficiently promising, bill of goods.

To pass from legend to geography, Greater New York is divided into five boroughs, which are synonymous with counties. The Bronx is the home of the cheer discourteous, and that poisonous cocktail. Queens is where the race tracks are. The borough of Richmond is Staten Island. Brooklyn is where baseball becomes most aggressively vocal, and where the Navy Yard and Coney Island are. (Will Rogers said New York's subways were built so Brooklynites could get home without being seen.) Manhattan, of course, is what people usually mean when they say New York. Long Island, Westchester County, parts of Connecticut and New Jersey are where the commuters live, where New Yorkers weekend, and where the New York complexion, which in the summer is pasty on Friday, pink on Monday, often gets its ephemeral color.

Politically, New York City is traditionally Democratic. So far as the state is concerned, there is the usual struggle between the metropolitan and non-metropolitan area, for upstate New York is Republican and the fight for its forty-seven electoral votes in presidential elections is always desperate and often crucial.

In physical pattern, Manhattan is a striped town. The island is a little over twelve miles long and, roughly, the shape of a "weenie." Its avenues run the long way, its numbered streets the short way. Generally speaking, Park Avenue is its stripe of residential elegance. Central Park West is a similar stripe, and from its apartment-house towers, around Ninetieth Street, one of the best views of the town can be had. Here, from a prospect thirty or so stories high, Central Park seems a pleasant, green patch with one of the city's early reservoirs a central puddle, with the Battery skyscrapers visible on one's right and the flat plateau of uptown New York spreading, five or six brownstone layers thick, for miles in every direction. Here everything comes more convincingly into focus in the mind of the spectator than any map could possibly bring it. Yet if you've lived in the rushing immediacy of the canyons at the base of the city's towers, the view is apt to take on a too-encompassing papier-mâché quality, as if what your eyes saw was perhaps an exhibit thought up by General Motors for a World's Fair.

Fifth Avenue is the town's stripe of most splendiferous stores, though much of its art and high fashion turns off onto Fifty-seventh Street, and dribbles down a parallel thoroughfare, Madison Avenue. Fifth Avenue is also where lonely but decorous girls, in search of tentative adventure, walk in pairs at eleven o'clock at night, whereas their more totally committed sisters venture Broadway alone after midnight. Blaring, blatant Broadway, an individualist to the last, runs catawampous from one end of the island to the other, and everything meets head on in the West Forties.

Aside from lunch, most New Yorkers eat at home. In case they wish to eat out, there are of course fine restaurants serving food in almost every language and dialect. When you dine out in New York, the kind of food you get often bears no direct relation to the price paid. The most expensive thing is elbow room, not to be stampeded by large groups of the impatient hungry. Then come such other factors as *décor*, service, music, location, and, in some cases last of all, the quality of the food itself. There are probably no better roast prime ribs of beef in town than those served by the Automats. The food is good and cheap, but mealtime at the Automat closely resembles kickoff time at Notre Dame. In any case the Automat, where the coffee always knows just when to quit running, is an experience. At the other and luxurious extreme are the plushy restaurants of the Park Avenue area. When the check is presented here, have smelling salts ready.

One of New York's biggest businesses is the clothes you wear. Roughly three-quarters of the nation's clothing, nearly all of the

ladies' dresses which are not home sewn, are New York designed and
New York made. Its dress industry is a one-and-a-quarter-billion-
dollar concern. But its fashion and design people, despite all outward
promotion to the contrary, are still pretty self-conscious about Paris.
Anyway, the chic level of New York women, their grooming and
style, is justly famed.

From the standpoint of the nation, the three outstanding products
of New York are ideas, finance, and amusement. In the world of
American finance Wall Street now finds itself, to its embarrassment,
no longer dominant since Washington began putting controls on it.
Nevertheless, it's still down on the lower end of the island, and its
surrounding buildings are the ones you see when you steam into New
York harbor from the ocean in a seat at your local movie.

New York naturally finds expression for its ideas, aside from
those that are expressed industrially, through its publishing business.
It is an artesian source of daily journalism, the point of origin of more
famous columns than the Parthenon. Its papers with the largest cir-
culations are, of course, the tabloid *News* and *Mirror*, that are designed, both in size and news presentation, for subway reading. The
Times is the city's most famous paper; then, reading from left to right,
politically, there are the *Daily Worker*, *PM*, the tabloid *Post*, the
Herald Tribune, the *World-Telegram*, the *Sun*, and the Hearst-owned
Journal-American. There are many foreign-language newspapers published in New York, and *Variety*, which is Broadway's mouthpiece,
speaks an American patois all its own. The city's small, weekly-
speaking, fine-tooth-comb-edited voice in the magazine world is *The
New Yorker* magazine. During the war it was the city's suave, sin-
cere Pagliacci in its time of agony.

New York's export trade to the rest of the country in magazines of
almost every description is colossal. It is also the heart of the nation's
book publishing business, as well as the spiritual home of the bookish.
These folk are in full possession of several of the city's small interior
towns within the metropolitan anthology of villages. In these towns,
plain John American might wonder how people who talk so endlessly
would ever have anything left over to write, or how a single community could encompass so spectacular and diversified a collection of

neuroses. These are the towns wherein the citizens, if for the time out of pocket, can live six months on hot hors d'œuvres and the damp Martinis of the continually recurring literary cocktail parties.

Standing astride the line of demarcation between ideas and amusement is the theater which, as Mr. George Jean Nathan has observed, is what literature does after dark. Broadway and its endless visitors like best such high-quality, simple-glow shows as *Oklahoma!* and *Life with Father*. Its less spectacularly successful day-in-and-day-out menu, yet one which will pay the rent on a theater, is the mélange of bright tunes, pretty legs and sharp humor. But just as much at home on Broadway are the serious plays starring such people as Katharine Cornell and Helen Hayes, and the bright drawing-room comedies of the Noel Coward type. Plenty of box-office applicants respond with enthusiasm to what Margaret Webster and Maurice Evans have done with Shakespeare. Rowdy fifty-cent burlesque has been driven off the boards, and its equivalent is allowed solely in the night clubs and high-priced revues, the thesis apparently being that the pastime of ogling strippers is seemly only when pursued by those in the chips. New York also has its foreign-language theaters and movie houses spotted around town. But for regular movies, the legitimate theater, the penny arcades and freak shows, Broadway is the place. And of course radio, whose national chains largely headquarter in New York, draws much of its talent from Broadway.

New York is renowned for its many opportunities for free, or almost free, amusement. The principal one of these is simply the sight of the town itself. Such a show could hardly be staged for all the gold buried at Fort Knox. The most stereotyped, and a very good, way to see much of the town is from the top of a two-story Fifth Avenue bus. The ride costs a dime, that is sucked with astonishing suddenness out of your fingers by the peremptorily greedy tin piggy-bank the conductor carries in his hand. If you have an especial objective, and time is a factor, it's best to battle your way onto the subway, where the fare is a nickel. Maybe you're going to Chinatown, where dead ducks are blown up with a bicycle pump and sold dried, or to Coney Island, where, as you've seen by the papers, all of the bathers are not beauties. You may want to see Grant's Tomb on Riverside Drive, the Lower East Side, the Bowery, Harlem, the Hayden Planetarium, the Metropolitan Museum, the Museum of Natural History, Radio City, the Bronx Zoo, Wall Street and the Statue of Liberty, the Polo Grounds, where the Giants play ball, the Yankees' Yankee Stadium, and Madison Square Garden, where the rodeo and the circus come to town. But perhaps the town's most celebrated bargain, after the subway, is the nickel ferry ride to Staten Island.

Then there's always window-shopping at the nation's most legendary stores: Tiffany's and Saks Fifth Avenue, Abercrombie's for the sportive male, Brooks Brothers for his more sedate brother. Children love F. A. O. Schwarz's, the big toy house, but two of the most interesting and variegated stores in town are R. H. Macy's, where you can buy everything from a mink coat to a setting hen, and its near-by heavyweight-championship competitor, Gimbel's.

Too, there are the widely known hotels, where the curious but maybe busted visitor can drop in and look around, such as the huge Waldorf-Astoria on Park Avenue, the Algonquin on Forty-fourth, where the publishing folk hang out, as well as at the Ritz. Perhaps the most quietly elegant hotels in town are the Pierre and a few of its lower Central Park neighbors. But if the doer of the town insists on night clubs, there's no inexpensive way to make their acquaintance. An evening for two at El Morocco, the Stork, and a few of those which are lined up on Fifty-second Street—an evening consisting of a couple of rounds of cocktails, a decent dinner, and a moderately moist post-dinner whistle—will make mincemeat out of a fifty-dollar bill. The biggest merging in town of the show and night-club business is at Billy Rose's Diamond Horseshoe. And 21 is the spot where the expatriate from Hollywood comes back to take out his Manhattan naturalization papers.

But if 21 is the Hollywoodite's port of entry, millions of others, some of them just as extraordinary, have entered via Ellis Island. New York's port is, of course, the greatest and most fabulous on earth. It handled 60 per cent of the wartime tonnages leaving the United States by water. Much of Manhattan Island's shore bristles with piers and jetties, like the teeth of a two-edged comb. It is at these piers that the great and famous liners hold their sailing parties, which are such a feature of New York's social life. The Hudson, the East and the Harlem are the rivers that the mighty bridges so majestically span and the tunnels burrow under. Yet even these extraordinary means of ingress and egress are insufficient to handle the daily, almost tidal, influx and exodus of commuters, hordes of which come and go on the busy ferryboats. New York's Grand Central Terminal and Pennsylvania Railroad Station are bedlam at the come-to-work and go-home time, a kind of hell overworked people have to endure twice a day.

One of the worst things World War II did to New York was to present it with a crushing housing problem. True, there are thousands of vacant cold-water tenements, but, understandably, nobody wants to live in them. Virtually every other square inch of dwelling space in the town is occupied. When, during the war, civilian America got war jingles in its pockets and war jangles in its nerves, it sought relief in New York's amusements, and swamped the place. Even now, only those who are in possession of pugilistic talents can accomplish much in getting around Times Square on Saturday nights, where the wide sidewalks are wholly unequal to the crowds which spill out into the streets. Another war casualty was New York's taxis. They were victims of combat fatigue, and for a time nobody was surprised when, on entering one of them, the door came off in his hand.

But while Manhattan's sassy cabbies have got some relief from their spavined vehicles, they will probably never be rid of "New York's Finest," the name the town sometimes uses for its 19,000 coppers. The Force is not merely the biggest but is actually one of the most efficient police corps in the world, despite the fact that many of its members are allergic to taxi drivers.

Yet, if the clangor of traffic and whistle of cops make up the dominant note of Times Square, there are other places of wondrous quiet, such as Sutton Place on the East River; Gramercy Park, which is fenced in and to which only the families of its neighborhood have keys; Washington Square, home of New York University, which fringes on Greenwich Village; and up on Morningside Heights, the Columbia University vicinity. But where the city becomes downright pastoral is in beautiful, 840-acre Central Park in the heart of Manhattan. At the Park's lower end are top-hatted drivers of horse-drawn hansom cabs and victorias, which people hire to ride through the park, people wearing self-conscious expressions on their faces and usually appearing to be struggling against an impulse to leap out of the carriage and back into the sheltering anonymity of the park's pedestrian world.

Should a contest be held to find the average New Yorker, the fellow who won it would probably be a white-collar worker who likes simple things such as walks in the parks, dogs—New York has the most dogs, and the lowest dog mortality rate of any city in the nation—newspapers, movies, which he usually sees at his neighborhood movie house, and, above all, conversation. The average New Yorker reads more than the average American, is more socially conscious, more articulate, slightly more critical of his surroundings, slightly more irritable. He lacks the simplicity of environment of rural folk, and yet if he disapproves of you, he is far less likely to knock your brains out than a Southerner or a Southwesterner, but he is more likely to take legal action when aggrieved. He responds more audibly to newsreels, is more apt to hiss or cheer, than the ordinary moviegoer.

This average New Yorker pays more for almost everything than the rest of the nation. His rent, and the rent of the man who sells to him, would be reason enough for these high prices. And since space and time are the ore from which he smelts his living, he is naturally busy trying to wedge sixty-five seconds into a minute, fourteen inches into a foot. Surely no town on earth is more briskly paced. And for this pressure the New Yorker pays in something besides money, something that is drained out of himself. Unless he has the wire nerves with which a slum upbringing may have endowed him, he pays something that is not compensated for by the blare of light and sound, the fundamental doom of bars late at night, or a higher income bracket. New York's "successes" in art, literature, the stage, business or politics seldom refuse to pay the self-consuming price that is the utility bill for Manhattan's limelight. They cling to it as, to what nameless aspiration, do the derelicts who are to be found lying unconscious, filthy and ragged, in the doorways on Sunday morning, their defeat screaming out to everyone except to their own momentarily blotted-out selves.

There is enough hideousness and tragedy in New York to fill a hundred books. But the average New Yorker, being among other things normal, has eyes that do not dwell upon them. He seeks, instead, the curious, the amusing, the glittering, the splendid—the sights that serve his own needs and ends. He knows intuitively that New York's magic-quotient is high and that for human uses, his own in particular, even reality has its limits.

If the average New Yorker is a Manhattanite, he's proud of the city, and of being a part of it. In his mind Brooklyn, Queens, Richmond and the Bronx are the semi-finals in the contest to see who is going to live in what to him is the most exciting spot on earth. Finally, he is proud of, as is that part of the rest of the nation which will admit it, his skyscrapers. He has seen them, from a distance on a faintly hazy winter night, appear not as a geometric patchwork of lighted windows, but as if the structures themselves were breath-takingly translucent and luminous. He feels a thing about them, the reality of which outlanders may hesitate to believe. He sees and recognizes them as human emotion, exuberance, egotism, an almost mystical manifestation. Many of the highest of these buildings were built against the advice of financial consultants, against the wishes of city planners. They would hold more people than the streets could funnel into them. Some have been almost continual money-losers. That they were built was a kind of voluntary keeping of faith with the New York myth, an expression of its vitality and richness and, on occasion, of the urge to do huge and stupendous things just for the hell of it.

Things too dramatic, too spectacular, too pat to be true usually aren't. Especially when a thing deals so much in make-believe as does New York, it's easy to begin thinking of it as the setting of a fairy story, an over-sold thing that perhaps will one day, like technocracy and the zoot suit, pass away and leave us to the consideration of more sensible and plausible matters. Perhaps the most astonishing thing of all about New York is that a large percentage of its myth is true. The steel-and-stone bean-stalks, the bewildering problems so often solved, the human ache, the deathless hope are really there. Writers more intellectually pretentious and less emotional than Walt Whitman have chided him for dynamically expressing what was there, rather than how it ought to work, for not supplying the combination to its secret soul. I can only say that the brains and vitality, the striving people, are there, expressing themselves through endlessly complex, yet surprisingly unobstructed sleeves of transit, of commerce, of industry and communication, expressing the human spirit in every shade from despair to exaltation.

And the myth, which in reality is the town's personality, will get you if you don't watch out.

3 : *Salt Lake City*

SALT LAKE CITY is a strange and somehow lonely city in the high fastnesses of the Rocky Mountains, out where the water, when there is any, runs west. It is endlessly intriguing in its oblique contradictions, in the interplay of spiritual and wholly practical considerations. Like Rome and Jerusalem and Mecca, it is a holy city. It was the final refuge of a people who attempted two things that are impossible in the United States of America: to be fundamentally and continuously different, and to be sufficient, spiritually, economically and socially, unto themselves. The basically different aspects of their life, such as polygamy, isolation and socialism, have, over a period of a hundred years, been hammered out of them. As their differences decreased, so cooled the hatred in their neighbors' breasts. Today they live in tranquillity among "the Gentiles," as they call all their non-Mormon neighbors, be they Catholic, Protestant or Jew. And every now and again one reads in the church-owned daily, the *Deseret News*, of this or that person having been excommunicated from the Mormon Church for plural marriage as unlawful cohabitation.

Now, even more than in the past, the Mormon Church, aside from its ecclesiastical character, is one of the greatest mutual-aid societies on earth. And the city which it founded is, except for its sacred aspects, a robust Western business town, where you can still pick the right spot and make a fortune selling hamburgers. Here in the priesthood of the church are some of the most level-headed, as well as devout, men in town. One Salt Lake City Gentile, and one who, incidentally, has found the Mormons to be fine neighbors, points out that the Mormons had for many years to rely on barter, that they are gifted traders and had rather beat you on a horse trade than eat a Utah apple. For Salt Lake City is a place where shadow and substance have at times not only merged but, more often than not, made sense. Again, this mountain-ringed valley, where old Jerdan doth sweetly flow, has been a fitting stage for one of the most dynamic tributary dramas in American history. It is here, and in reaching here, that that colorful and able American, Brigham Young, demonstrated himself to be one of the great colonizers of history.

On Salt Lake City's wide streets, the beard-and-bonnet Mormons of an earlier time are seldom seen today. The people dress like those of any other American city. Most of the many Mormons that I met were healthy, energetic, quietly merry, incredibly dutiful people. They love to dance, and the church thinks it's good for them. The same goes for the theater. About these people is a sort of practical kindness, as shall be later shown, that gets you.

The only particular differences I could see between the Mormons and anybody else were their extraordinary interest in genealogy and their astonishing longevity, their long-haul pep. This durable hardihood may well be due to "The Word of Wisdom," the Mormons' health code, which, among other things, prohibits tobacco, alcohol, tea and coffee. Mormons think nothing of living well into their nineties. For example, Mabel Young Sanborn, a daughter of Brigham Young, whose eyes are as bright and brimming with warmth as a girl's, still works five hours a day in the church offices. Then, come nightfall, Mrs. Sanborn, an all-out fan, heads for the movies. As this is written, she is busily trying to sell her house in order to take an air trip around the world. Mrs. Sanborn is eighty-three.

As a result of the persecutions of the past and a certain unfortunate tendency on the part of the press to present the Mormon patriarchs as orgiastic old billy goats, a few devout Mormons, understandably, have slight persecution complexes. Locally, the Salt Lake *Tribune* consistently, in the old days, gave the Mormons the back of its hand, though by now both the *Tribune* and its stable mate, the afternoon *Telegram*, treat the church with full consideration. One former *Tribune* reporter, Louis Sherwin, later wrote that instead of being immoral, the Mormons' sole defect, at least from the standpoint of companionship, was their puritanical morality. He added:

"The man with five wives behaves himself with exemplary propriety. It is the man with only one wife who spends all his spare hours looking for the five he has not."

Most Salt Lake Gentiles have a healthy respect for the Mormons and their church. Every now and then in any community there are hard jobs to do. And on a city- or state-wide basis, the participation of the Mormon Church in any project means that the job will get done. When a flash flood left a substantial part of Salt Lake City buried in silt, it was the Mormon Church that dug the city out, cleaned the property of Gentile and Mormon alike.

While a majority of Utah's people are Mormons, they compose only 40 per cent of the 175,000 souls in its capital city's corporate limits. Some quarter of a million people inhabit Salt Lake City's metropolitan area. And the city is the wholesale distributing point for all of Utah's sparsely settled 600,000 people, plus about as many more customers outside the state. Salt Lake City, to pin it down geographically, lies 940 road miles southeast of Seattle, 779 northeast of San Francisco, and 538 west of its closest large neighbor, Denver. From sea level it is 4,354 feet straight up. It is built in the cathedral-esque Salt Lake Valley at a spot that was once about a thousand feet under the surface of the lake. One of the city's slogans is: "The most beautifully situated city on earth."

Located principally in the flat valley, the city, outside the business district, has a low, widespread appearance. The predominant dwelling architecture is expressed in simple, apparently purposefully plain, little Mormon bungalows with low-pitched roofs and, because of the lumber scarcity, usually constructed of brick—some of the older ones of handmade adobe blocks that the years are gently melting away. One very utilitarian Salt Lake oddity is the cellar-house. Young couples with just enough money for the underground part of their houses build that, roll some tar paper over the ceiling and move in. Some of these dwellings, reaching only a couple of feet above the ground, are tastefully surrounded by bright flowers and pretty lawns, quietly awaiting the time when another story or two can be added. The section of town overlooking Memory Park, called "The Avenues," has the most beautiful view, while the neighborhood with the most luxurious homes is called Federal Heights. There are lots of trees, all man-planted, maples, elms, sycamores and cedars, but most of all poplars, which grew quickly and made good wind-breaks, but are now old and heavy and brittle and a little dangerous.

Salt Lake City is the home of old Fort Douglas, as well as of the University of Utah. The university, with a normal enrollment of 4,200, frequently dominates the Big (though not very) Seven in football, and has won the intercollegiate championship in basket-ball. Its Department of Drama is its pride and joy. In fact, drama-struck Salt Lake City, in whose scenic environs some thirty pictures a year are filmed, is the birthplace of Maude Adams and Loretta Young.

In the "feel" of the town there is a pleasant admixture of the spirit-ual cast of its religious groups, plus the natural exuberance and con-fidence of the West. Though it's big enough to be a city, it's still the kind of place where everybody knows most of the people around town, and where the service in the stores and filling stations slacks up in the fall because lots of the employees have slipped off to go deer, duck or pheasant hunting. It's also the kind of place where a hook-and-ladder truck is named "Big Dan" for Dan Cunningham, one of the most popular of the city's thousands of railroaders, who work for the Denver and Rio Grande Western, the Western Pacific, the Southern Pacific, and that mountain-jumping giant, the Union Pacific.

But in a world full of desperate problems, perhaps the nicest thing about Salt Lake City is its lack of major local problems. Cupped, as it is, in the mountains, it has a messy winter smoke problem, but already it is building plants for the production of smokeless fuel. Too, it has a rubbage-disposal problem and is, sooner or later, going to have to find some alternative for just piling it up on the edge of town. It also has a juvenile-delinquency problem which, for well-behaved Utah, is new, but which, compared to that of most of our other cities, is slight indeed. But the striking thing is that it has no real slums and, relatively speaking, no race problem. There are only a handful of Negroes in Salt Lake City, and one of the state's former governors, Simon Bamberger, was a Jew. There are a few extraordinarily rich people, but few that are desperately poor. And it's almost impossible for a child to swing onto his ignorance in Salt Lake City. Its schools are celebratedly good, and the truant officer rides herd on the kids until they have either graduated from the city's twelve-grade system or reached the fairly ripe age of eighteen. Salt Lake City claims the highest percentage of literacy of any American city. Two of the lads who learned their three "*R's*" here were John Held, Jr., and Jack Dempsey.

As for the lake which once covered the present site of the city, it is still receding and in recent years has gone off and left the famous old beach resort of Saltair sitting high and dry. As you've no doubt heard, the difficulty in swimming here is not in keeping your body up, but your feet down, and the stinging water out of your eyes. The great Bonneville salt flats, where the automobile racing is done and where Salt Lake's former mayor, Ab Jenkins, set 148 world's records, lies 125 miles away. Yet right out on the edge of town, the Royal Crystal Salt Company makes salt commercially by simply pumping the lake water, which is seven times as salty as that of the ocean, out onto the flats near the lake. The sun pulls the water up into the dry summer air and leaves the brilliant white fields of salt, which is harvested by bulldozers in the fall. There's no danger of its getting washed away. Dry Salt Lake City has to depend principally on snow for its water supply. And the mineral-enriched melted snow from the dammed canyons will probably chap you in the bathtub unless you are used to it.

Salt Lake County is the world's largest nonferrous-smelting center, and a good half of Utah's population lives off its great extractive industries in which people are busily digging things out of the ground: iron, coal, copper, silver, gold, lead and zinc. Near Salt Lake City are the colossal diggings of the Utah Copper Company, the largest open-cut mine in the world, which produces 30 per cent of our domestic supply of copper and 10 per cent of the world's. It is said to make enough off the gold and silver it finds in its ore to pay for its entire operation. And anyone with an ounce of rubber in his neck will drive out to see the daily blasting, which occurs in the afternoon and looks like an artillery duel.

Utah Copper performs many engrossing functions. In the first place, it grinds the gray-green ore to powder, mixes it in a kind of greasy dishwater, floats the metal to the top, skims it off, and cooks it into hunks of blister copper. Thereafter, it is shipped to the East for further refining. But the biggest cinch Utah Copper has got is just catching the copper-laden water that runs off its vast diggings. This water is guided through great vats filled with tin scrap; the tin is eaten away by the water, and the copper deposited, in red granules, at the bottom of the trough, where the copper company has merely to shovel it into a boxcar and send it off to be made into high-priced boat-bottom paint. This copper-from-drain-water process is carried on at the mine town of Bingham, in the bottom of a narrow canyon. The mean width of this two-mile-long town is 150 feet.

There are other great extractive possibilities for the future. In Salt Lake City's bailiwick lies a vast proportion of the earth's fund of bituminous coal and oil shale, both sources of gasoline in a world where the supply is fast dwindling. Also there are mountains of phosphate, which will one day give renewal to America's tiring fields. It is further believed that the lake will eventually give up a fabulous variety of rich chemicals.

But all this direct mining and sale of raw wealth seems to many a Salt Laker a kind of selling of his birthright. For mining is a depleting industry, and many of the deep mines which produce lead, zinc and silver have already begun to peter out. There are, therefore, rumblings about voting a severance tax on all Utah minerals that are exported without being locally processed. The sad fact is that Salt Lake City has no near-by pools of population to serve as customers. This is probably one of the main reasons why U. S. Steel was so hesitant about buying the $200,000,000 war-built steel mill at Geneva, thirty-five miles from Salt Lake City. Then there is the related fact that the railroads have got this inland, isolated metropolis stretched over a tub. It's cheaper to ship a thousand flat-irons from San Francisco to New York than from Salt Lake City to New York, since Salt Lake City's railroads have to meet no water-rate competition. And the fact that all the central transcontinental airlines radiate out of Salt Lake City won't solve the problem of a man who wants to make cookstoves or crowbars and sell them nationally.

But Salt Lake City holds some advantages, and means to use them shrewdly. In the first place, the people of the Bee Hive State, who make a fetish, almost, of personal industry, education and honesty, are, as workers, a very solid starting point in the attracting of industry. Gus Backman, who runs the Salt Lake Chamber of Commerce, has a brother, Ralph, who directs the city's cracking-good adult-education program. In one recent instance, Gus got a clothing factory to move to town with the promise that Brother Ralph would (1) recruit, (2) screen and (3) train the three hundred workers the factory would need. The same scheme was worked with a radar equipment company and a watch company, in both of which cases, it's worth noting, Salt Lake City's geographical position has little bearing. For the transportation bill on a wrist watch from Salt Lake City to Timbuktu would leave a very slight dent in anybody's purse.

Salt Lake City does some milling of its farm produce, making flour out of its dry-farmed winter wheat, and sugar out of Utah beets, as well as knitted goods out of Utah wool. But even though Utah farmers are wizards at irrigation, there just plain isn't enough water for the complete irrigation of more than about 1,350,000 acres. Utah hopes to get Colorado River water that will bring another 600,000 acres under varying degrees of irrigation. But with the mechanization of farming, plus the extraordinarily tiny size of present irrigable farms, Utah agricultural experts believe that this additional land will be needed merely to hold, and not to increase, its present farm population.

Incidentally, if you want to make everybody in Utah happy, go out and buy a stalk of Utah bleached celery. Utahns cover the stalk with dirt, let snow cover that, and the temperature drop to zero. The liquid inside the celery gently crystallizes, and Utahns rhapsodically declare its equal for crunchiness, plus a faint salt tang from their salty earth, is not elsewhere to be had. Salt Lake City even organized a post-season football classic to be known as the Celery

Bowl. But since there was no one to pile dirt up around the spectators, this festival had a hard rigor and froze out.

In the prewar years, the tourist pickings in this state that is studded with tourist attractions, was a piddling $30,000,000. But the state has scratched up about a half-million dollars to spend in luring tourists and in opening new roads to those of Utah's hitherto inaccessible wonders. The state, the city, and the Mormon Church are jointly planning a big-time 1947 Centennial celebration. This summer-long shindig will include every sort of national championship sporting event from clay-court tennis to golf, as well as skiing at near-by Alta, than which, Salt Lakers contend, there is no finer ski range on earth. The Utah Symphony will be bolstered with numerous ringers from both the East and West. Dramatic stars from Hollywood and Broadway will carry lead roles, supported by University players, in local productions. Every community will turn its particular days of celebration into all-out spectacles. And, finally, the Mormon Church will undertake to tell in pageantry the story of the coming of the Mormons to Zion, the holy city of Salt Lake City.

They've got a powerful story to tell.

The Mormon religion or, more exactly, the Church of Jesus Christ of Latter Day Saints was founded by Joseph Smith in 1830, at Palmyra, N. Y. He declared that a heavenly messenger, the angel Moroni, had led him to the hiding place of a book with golden pages, inscribed in a strange tongue. He claimed that in the stone box with the book he found a set of magic eyeglasses which made the writing intelligible. From behind a curtain Smith translated and dictated the golden tablets to a secretary, after which he said they were carried away by a heavenly messenger. Smith's transcript was called the Book of Mormon, and his followers accepted it as a new book of the Bible and the foundation of their religion.

Most of his converts were extremely zealous. They pooled their resources, worked harder, lived more frugally, and prospered more, than their neighbors. And this was resented by their neighbors. Moreover, with profound tactlessness, the converts, though living in a world of sinners, called themselves "Saints." That too, along with their clannishness and the fact that Joseph Smith claimed the power of continuing revelation, was resented. Smith finally organized a church army, the Nauvoo Legion, and affected a general's uniform.

Feared economically, considered arrogant in their religious pretensions, and a local threat militarily and politically, the Mormons were then discovered to be practicing polygamy, in obedience to one of Joseph Smith's revelations. Here was the excuse, more than the reason, for the brutal persecutions that followed. Time and again they were driven away from their land and property, which was confiscated by their tormentors. State and federal governments gave them no protection or succor. Finally, in 1844, Joseph Smith was murdered by a mob while he was in jail in Carthage, Illinois. In this black hour, a new leader assumed command of the Church of Jesus Christ of Latter Day Saints. That man was Brigham Young.

Brigham Young possessed clear vision, great courage, and an iron will. He was further blessed with the powers of leadership and the quality of command to extraordinary degree. Physically—and this, under the pioneer circumstances, was of profound importance—he had the power and the stamina, the vitality and virility, of a ram.

After the Saints had been driven out of Nauvoo in 1846, Brigham Young led his harassed and impoverished people out of Missouri and Illinois to the Great Salt Lake Valley, 1,200 miles away. First he established temporary settlements along the way and winter quarters at what is now Council Bluffs, Iowa—quarters which at one time harbored 12,000 souls. He organized companies of wagons and spaced their departures so that the grass along the trail would have time to recover between the passage of one company and the next, sent certain groups forward to break land, others to follow and plant seeds, still others to harvest the crop. There was every reason for this fantastic venture in long-range logistics to fail: hostile Indians, deserts, uncharted mountains, merciless winters, human frailty, indecision and despair. The reason it did not fail was because Brother Brigham would not let it fail.

And on July 24, 1847, a year and a half later, Brigham Young, himself racked with mountain fever, led his advance guard, three quarters of them barefooted, out of the mouth of Emigration Canyon. The Great Salt Lake Valley stretched, majestic but desolate, before them.

Other Saints by the hundreds followed, many of them afoot, hauling their belongings in pushcarts. The first detachment of the Mormon Battalion that had marched 2,000 miles to help in the Mexican War, and whose pay allotments had materially helped the Western migration, arrived in Salt Lake City.

To telescope the events that followed Brigham Young's arrival in the valley, he had a stream diverted and crops planted in the moist earth. He built a mud fort, a brush-arbor tabernacle, and, with almost unique foresight, laid out a great city. That first winter the food was exhausted. The people dug sego-lily roots and thistles to keep themselves alive. They boiled the buffalo hides they had brought for bedding. One man offered a pound of gold for a pound of flour and found no takers. Next spring a horde of crickets descended on and were devouring the first crop. The people prayed, and, miraculously, a flock of sea gulls came and devoured the crickets.

Brigham Young formed the provisional State of Deseret with its own judiciary, legislature, currency, coinage and so forth, with himself as governor. When the United States made Deseret the Territory of Utah, Brigham Young became its first governor.

In 1857, false rumors reached Washington that the Mormons were highjacking immigrants on their way to California's newly discovered gold, that, in fact, the Mormons were in a state of rebellion. A small army under Albert Sydney Johnston was sent out from Washington to occupy Salt Lake City. Brigham Young's spies brought word that the motto of the soldiers was "booty and beauty," Mormon wealth and Mormon girls. Brother Brigham decided his people had been plundered enough already. He rallied his own army, burned the prairies ahead of Johnston, attacked and destroyed his baggage train, drove off his animals. Young evacuated his people to the south, had dry straw piled against the buildings, and stood ready to burn the city to the ground if Johnston tried to occupy it. Johnston finally agreed to bring his army through the city without stopping and park it at a respectful distance in Cedar Valley, thirty-six miles from Salt Lake, and the "Utah War" was over.

Although a carpetbag Gentile government and a growing population of Gentile miners made life miserable for the Saints, taking both legal and literal potshots at "the big Mormon," Brother Brigham, he was constantly guiding the fortunes of the church and of himself to ever greater heights. He built mills, a theater, banks, a newspaper, a telegraph system, great temples, schools and universities. He did not merely conceive these things, but determined the details of their execution, even to the curve in the tabernacle pews. He colonized all the irrigable valleys with Mormons, and built adequate dams. Finally, in 1877, he departed this life, having married some twenty wives, fathered fifty-six children, and amassed an estate worth more than a million dollars. The community he founded had become a proud city, and the church was indestructibly established.

But its troubles were by no means over. After the church's public avowal of plural marriage in 1852, the clamor against that practice —and Mormons—had mounted steadily. Congress, under pressure from the public and various special-interest groups, had passed several laws against polygamy. Finally it put the United States marshals after the "co-habs," as the polygamists were called. The patriarchs took to the brush and the mountains or were captured and thrown in jail. Ultimately, the church disavowed polygamy, and in 1896 Utah was allowed to join the union as a state. Yet even after the century turned, there was a nationwide drive that kept Utah's Reed Smoot out of his seat in the United States Senate for three years. Smoot was an apostle in the church, and the nation was still not convinced of the church's stand on plural marriage.

The church Brigham Young built has, today, a million members. Materially it owns many millions of dollars' worth of office buildings and other property in Salt Lake City. It owns banks, insurance companies, mills, and a substantial interest in the huge Z.C.M.I. (Zion's Co-operative Mercantile Institution), the biggest department store from the Missouri to the West Coast, which does more than twenty million dollars' worth of business a year. The church developed the large Utah-Idaho Sugar Company primarily as a means of giving employment to its people. Besides its newspaper, it has its own radio station and its own hospitals, where an impecunious Mormon can get his mortal envelope repaired for what he can afford to pay. In addition to unknown amounts of securities, it owns the controlling interest in Salt Lake's superlative Hotel Utah, whose Empire Room in winter and roof garden in summer are the social centers of gravity in the city. Then there are those million tithing Saints. The chairman of the financial board, the church's high chancellor of the exchequer, is able, energetic Orval Adams, former president of the American Bankers Association, whose golf form is bad but whose scores are good. More specifically, he runs the Utah State National Bank, one of the church's string of three Salt Lake City banks.

The only religious functions in which the Gentiles may not participate are the Temple rites. Although Gentiles are welcome in the great elliptical Tabernacle on Temple Square with its huge organ and mighty chorus, even "jack-Mormons" (backsliders) are barred from the Temple.

The thing that makes the Mormon Church able to accomplish so many complex jobs in Salt Lake City and elsewhere is its tight organization, the obedience of its people, and its centralized authority. For administrative purposes, the church's domain is divided into religio-geographical areas. A ward contains about 800 people. It has its own meeting house and recreation hall, and is presided over and looked after by a bishop who has a card index containing everything about everybody in his ward. So many wards comprise a stake, and so on. Every male member over twelve years of age is an officer of some kind in the priesthood, that pyramid of soviets that goes up to the twelve apostles and finally to the president of the church.

On the theory that idle hands are the devil's workshop, a good Mormon is given enough time to earn his bread—most of the jobs in the priesthood are nonpaying—and the rest of his time is pretty well taken up by the church. Even Mormon children must find time each day to put in an extra class period at the Mormon seminary, which is invariably built beside Utah high schools. There are endless church societies, duties and meetings, at least one night a week being devoted to ward socials or recreational meetings. And if a young man is making a brilliant start in business, it is not at all unlikely that his elders will call upon him and inform him that he has been selected to take up a foreign mission—at, it goes without saying, his own or his parents' expense—and the good Mormon obediently goes. In normal times the church keeps some 2,000 missionaries dotted over the globe. And it is the foreign languages and cultures which these people are constantly bringing back to isolated Salt Lake City that make it oddly cosmopolitan.

But where the church has been most brilliantly successful is in its vast Welfare Program, which, manifestly, is an important factor in Salt Lake City life. This is the program that means simply that no Mormon need ever be in want. It worked during the depression, and it's working better all the time.

Each year the Mormon Welfare people estimate conservatively how many persons they may have to care for in the coming year. In good times, for example, the Welfare Program plans to have to care for only 10,000 people. A meeting is called, and it is determined how much of each product will be needed for the over-all program. Long experience has taught them how much of what a destitute person requires. In the case of flour, suppose it's decided that the yield of 5,000 acres of wheat will be needed. The stake presidents in the wheat-growing areas will divide this burden among them. Each stake president will parcel out the acreages he has agreed to accept among his bishops, and each bishop will divide his commitment among the Saints in his ward, who must voluntarily furnish the land and seed and labor necessary to raising their portion of the crop. It is the same with almost every other commodity.

For processing these raw materials for the Welfare, the church has its own mills and elevators, canning plants, garment factories, dairy plants for bottling and condensing milk, soap factories, meat-processing plants, and coal mines. The church, for Welfare purposes, is even in the junk business: rehabilitating castoff clothes and furniture. After this great variety of products is processed, it is portioned out among the various Bishops' Storehouses.

But the ingenuity and labor don't end here. In Salt Lake City the very Storehouse itself, an imposing brick-and-glass structure, is the result of an alert disciple hearing that five brick buildings were to be demolished. He hurried to the owners, offered to get the church to handle the demolition for the junked material, and to leave the lot clean. These same materials today compose the big Central Bishops' Storehouse.

Inside, the Storehouse looks like any top-notch, super-market and department store combined. Here, smartly packaged and labeled under the proud brand name "Deseret," there is everything from marmalade to bluing. There is fresh meat from the church ranches, fresh eggs from the poultry farm. But nothing is for sale. Goods are removable only on written orders from the various bishops or the Ladies' Relief Society.

Each bishop keeps a careful eye on changing conditions in his ward. If one of his flock is heading into trouble through sloth or folly, it is up to the bishop to straighten this brother out, but if the brother be in real trouble, the bishop has to see that he and his family are not in want. If the trouble is unemployment, that is quickly remedied. The down-and-out brother is put to work in the Bishops' Storehouse or associated enterprises, and supplied, until a job in regular commercial channels can be found for him by the church employment agency. The whole idea of the Welfare Program is to help the Saints to help themselves.

Consider one example. A Salt Lake City barber had some trouble with his back, could no longer stand to his work, and lost his job. He was invited to appear before his elders. They said since he couldn't stand and work, why didn't he get a high stool? The man said no one would hire a sitting barber. One elder remembered a small frame building in a residential section where the rent would be cheap. They arranged for the Welfare to lend the man enough money to buy his equipment. But in addition—and this is the touch that seems to make so many Mormon enterprises work—all agreed to let Brother So-and-so cut their own hair thereafter.

At first the going was hard. The barber had to be supplied out of the Storehouse. That being the case, the bishop in charge of the Storehouse, who was seeing the unshorn young'uns of the poor every day, let the barber cut their hair as a kind of repayment for goods received from the Storehouse. Business picked up. Another barber—this one having only one leg—was taken in; finally even a manicurist. The story ends with the barber's running a prosperous business in downtown Salt Lake City.

True-story variations on this theme of intelligent mutual aid that involves little or no money, only the sweat and brains and perseverance of the Saints, could go on endlessly—the kind of teamwork that, according to First Counselor J. Reuben Clark, Jr., does not debauch character with mendicancy. Or again, to quote Elder Harold B. Lee of the Council of the Twelve Apostles, "There's a world of difference in a sack of flour our people have made for themselves against an emergency and a sack of flour that comes from Washington."

At the moment these good folk are busily packing and sending boxes of restored clothes, canned mutton and the like, to the hungry Saints in Europe.

To give you some idea of the magnitude of the Mormon Welfare Program, the late president of the church, Heber J. Grant, reported in 'Forty-three that the church Welfare Program had 14,587 acres of land under cultivation by voluntary labor, maintained 90 Bishops' Storehouses, 65 canneries, 598 livestock projects, over 300 processing plants. And he added, since the purpose of the plan is not merely to succor, or increase dependency, but to rehabilitate, that 1,200 down-and-out families had been established in farming or some sort of business.

The idea for all this, and in a more primitive way the practice, originated with Brigham Young.

As is only natural, two of the first things most contemporary visitors to Salt Lake City want to see are the Lion House and the Bee Hive House, the apartment buildings where Brigham Young housed his families until these large buildings simply became swamped with wives and progeny, and auxiliary structures had to be obtained. From available records and discussions with various ones of his 2,500 descendants, it would appear that these families came about as near as most to getting on well together and living happy, useful lives.

But what will probably strike the visitor most of all is the continuing influence of Brigham Young in the city's life today, for it is almost impossible to spend even a few days there without feeling the impact of his ideas and character in a dozen different ways.

And, unless the visitor bring with him his own cast-iron prejudices, he'll very probably conclude that Salt Lake City and the man who built it have ample right to be proud of each other.

4: *Baltimore*

IF YOU had a trowel sufficiently wide and an arm sufficiently strong simply to scoop up both New Orleans and Boston and set them down, mingled together, on some more central piece of American topography, preferably beside a meadow that had sunk a little beneath tidewater, the result would, in a number of ways, approximate Baltimore.

For you could hardly bring Boston without its copious statuary, narrow, bewildering streets, its modified English ways, its Revolutionary history, and its polyglot population. Nor, on the other hand, could you bring New Orleans without its love of horse racing, its great cuisine, and its relaxed tempo. And since Boston and New Orleans more or less mark the extremities of the ancestor belt, their upper crusts could go right on, just as Baltimore's does, snubbing their less blue-blooded neighbors. The fact that Boston and New Orleans might have trouble seeing eye to eye on the Civil War wouldn't particularly matter since, when that war was fought, Baltimore was pretty much caught in the middle and was herself of two minds about which way to jump.

Yet it would be difficult for either Boston or New Orleans to dig up a substitute for Baltimore's own sharp-spurred Henry Mencken, who exuberantly raked his more smug countrymen from shoulder to flank throughout the 'Twenties. Speaking of Baltimore, where he still lives, Mr. Mencken, in his book of reminiscences, *Happy Days*, has remarked:

The city into which I was born in 1880 had a reputation all over for what the English, in their real-estate advertising, are fond of calling the amenities. So far as I have been able to discover by a labored search of contemporary travel-books, no literary tourist, however waspish he may have been about Washington, Niagara Falls, the prairies of the West, or even

43

Boston and New York, ever gave Baltimore a bad notice. They all agreed, often with lubricious gloats and gurgles, (*a*), that its indigenous victualry was unsurpassed in the Republic, (*b*), that its native Caucasian females of all ages up to thirty-five were of incomparable pulchritude, and as amiable as they were lovely, and (*c*), that its home-life was spacious, charming, full of creature comforts, and highly conducive to the facile and orderly propagation of the species. There was some truth in all these articles, but not, I regret to have to add, too much.

Yet Mr. Mencken would probably have a hard time convincing the people of the British Empire that Baltimore girls haven't got what it takes, since Baltimore's Wallis Warfield succeeded so gloriously in getting King Edward's mind off his business—or for that matter, the French, when, in an earlier day, Baltimore's Miss Betsy Patterson picked off Jérôme Bonaparte, whose big brother was so fond of wearing his hat sideways and scratching his chest.

But in suggesting that Baltimore may have one or two aspects inferior to those of the city with the golden streets and the Pearly Gates, Mr. Mencken is enjoying a special Baltimore pastime. For Baltimoreans, who are affronted when the city receives anything short of adulation and obeisance from strangers, themselves enjoy nothing more than pointing out its faults. When the wind comes riding down from the fertilizer plants, enriched with the blended perfume of tankage, guano and fish scraps, they yelp with great authenticity that the old burg stinks. When there is no wind, they bemoan the fact that smoke engulfs the Basin. They love to complain that the city is dirty, that traffic moves at a crippled-snail's pace, and that the weather is lousy. Few things entertain Baltimoreans more than to have a good gripe about the narrowness and want of smoothness of their streets. Even the city engineer, according to columnist Louis Azrael of the Baltimore *News-Post*, says a great number of the city's streets are no longer worth repairing.

Ernest Hemingway once lamented the substitution of concrete for paving stones, feeling that, with the passing of those readily available missiles, the public was losing its last effective means of protest against the police. But in much of Baltimore, this instrumentality of democratic expression remains inviolate—and daily shakes out the less-securely-fastened dentures of motorists.

But despite the heavy out-of-town motor traffic that bounces through Baltimore and the millions who zip through on trains, Baltimore is, in many ways, one of the least realized of the great American cities. Though its metropolitan population is in excess of a million souls, it has not, for a long time, been much worked up, so far as tourists are concerned, about tooting its own horn. Again, there are physical reasons for its lack of impact upon the national consciousness. If you drive through Baltimore in a car, you are routed around through the peripheral furrows of row houses where the most recurrent sight is the posterior of a housewife swabbing away at the marble steps. You may also notice that these householders, in great numbers, take the trouble to keep their windowpanes shiny-clean and the lace curtains behind them white and starchy. But that's very little to see of so many-sided a city.

If you come through Baltimore on the train, about all you see is the somewhat uninformative interior of a tunnel or a trench. In fact, Baltimore pretty much has to be stalked to be seen. Its extremely cunning port—in prewar times Number Six, business-wise, of all the ports on earth—is probably Number One in unobtrusiveness. Yet only by getting out into the harbor in a boat do you really see the city at its most impressive. Almost all of central Baltimore, except its downtown area, is old and not particularly startling. But a $125,-000,000 fire in 1904 burned for ten days and razed the downtown section. Thereafter, this area began to blossom with modern buildings, many of them skyscrapers, so that today its silhouette is a very flossy sight indeed.

A large part of the fun of making the acquaintance of Baltimore lies in trying to unravel its endless contradictions. Unlike the easily typed characters in trivial fiction, Baltimore much more nearly resembles that baffling thing which is a normal human being. It is so delicately complex, and so enjoys that complexity, it's willing to bet you that almost any sweeping statement you make about its character will be wrong. Most of its inconsistencies are not simple, direct paradoxes, but oblique, chain-stitched contradictions which in the end lead one not merely around but over and under Robin Hood's barn.

It has a Democratic boss, erudite Billy Curran, who in his spare time sometimes writes book reviews, and a Republican mayor, Theodore Roosevelt McKeldin. It's a town where, in recent years, a thousand-dollar bribe, to facilitate your affairs, might very well land you in jail, whereas to fail to buy the goods or services of this or that strategically located politician could be an important blunder. It's a town where thousands of people have purchased their homes outright—on rented land. Its *Sun*papers have the quaint habit of starting news stories on the back page and continuing them up toward the front. The *Sun*'s Richard "Moco" Yardley—though not so well known nationally as political cartoonist Edmund Duffy—enchants Baltimoreans by making sport of their unprogressive ways, old ways that they love and haven't the faintest idea of changing.

Baltimore is an important steel city known, unlike many steel cities, for its grace, though in an earlier time when it was only moderately industrialized, it was known with good reason as "Mobtown." It is a much more than commonly cultured old city, which has produced next to no great literature, even though Edgar Allan Poe died and was buried there.

Baltimore's port, on the Patapsco estuary, is the most southern of the Northern ports, the most northern of the Southern ports and most western of the Northeastern ports—and may well be the port hardest hit by the completion of the St. Lawrence Waterway. Baltimore is thought to have its strength sapped by the cordon of surrounding great cities, which may be presumed to act as pickets in shutting it off from the interior. Yet life in Baltimore wouldn't be half so pleasant without New York, Philadelphia and Washington so conveniently visitable, according to one's mood. Besides, the port would be less busy without the patronage of rich Washington, which is too busy talking to produce goods.

And while Washington's ex-resident, Lincoln, would still pull a heavy vote in Baltimore, it is, nevertheless, a town where, on Jeff Davis' birthday, the Confederate Stars and Bars are unfurled in an occasional window. It's a city where the industrial expert of the Association of Commerce has done his spot of poetry for Mencken's

Journals, and where the manager of the Association directs plays. Though its traditional commercial forte is transportation, having launched not only sea- and air-borne Clippers but the B. & O. as well, its municipal airport has drowsed into obsolescence, and a good many of its harbor installations are apparently still standing because no one ever walked squarely up to them and hollered boo. Yet elsewhere about the harbor are such monuments to efficiency as the giant gadget that grabs up a full-size coal car, turns it over and dumps out the coal as easily as any early-rising Boy Scout ever tipped over his comrade's cot and dumped him out on the dewy ground.

This moderate old city, which is allergic to ballyhoo, has a kind of sly effectiveness. When it was really convinced that the airplane was here to stay, it decided it needed a company of its own. Its industrial experts, knowing nothing of aircraft design, simply looked about to see which company had, in their opinion, the soundest manufacturing techniques. They decided Glenn Martin was the man, and quietly lured him away from Cleveland to Baltimore. Mr. Martin built forty million dollars' worth of planes in 'Forty-six, and is building a hundred million dollars' worth in 'Forty-seven. And the way that, just now, he loves Baltimore and it loves him is almost embarrassing. Mr. Martin thinks the quality of Baltimore labor cannot be surpassed. Most of it, for all its earlier origins, is now very solidly American, and there are some Baltimoreans who believe that a part of the stability of Baltimore working folk can be attributed to ground rent and the row house.

Most of these row houses, which are one room wide, contain six rooms, three upstairs and three down. They originally cost their owners something like $2,500, often with a down payment of as little as $50. This low price was possible because they were mass-produced by the row and because the purchaser only rented the land beneath them, usually with an option to buy it outright at the end of five years. This amounted to a kind of uncallable mortgage. For if, at the end of five years, the householder found himself not in a position to buy the land, he could go right on renting it. Through this device, the majority of Baltimoreans came to own their own homes.

Today some of these rows of houses are seventy or eighty years old, yet, being constructed of brick, they still stand firm and strong. Sandwiched in, as they are, there is no leakage of heat through the side walls, and there is nothing to paint except the front door and the window frames. Therefore, a minor paint job on the outside woodwork and a little soap and water on the marble steps perks them up wonderfully and makes them look as good as new.

On the north side of town are several real-estate developments, such as the Guilford district, where homes are massive, expensive, and many of them beautiful, where both private and public gardens are aglow with flowers in spring. But since most rich cities have such developments, it is really the trim, unpretentious little T-Model row house that is most distinctively Baltimore.

Baltimoreans do not pronounce the name of their city as it is spelled. They call it "Bawlemer," with the accent on the "Bawl." This name derives from the titular seat of Maryland's first men of distinction—whose family's name was Calvert by the way—the Lords Baltimore who were Maryland's Lords Proprietory in Colonial times. Since the Baltimores were Catholic, the city which bears their name built the first Roman Catholic cathedral in America.

During the American Revolution and the War of 1812, Baltimoreans had a wonderfully exciting time making a nuisance of themselves to the British. They built hundreds of the famous Baltimore Clippers which sallied forth as privateers. Most everybody in town who had a little cash bought shares in these vessels, which could with such ease run rings around the British. And the shareholders often lay awake at night dreaming of what manner of prizes their ships would bring in next. In any case, throughout this period, Baltimore seamen captured fabulous quantities of stuff from the British—and the wealth derived from this booty was re-invested in Baltimore business.

It was during the War of 1812 that the British made their most determined effort to get their hands on "this nest of pirates," as they thought of Baltimore, and to put a stop to the building of those pesky Clippers. But on the day that the commander of Britain's land forces, General Robert Ross, declared he was going to eat dinner either "in

Baltimore or in hell," he got fatally plugged by a local marksman and, wherever he dined, it was not in Baltimore.

Throughout that night Francis Scott Key, who was watching the naval attack on old Fort McHenry, not only saw the bombs bursting in air and that, at dawn, the flag was still there—but, moreover, he had the wit to write it all down in verses that would fit an old melody. Baltimoreans found it fairly hard to get the hang of the tune, yet they were so happy over the victory that they had to sing something, and the new song caught on fast.

Baltimore's participation in the Civil War was a little less single-minded. The town was so divided that the Federal government deemed it expedient to mount cannon on the heights and keep them trained on the citizenry, in order to dispel any little wishy-washiness in the Baltimoreans' zeal for the Union cause.

When the war was over, Baltimore's good customer, the South, was busted. But at the same time there came an influx of Virginians into the city. And since Baltimore is a place where business is done largely on a basis of knowing the fellow you're dealing with, these Virginians, being widely acquainted in the South, were able to tell Baltimore merchants precisely who was and who was not a good credit risk in the South. With this special information, Baltimore was enabled to extend longer term credits to the South than Philadelphia or New York could, and in that way got more than her share of the business.

Up until World War I, the character of Baltimore was a somewhat more cohesive and integrated thing than it has subsequently become. Until that time it had been principally a shipping and distributing center, with easy, old-fashioned ways, with hand and heart just as open as were its sewers. It was moderately, but only moderately, industrialized. Having started out as a tobacco-growing and milling center, it had later come to manufacture some textiles and to smelt and process metals. In fact, it was over a length of Baltimore-made wire that the first official telegraph message was flashed. The town had for many years processed such traditional products as the canned oysters with which it led the world and gorged the West. To keep the rain off the straw hats it so copiously produced, it made innumerable umbrellas, a product it claimed to have introduced to America and about which it crowed: "Born in Baltimore, raised all over the world." Besides, since it was located a little north of the bourbon belt, it was necessary to run off an occasional drap of Maryland rye.

Nevertheless, the decade following its great fire in 1904 found Baltimore in the doldrums. Its industrial expansion was by no means keeping pace with that of Philadelphia and New York. To most Baltimoreans, this seemed inexcusable. Baltimore, as a port, not only had a definite geographical advantage, in being closer to the inland marts of the Middle West than her other two principal competitors, but she had an overland freight rate that was made in heaven. Comparatively speaking, her taxes, from the standpoint of attracting industry, were not out of line. After considerable surveying and public meeting, Baltimore leaders decided that what kept the gold out of their till was the lead in their pants. They went, albeit quietly, over onto the offensive.

Twenty-five years later, they took stock to see what, if anything, had been accomplished. In the meantime of course there had been a World War, but that could be canceled out by the great depression in the Thirties. The result seemed to reflect not merely progress or healthy evolution but what amounted almost to revolutionary advancement. Light-industry Baltimore had become heavily industrialized. Both wages and value of products had tripled and the city's business had well outstripped the rate of growth of either Philadelphia or New York. Her range of products encompassed almost everything from rails to spices, while her bonding and insurance houses, despite ups and downs, had kept right on growing. Between that time, 1939, and this, Baltimore has of course been producing full tilt.

Of all Baltimore industries the biggest today is the Bethlehem steel plant on Sparrows Point. This plant, America's only huge one on tidewater, blithely ignores the old rule that one must set up in the steel business where coal, ore and limestone are locally plentiful. It buys its limestone from the Maryland-Pennsylvania border, its coal from West Virginia or most anywhere. Its ore comes from such unlikely places as Chile and other South American republics. Yet, because of the mill's close proximity to the Eastern market, along with other factors such as access to the sea, it is said that this plant is the most economical in the Bethlehem empire when all costs, distributing as well as producing, are taken into account.

The fortunes that have grown out of Baltimore's industry and commerce have by no means all been frittered away on yachts and cuddly chorus girls, but have often been devoted to the cultural enrichment of the city. Baltimore has received such priceless gifts as the Peabody Institute from George Peabody, its beautiful Pratt Library from Enoch Pratt, and, its brightest diadem, the beginnings of its great hospital, medical college and university, Johns Hopkins, from its late citizen of that name.

Baltimore is a city with a truly fine and proud heritage in medical research, medical education and just plain curing sick folks. The huge and famous old Johns Hopkins hospital and medical school are, architecturally, mostly very 1880, made of smoked red brick and topped by domes of slightly less than Byzantine fatness. More modern are such later additions as the Brady urological wing, donated by Diamond Jim in a fit of appreciation for some timely plumbing repairs. The academic department of the university is entirely separate and housed in charming, Georgian buildings which take their architectural tone from adjacent Homewood, the lovely old house built by Declaration-of-Independence-signing Charles Carroll of Carrollton and which now contains the office of the president of the university. But for all its beauty and excellence and the incidental fact that it is frequently a national champ in lacrosse, it's hard for the academic school to attain the enormous prestige that the Johns Hopkins medical department commands not only over the nation, but even in its own home town.

For just as Cheyenne is a ranchers' town and San Antonio a soldiers' town, so Baltimore is, to a considerable degree, a medicine man's town, where such names as Osler, Welch, Kelly and Halstead are still magic words. It's a town where the cops recognize the automobiles of and wave at such distinguished physicians as Dr. Louis

Hamburger, who, by the way, was the first student to register at Johns Hopkins.

As it happens, medicine is also the strong point of the University of Maryland, which has the oldest dental school in the nation. Likewise, it has its own modern hospital, beside which Johns Hopkins would look seedy if it happened to have another name. But the municipally owned Baltimore City Hospitals compose the city's largest refuge for the ailing.

Yet Baltimore has other facilities conducive to health that involve no pills or thermometers. Most important of these is, of course, its own inland sea, Chesapeake Bay, for bathing, fishing and sailing. There are special types of Chesapeake boats such as the skipjack and the log canoe, both of which sport sharply raked masts. But it is by no means necessary to own a boat to cruise on the Chesapeake. A Baltimorean with fifty cents in cash and his lunch in a shoe-box can make a day of it in a passenger steamer. And finally, Baltimore's got a bill of fare full of items that should contribute not only to health but to happiness.

Many Baltimoreans feel that Chesapeake Bay oysters are the finest in the world. Perhaps that claim is excessive, but it can be accurately said that they are absolutely wonderful. In fact Baltimore politics are built around the oyster roast in winter and the crab feast in summer. Many modern Baltimoreans have lost their taste for bloody duck— mere singed raw duck which some of their aging forefathers felt tended to accent the caveman in those who partook of it. In the same way, these moderns have largely abandoned the time-consuming old Maryland custom of whaling biscuit dough for half an hour with a club or the flat side of a hatchet, even if beaten biscuits were all the rage in their mothers' time. But they still go for Maryland oyster fritters, which they call "flitters." There are cooks from points more southerly who do not regard fried chicken Maryland as the last word in this department. But there are few sections that would dare to claim a greater understanding of what to do with a diamond-back terrapin.

Terrapin is not a dish one sees as often in Baltimore as, say, turnip greens or its good unsweetened cornbread. Terrapin is a party dish usually reserved for champagne occasions. Local connoisseurs say it's best prepared in Baltimore's exclusive Maryland Club, which is not late but early George Apley. Yet even more exclusive, if that be possible, is the Bachelors' Cotillon. It is at this club's germans that the daughters of Baltimore's bon ton make their debuts, and there are not enough strings to be pulled in Baltimore to get you invited to one of these functions unless, in the eyes of the club members, you belong. Money is entirely beside the point, so far as invitations are concerned, and some Baltimoreans regard the Cotillon as a monopolistically restrictive social holding company, since failure to receive an invitation has broken many a poor little rich girl's heart. However, this Cotillon is a perfect means by which an old but momentarily strapped family may launch its dimity debutante. At these functions social Baltimore is on its best behavior and is squired by liveried footmen. These attendants, unlike those at the Maryland Club, are not black, but white.

Baltimore's Negroes, who compose about a quarter of its population, have not as yet been heavily absorbed into industry. Nevertheless, despite the overcrowding of all races and the tensions which such a situation breeds, Baltimore had no serious race flare-ups during the war.

Baltimore is the headquarters of the large, shrill Negro daily, the *Afro-American*. But Baltimore is also the home of hoary G. Lake Imes, a Negro colleague of Booker T. Washington. "There are two kinds of people working for the Negro," Dr. Imes says. "One I call 'the smart boys.' They say, 'I'm going to hit you on the head and take what's coming to me.' The others, the side I'm on, want to work for the recognition we really deserve."

Though Baltimore is part of a state which considers itself Southern, her Negroes vote freely at the polls. Yet the town as a whole may legitimately complain of taxation without adequate representation since, through a rotten borough system, it is the counties that control the state government over in lovely, near-by Annapolis—this, despite the fact that over half of Maryland lives in Baltimore.

Baltimore is, of course, the place where the Middies play their "home games" when they want to draw a crowd and make some money. These games are held in Baltimore's Municipal Stadium where until, embarrassingly, a number of the seats rotted away and fell down, 90,000 people could be wedged in. The Baltimore Orioles also play in the Stadium these days, since their own establishment has burned down.

But what sporting Baltimore loves best of all, as much almost as it loved the perennial lotteries that were held in the old days, is to see a fast horse switch his tail and come charging out of the starting gate at Baltimore's own Pimlico track, where the nation's Number Two racing attraction, the Preakness, is run in May. When nothing is going on at Pimlico, it's not too much of a trip to run up to Havre de Grace or any of a number of other Maryland tracks, which, it is estimated, pay the state enough taxes to buy each of the counties ten new fire wagons per year.

Horsy Marylanders also love to bang themselves up steeple-chasing in such spring classics as the Maryland Hunt Cup, the Grand National, and the Milady's Manor Point-To-Point races. Many of these same folk like, on Thanksgiving, to don the old pink coat, have a spot of hunting breakfast, get the hounds blessed, and, emitting now a discreet "Yoicks!" and again a spirited "Tally-ho!", tear out in pursuit of Br'er Fox. Also, in the counties, are held tilting tournaments in which riders spear little rings en route and, to add to the fun, observe a good many of the customs followed by the King Arthur set at an earlier time.

Less exalted Baltimoreans find amusement after dark in the haunts of East Baltimore street, known as "the Block," an area inhabited by burlesque shows and crummy honky-tonks. One of these, the Oasis, proudly advertised itself as "the world's worst night club." But in general, Baltimore, which sailors consider a graveyard, doesn't go in much for night clubs, and usually manages to entertain itself with more civilized devices, such as its Symphony Orchestra or the Vagabond Theater, the oldest noncommercial dramatic group in the nation, which has not missed a lick for thirty years.

Baltimore's Walters Art Gallery has a larger, and some feel better, art collection than the newer Baltimore Museum of Art, but the Museum has by far the more impressive plant and has fallen heir to the private collection of Baltimore's late, lively merchant, Jacob Epstein, a collection which experts declare is worth in excess of a couple of millions. Eventually, the Museum is due to inherit the Cone Collection, said to be the finest private collection of modern French painting in America.

The city's art urge has found additional expression due to considerable local deposits of marble, which it not only fashioned into doorsteps but carved up into statues. Baltimore, which is sometimes called "the monumental city," even has a monument to the repeal of the Eighteenth Amendment. Baltimoreans can entertain themselves by looking askance at a couple of rather extraordinary monuments to Francis Scott Key and perhaps with more solid pleasure at the Battle Monument, which commemorates the Battle of North Point, when the townfolk chased the British away in 1814—not that any physical reminder is needed to make Baltimore recollect that it's the only great city on the Eastern seaboard that has never fallen into the hands of an enemy. Baltimore has a Parthenon-like World War I memorial, but the most impressive statue in town, the one known simply as "the monument," is on Mount Vernon and Washington Places, where George Washington stands atop a massive marble column, the whole structure towering 204 feet above the four handsome esplanades that lead to its base.

It is here in Mount Vernon Place that Baltimore holds its annual Flower Mart in May, a kind of one-day county fair in which the ladies sell flowers and homemade pies and cakes, the kids ride ponies, and local artists hopefully display their work, the while a merry-go-round chases its tail with springtime abandon.

When in an outdoor mood, Baltimoreans may simply go picnicking in the city's 3,700 acres of parks or in the cooler, near-by hills. But whatever they do for pleasure, they seem to do with a lack of the haste and/or hysteria that sometimes characterizes the actions of people living in higher-keyed cities where the remorseless pace and pressure tend, in some degree, to dehumanize them. For while Baltimore is neither a lazy city nor a decadent city, it does have poise. Its people generally seem to have learned that, although it's absolutely essential to earn a living, it's also a good idea to get a little fun out of life—and to have that fun casually, simply, and without straining or working at it.

In the long run, when all Baltimore's factual contradictions are forgotten or ignored and when the agreeably evanescent quality of the old town is felt rather than discussed, this probably least spectacular and least caricaturable of great American cities seems to amount to an especially harmonic whole. And after even a relatively short stay, the visitor is apt to regard the Baltimorean a little enviously, having come, even during a brief visit, to believe, like his host, that Baltimore is a wonderful place to live in—and complain about.

5: *Dallas-Fort Worth*

THE MOST dangerous man that ever lived in Texas was named Jim Bowie. He rode alligators bareback, and when he fought a knife fight he liked to hold one corner of a handkerchief in his teeth while his opponent bit into and held the opposite corner. When either duelist got enough, he could stop the fight by turning loose the handkerchief.

But in the long fight between Dallas and Fort Worth, the thirty-mile strip of land that inadequately separates these cities can't be turned loose. Both towns are built immovably into the earth, tightly entangled in each other's hair. They stand belligerently facing each other at close quarters, like two bull chickens in a pit with hackles blooming. And nothing so enraptures either combatant as to plunge his gaff into his neighbor.

More often than not it has been a healthy, actually a profitable, rivalry. Just as two pigs in the same pen will gobble more corn and gain more weight than if they lived separately, so have these cities extended themselves to extraordinary degree, spurred, even after their own self-interest had been served, by a gnawing, wagon-green jealousy. Certainly this brawl has been carried on so noisily that the Southwest has been made much more conscious of these cities than it otherwise might have been.

At times, however, this rivalry has resulted in antics that were peevish and detrimental to both. For example, according to Tom Gooch, of the Dallas *Times Herald*, a Dallas coffin manufacturer once had to ship his wares for Fort Worth via St. Louis because people in Fort Worth wouldn't be caught dead in anything from Dallas. In later times there could have been a great airport halfway between Dallas and Fort Worth, and convenient to both. By combining to build one great central field, each combatant could have saved half the cost of an airport. But once a squabble developed over whose side the administration building should be located on, negotiations were broken off, and each city had to supply its own facilities. As a result, the transcontinental air service of each has been precisely halved. Instead of stopping all planes at the midway airport, the trunk airlines employ skip-stops, landing half their planes in Fort Worth and the other half in Dallas.

Much of this conflict undoubtedly derives from the antipathetic natures of the two cities themselves, as in the case of Sparta and Athens. Down in his secret heart, the zealous Fort Worth citizen thinks of his Dallas neighbor as a pallid, money-changing, road-show Texan, and the particularly sophisticated Dallasite may admit, in the bosom of the family, to the belief that his Fort Worth brother is a barbarian.

There are natural reasons why Fort Worth, along the old Chisholm Trail, should have a Western flavor and why a man in Eastward-looking Dallas can wear spats in comparative safety.

Fort Worth, "Where the West begins," is a cow town, a big-hearted, loud-mouthed, "Howdy, stranger" town. It is the capital city of that magnificent realm of Western ranch lands that stretch west to New Mexico and northward almost to Kansas and Colorado. In much of this land rain is a curiosity and everything either "sticks, stings or stinks." And the sturdy Western folk with the rawhide hands and the high-heeled boots rub off on a town where they bank and buy and frolic. Fort Worth probably comes nearer expressing what the word "Texas" signifies to most outlanders than any other city in the state. In its efforts to make a hit with the outside world, its problem is simple: it has simply to be itself, exuberant and whooping and friendly, since nearly everybody loves a Western story.

Dallas has a much more complex problem. "Big D," as it likes to be called, reflects an altogether different region and way of life. In earlier times it was shut off, even shielded, from the frontier by the outpost city lying just to the west. Dallas grew up in a more orderly fashion into a town with a metropolitan population of a half-million plus, and where the natural emphasis was upon the virtues of the account book instead of those of the open range. It became the happy hunting ground of the farmers of North Texas who, with tame mule rather than fiery bronc, processed the fertility of the great ribbon of black land that stripes the state from north to south.

The demands of Dallas' vanity and pride will not allow it simply to relax and be itself. If it did, it would be a routine, branch-house, insurance and banking town—prosperous no doubt, but boring. And Dallas, with as much of a flair for the theatrical as Sam Houston ever had, will die and be damned before it will submit to being routine and uninteresting. Though in actuality it exists under the icy control of its banks, it's determined to be human and interesting, even compelling. In this direction it has, to understate the case, done a job that is absolutely remarkable.

Dallas has undertaken to become the Athens of the alfalfa fields, the cultural capital of the Southwest. For a raw Texas business town, that was a big order. This municipal aspiration was bound to be confusing to many a hitherto poor family that had got rich on East Texas oil or who had happened to snag the wholesale agency for a good line of farm equipment. But in a way that's really amazing, they all pitched in and played the game, even if some of them had no very definite idea of what the score was. They just knew that, culture-wise, Dallas had climbed into the saddle, and they meant to keep it there. For though Dallas is, in essence, a Southern city, rather than a Western one, still it is bathed with the rampant emotional juices of Texas and is, therefore, Southern in a more than ordinarily virile way. And in Texas, it doesn't matter what you are so long as you're the best of the breed. When Dallas puts on a concert or an art show, it does it in precisely the same way its sister city stages a rodeo. It's playing for keeps. A few musicians or painters may get trampled in the rush, but everybody will know he's been somewhere.

Whether Dallas culture results from a yearning in the souls of the people for the higher things of life or, as some skeptics charge, from a desire on the part of the local Medici to show their muscle, its achievements are actual and real. Those who think of Texans with a six-gun in one hand and a chili bowl in the other, both smoking, may be surprised to learn that Dallas is one of the biggest book towns in the nation. While the average per-capita expenditure for books in the United States is about $1.50 a year, that of the average Dallasite is six dollars. Dallas' Cokesbury bookstore, from a standpoint of elegance and size, need take a back seat to none on earth. Annually this store sells one and a quarter million dollars' worth of books, which is said to be more than any other American store dealing exclusively in books. Elizabeth Ann McMurray, whose bookshop is totally unimpressive in size, is a potent factor in American publishing. Perhaps the keenest point of competition between the two Dallas newspapers is the rivalry between their book sections.

Not only is Dallas a town that visiting authors love, because it makes such a pleasing fuss over them, but it's downright sympathetic to struggling young artists in a way that Paris and London, San Francisco and New York, have been at varying stages of these cities' careers. Dallas' first Book Fair, a huge success, left home-town book folk laid out in rows of emotional exhaustion.

Some of the town's leading patrons of the arts are members of Dallas' rich Petroleum Club. Here you are apt to encounter such distinguished men as E. DeGolyer, often spoken of as the world's leading geologist. He not only has had the foresight to pick up a few millions in the oil business, but is also an historian. One of the liveliest spots in the Petroleum Club will be the table where Tom Knight, one of Texas' most brilliant lawyers and conversationalists, is noisily playing gin rummy. And if you're from out of town and he likes you, he may take you to the Thirteen Club, Dallas' most exclusive, where for thirty years thirteen local men, among them, John H. McGinnis, the dean of Texas letters, have met once a month to dine and discuss the problems of the day.

One of Dallas' latest cultural upheavals has been the relaunching of its Symphony orchestra, which the war had temporarily put out of business. To get it going again, D. Gordon Rupe, Jr., a young Dallas investment banker, sold 150 founder memberships at $1,000 each, and 1,000 sponsor memberships at $100 a throw. The city itself kittied in $10,000.

Approximately three months after the agitation started, the new

Symphony made its debut under the baton of handsome, smartly tailored Antal Dorati. By that time so much work, suffering and spiritual torture on the part of everybody had gone into getting ready that Dallas was already worked up to concert pitch.

To begin with, Dorati and his eighty-three-piece orchestra cut loose on Beethoven's *Eroica*. When John Rosenfield, amusements critic for the Dallas *News*, got hold of his typewriter, he let go with both hands. He wrote that the crowd was "stirred by the excellence of the ensemble that will bear Dallas' name. To many, grown realistic and cynical during the year's cultural struggles, the new orchestra was an unbelievably precious gift. . . . Dismissing the feelings caused by the impact of the occasion, the more casual listener, if there was one, heard a splendid new orchestra that is, already, a big-league operation. . . . The dainty dynamic scale and gossamer delicacy of the scherzo was the first breath-taking disclosure of the orchestra's virtuosity. . . ."

Almost immediately after this triumph RCA Victor invited the fine new orchestra to join with Yehudi Menuhin in cutting an album of Red Seal records and, with a delicacy as gossamer as that of the scherzo, beatitude settled down over Dallas.

The town is rabid about all branches of the arts. It turns out in force for such exotic spectacles as the ballet and the opera. However, Dallas' detractors enjoy pointing out that desperadoes Bonnie Parker and Clyde Barrow were both manifestations of Dallas' vaunted culture, as is the "East Dallas Special," a kind of curving blade with which to treat thy neighbor to sudden evisceration. Some Texans also charge Dallas' elite with an inordinate love of expensive display, particularly in regard to raiment.

There's some truth in that. It is the conviction of many qualified observers that Dallas has, as a whole, the best-groomed women in America—which, these days, probably means in the world. In the first place, it's easy to keep clean in smokeless, natural-gas-burning Dallas. Secondly, it has what even New York and Paris haven't got: a single style dictator, Stanley Marcus, of internationally famous Neiman-Marcus Specialty Store. To show the length to which this influence spreads, chain-store buyers buy one class of goods for their other Texas stores, but a simpler line for Dallas, so that their customers can look as if they bought their clothes from Neiman-Marcus.

Almost as swank as a Neiman-Marcus label is a Highland Park address, which means you live in one of the most beautiful residential sections in America. For that matter, Dallas even has a highly restricted industrial park where the more refined types of industry can go, with assurance that forthcoming neighbors will make neither smoke, noise, nor unpleasant smells.

Dallas can afford to pay for all these things and live on this lofty scale since, so far as the Southwest is concerned, it is first in total business volume, wholesale distributing, number of manufacturing plants, bank deposits and insurance. It is the biggest inland cotton market in the world, and it sits squarely in the middle of some 70 per cent of the nation's oil production. With a per family income of $3,597 in 1940, it had the sixth highest family buying power of any city in the land. In fact, only recently it passed a $40,000,000 bond issue for the purpose of making itself still more beautiful and better equipped with cultural plant, thereby substantially furthering its ambition to become the Versailles of the Trinity Forks.

But all this wealth and power and flamboyance does not even dent Forth Worth's brashness or its determination to get the jump on Dallas at every hand. In some respects, it can move faster, since it's pretty much of a one-man town. Indeed, the three principal historical events in the Fort Worth story are (1) when the Texas and Pacific railroad came to town in 1876, (2) when the stockyards were built at the turn of the century and (3) a dozen or so years later when Amon Carter moved in.

And there are no two ways about it. Amon Carter is Mr. Fort Worth. He has been its dynamo for so long that he has come to resemble the town and it to resemble him. They both wear good Justin boots and Stetson hats. For years Amon Carter has given visiting firemen these big Western hats as a token of Fort Worth hospitality—in two sizes: three-inch brims to medium shots, and five-inch brims to thoroughgoing big shots. His newspaper, the *Star-Telegram*, is a highly vocal spokesman for the Fort Worth cause (as, for that matter, is the Fort Worth *Press*), and when Mr. Carter has to go to Dallas on business, he carries his own lunch, in order to avoid making even so small a purchase as a hamburger from the Philistines.

In this rivalry, it's natural that Forth Worth's teeth should be sharper since, population-wise, it is still the underdog with a metropolitan population of only 288,000. When the war came, Fort Worth out-hustled its rival in acquiring war contracts, got the forty-acre, four-fifths-of-a-mile-long Consolidated plant, that noticeably outbulged any in the area.

Today Fort Worth not only builds 200-passenger planes and processes much of the nutriment that sustains a skillet-happy Texas, but manufactures chemicals, oil-field equipment, textiles, etc., which had an over-all value of a quarter of a billion dollars in 1945. Though Fort Worth's T.P. yards are enormous, the railroad's handsome twelve-story office building remained empty until the war started and the Army occupied it. The company had built it to house its own general offices but, according to the Fort Worth Chamber of Commerce, Fort Worth's arch-enemy just wouldn't let the T.P. head offices out of her clutches.

There is, however, one fundamental trend in Texas agriculture which nobody can stop, and which plays straight into Fort Worth's hand. That is the continuing movement in Texas away from cotton and corn and toward cow, sow and hen. And every North Texas farmer who switches to ranching has his thinking and business re-oriented to fall within Fort Worth's orbit. In fact, the first two things a man wants to know when he is buying a ranch in this region are: (1) the annual local rainfall and (2) the distance to Fort Worth's one hundred acres of stockyards, where, daily, a thousand truckloads of livestock arrive at their last roundup. To live farther than a night's haul away from these yards means an expensive and troublesome stop-over at some intermediate pasture, with all that implies of vexatious unloading and reloading. This is especially true these days since India's sacred but all-fired rambunctious cows, the Brahmas, are becoming more numerous in Texas, where they are still willing to be worshiped in the open, but will fight you like a prong-horned tiger if you try to hem them in.

Fort Worth's Western tendencies are expressed in the way the town itself is built. In the first place, its city limits are of the wide-ranging Los Angeles type, and it's not too unusual to find a cow pasture or a copse of scrub-oak woods here and there. Yet these pastoral touches are minor indeed compared to the city's 10,400 acres of rambling parks, which is claimed to be the largest per-capita park acreage of any principal city in the United States. But even that's not enough to satisfy Fort Worth's outdoor-loving people. In a recent $20,000,000 bond issue, $1,200,000 was earmarked for more parks and playgrounds. Its flower-smothered Botanic Garden in Rock Springs Park would make cow town Fort Worth the Elysian fields to Ferdinand the Bull. Its heifer-built Rivercrest section and its more brand-spanking-new oil-built Westover Hills are, if not the biggest fine residential sections in Texas, still beautiful and beyond the reach of the likes of you and me. But you don't have to be a millionaire to enjoy the fishing and boating and other water sports on the forty square miles of artificial lakes in Fort Worth's immediate vicinity.

Characteristically, Fort Worth's biggest yearly festival is the Fat Stock Show. Right before God and New York's Madison Square Garden, Fort Worth declares its own rodeo, held in conjunction with the Stock Show, is the biggest indoor rodeo on earth. For that matter, many of the broncs and Brahmas that appear in rodeos the world over have been able to see the tops of the Forth Worth skyscrapers throughout their colt- and calf-hood, and many a leading roper and rider calls Fort Worth home.

For nearly fifty years the Stock Show was held in the North Side Coliseum, out by the stockyards. Lots of Fort Worth people grow misty-eyed at memory of the color and excitement and huge smells that always filled Exchange Avenue at Stock-Show time in March, when hat brims were sombrero-wide and every heel was raised three inches off the ground, when drinking and fighting and wild horse riding were the order of the day.

Certain progressive citizens had tried for years to move the Stock Show to the more elegant Will Rogers Memorial Coliseum and Auditorium on the other side of town, but the result had been open insurrection. Ranchers from all over Texas swore they would not send their cattle to such a high-toned neighborhood where neither they nor the cows could be properly relaxed. But when the war came, the North Side Coliseum became a war plant and the Stock Show moved to the more elaborate quarters.

These buildings are a memorial not only to Will Rogers, but to the climax of the rivalry between Dallas and Fort Worth. To reduce the focus, it was an all-out head butting between Amon Carter of Fort Worth and Banker Robert Thornton of Dallas. In the early 'Thirties, the Texas legislature was trying to decide where to hold the state's official Centennial Exposition in 'Thirty-six. Every city in Texas fought hard to get it. But Bob Thornton got it for Dallas when he told the legislative committee, "We've got the plant, we've got the money and, to show our pride in Texas, we've got the guts to spend it." The plant to which Mr. Thornton referred was the group of fine buildings where Dallas annually holds the Texas State Fair, "Show Window of the Southwest." And when he promised the committee that Dallas could get up $12,000,000 in public and private funds, he'd bought himself a centennial exposition.

Amon Carter was out of the state at the time, but when he heard Dallas would get the Centennial, it threw him in a hard bind. Had Houston or San Antonio been the lucky city, he would not have felt so directly invited into the fight. But he just couldn't stand by and see Dallas wallow, unchallenged, in all that glory.

He rallied Fort Worth's business people and found them ready for the fray. Then he made a public pronunciamento. Fort Worth, he said, would stage a centennial celebration on its own, and one that would make Dallas' look like a Sunday-school picnic.

Now that the fat was in the fire, the long distance phone lines began crackling like a Chinese celebration. Mr. Carter got hold of Billy Rose and offered him a thousand dollars a day for a hundred days if he would come to Fort Worth and put on a show that not only couldn't be beat but couldn't be tied.

Over in Dallas, Bob Thornton and his cohorts stood at the Rubicon. The question was whether to make their show cultural and dignified, thereby inviting grave risks at the box office, or whether to seize onto the sure-fire old carnival maxim of "kewpies, curiosity and sex." Uplift won.

Also in the Dallas camp, crafty Bill Kittrell, famed in Texas political circles for his ability to turn water into wine, was waging a powerful and successful campaign to bring big-time industrial exhibitors to the Dallas exposition. At the same time he was busily organizing a five-alarm pageant to be called *Cavalcade of Texas*, which was to have a typically dashing Kittrellesque flair. He persuaded D. W. Griffith, who'd done all right with *The Birth of a Nation*, to come to Dallas and lend a hand.

Both cities began to stump the nation. Amon Carter plastered the state with billboards and posters saying: "Go to Dallas for education. Come to Fort Worth for entertainment."

Dallas, with the full weight of the state of Texas behind it, staged a smash exhibition and, knowing how Texans love their own state history, chinned itself on each bar of the Lone Star flag. The price of admission was only fifty cents, and the Dallas show naturally sold more tickets than the Fort Worth Frontier Exposition which featured Billy Rose's show, a large and lavish night club called *Casa Mañana*, which cost the reveler a minimum of $2.20, with dinner included. Rose mounted his production on a hundred-foot revolving stage. It was loaded with pretty girls in various conditions of deshabille. There were no kewpies at *Casa Mañana*, but Sally Rand fanned interest in the other two carnival musts. What's more, the customers left singing the brand-new hit tune, "The Night Is Young and You're So Beautiful." Even today it's hard to find a Texan who'll admit that he ever saw a better show.

Of course both cities lost money on their spectacles, but that wasn't the point. The idea of each was to outdo its rival's show. Texas ruled that it was a draw. And both sides came out bloody but unbowed.

But if these municipal Kilkenny cats make the fur fly on every other problem, there is one at least upon which harmony has, in the nature of things, had to prevail. And that is with regard to the proposed canalization of the Trinity River, which runs through both cities and which Boyce House, Fort Worth humorist, says is the only river in the world where the catfish have to swim backwards to keep the mud out of their eyes.

Both cities are dedicated to the job of making the hundreds of intervening miles of the river navigable to the sea, and are supporters of the Trinity Improvement Association. Of course Amon Carter has virtually got a shovel in his hand most of the time. In fact, before his friend Will Rogers died, Mr. Carter spoke so lyrically and with such confidence on the outcome of this project that Will closed his eyes, leaned back in his chair and said, "Amon, I can see the sea gulls now."

But one of the most colorful figures in the canal project, or any other, for that matter, was the late great Commodore Basil Hatfield, to use only two of his eighteen names. He was a man with Buffalo Bill whiskers, a brave, round belly, and a dancing eye. He'd made and spent three fortunes, run guns to South America, organized the first standing Chinese army, once had a whole floor of Fort Worth's Neal P. Anderson Building for his oil company, from which he went, at the behest of the Federal government, to tend the roses in Leavenworth's gardens. But the Commodore was not a man to be disheartened by an occasional sojourn in the pokey. Eventually he built a scow and navigated it down the river from Fort Worth to the Gulf and back up again. He named his scow the "Amen" Carter, and when Mr. Carter complained of the misspelling, the Commodore said he knew what he was about. "In Fort Worth," said the Commodore, "you are the first word and also the last word. Therefore I have named my vessel the Amen Carter."

C. L. Douglas, managing editor of the Fort Worth *Press* and biographer of Texas' great sons, says that many a time the Commodore spent his last dollar for sweet-potato slips or castor beans or persimmon seeds, to hand out among the Valley people that they and the possums might fatten and prosper. He taught them to make filters of charcoal and sand for clearing the mud from their drinking water. He was the Messiah of the lower valley, and every man was his friend. He refused to cut his hair until the lower valley was canalized.

Recently, however, the Commodore passed away, and great numbers of the river folk feel bereft at his departure.

To open the river to barge traffic from the Gulf to Dallas and Fort Worth would require a system of locks that would lift the vessels 670 feet, would cost a good many millions, plus the political effort necessary to shout down the railroads who, understandably, do not want their freight rates imperiled by barge competition. But many a war-wise young Texan who has seen islands and harbors and cities remade under fire in a matter of days considers the job less awesome than at an earlier time. Too, there is in this whole Southwestern land a pervading spirit of youthfulness—with all that implies of boldness and rawness and lack of any real consideration for its minorities. Texans adore the strong, are impatient with the weak. They are willing to tackle almost anything, and tend toward a belief that whatever they tackle can be done.

These two young cities are, in effect, the two parts which might have formed a super Southwestern Kansas City. As it happens, they are slightly separated, and each has made itself agreeable to the temperament and tastes of the dissimilar regions that support it. But the character which each, in the beginning, assumed has since become frozen. Through the hundred years of their existences, the manner that each had acquired served to channel Western-minded immigrants into Fort Worth and those with slightly less wild and woolly interests into Dallas. Moreover, each of the several generations of children grew up with points of view shaped by their town's attitudes and aspirations. It's as natural that John William Rogers of the *Times Herald* and Lon Tinkle of the *News*, both Dallas boys, should grow up with an active interest in almost all the arts as that Fort Worth's ranching, horse-racing Waggoner boys should, at least for a time, pull out of Texas when pari-mutuel betting was outlawed.

Devoid of the broad buffer area that usually separates cities, it was in the cards that these virile, never-say-die towns should be intense rivals, and that they should slug in the clinches. Yet these cities have spread physically into broader confluence and have come more and more to resemble a single population pool. Many of their people are beginning to wonder how, in general, any new development that affects one city favorably could help being beneficial to the other—and especially so far as the Trinity project is concerned. Should the canal ever be completed, and one North Texan has said, "We'll sure as hell either canalize it or pave it"—it might become a symbol of unity overriding a sometimes chauvinistic intercity rivalry. For there are omens that Dallas and Fort Worth may have to pull together against the challenge of Tulsa and Oklahoma City, who have officially buried the hatchet and formed an entente to go after North Texas business.

Today there are many citizens in Fort Worth and Dallas, which together form the Souths' largest population pool, more interested in future co-operation than in past throat-cutting rivalry. Their attitude has been summed up by North-Texan Dr. George W. Truett when he gave the toast: "Hats off to the past! Coats off to the future!"

6: *San Francisco*

THE THING about San Francisco is not so much what it is as what it does to you. In the first place, it's in California, which to many Americans is a dynamic and intoxicating circumstance, else why the great and continuing hegira to this fastest-growing state? Secondly, it is a seaport, and any busy seaport, with its ships and foreign flags, its kaleidoscopic smells and dripping ropes, enlivens the imagination and laces it with fancy.

Then, whether a city be Boston or Bagdad, its traditions and the character of its past have a way of seeping into you, accenting your moods and tinting their flavor.

And if you find yourself in a place whose past has often been detonated with fires and gold rushes, vice and tong wars, if the sky is strung with bridges on which a man has much the feeling of a flea crossing the base of a concert harp, if the downtown street corners are ablaze with blossoms, if the more exuberant streetcars are virtually airborne, and if, every now and then, the very earth itself hauls off and does the jelly roll, then, friend, you're in San Francisco, the city where anything can happen, and most things already have.

San Francisco has the feeling of a Graustark devised by Bret Harte, Mark Twain, Jack London, and Robert Louis Stevenson, plus a couple of dashes of Saroyan—all of whose imaginations are woven into the emotional fabric of the town.

As a result of some kind of necromantic contagion, you find that, unlike the novitiate Los Angeleno who dons a purple shirt and cuts his britches off at the thighs to show that he has broken loose from the conventionality of his Eastern or Midwestern birthplace, you yourself, in your San Francisco incarnation, undergo a change that is entirely subjective. Your point of view becomes that of a cloak-and-sword character who, consciously pleased with the deceit, masquerades in plain clothes. Clothes, by the way, from which the fog, just in passing, has quietly eliminated the creases as it went about its more serious business of enshrouding the town in mystery and moist, but exciting, romance.

It's as fine a place to sit around and talk as Vienna was in the good days. It's civilized and robust, and its shoulder won't fit a chip. When you point out something wrong with the place, its people relish that defect too—because it's a valid part of San Francisco.

Unlike most American cities, much of its growth has been reluctant. Profoundly convinced it is the best town in America, it doesn't get worked up about trying to be the biggest. As a matter of principle, it judiciously resists mere change for change's sake, and seldom confuses commotion with progress.

In normal times San Francisco has a much easier gait than its hyperthyroid sister to the south. Perhaps it's natural that a financial center, whose Montgomery Street is called "The Wall Street of the West," should be in some ways more conservative. Not that Mr. Henry Kaiser, from the inboard side of the Bay, is wanting in showmanship. Or, for that matter, is A. P. Giannini, head of the Bank of America National Trust and Savings Association. And even though more conservative San Francisco financiers look down their noses at the ballyhoo Mr. Giannini has introduced into banking, he is nevertheless in a position now and again to claim that his Bank of America is the biggest on earth. Yet the accomplishments of these men are hardly a match for the aspirations of young Paul C. Smith, general manager of San Francisco's only home-owned newspaper, the *Chronicle*. He's all set to get a dam built across the Bay so that the San Pablo end will become a body of fresh water available for industrial uses. He also talks of building the dominant newspaper in the whole West, and of perhaps eventually giving Seattle ten-minute delivery service via radio-controlled rocket. But he says that his over-all ambition is to raise the per-capita income of the hundreds of millions of people living in the Pacific basin by two bits a year. This last, he says, is still in the laugh stage. But he wasn't laughing when he told it to me. He has settled West Coast strikes when nobody else could, has been petitioned by

48,000 San Franciscans to run for mayor. But at the moment there is the little matter of trying to whittle down the 100,000 circulation lead held by Mr. Hearst's *Examiner* which, by the way, was the first paper Mr. Hearst ever owned. The *Examiner* people somewhat condescendingly say, "We try to help the *Chronicle*. We're afraid that if they folded, some tough competition might come to town." The competition between the afternoon *News* and *Call-Bulletin* is another cat-fight altogether.

At present, San Francisco is experiencing some important sociological and economic changes. (1) It is emerging more and more from the dominant influence of its old families such as the Crockers, Phelans, Sutros, Fleishhackers, and, a name famous in every Pacific port, the Dollars. (2) It is going through the jolting process of changing over from a lumber-mining-farming-shipping economy into one where industry is of equal prominence. But its favorite period is still the roaring 'Eighties, and sentimental San Francisco warmly treasures and savors the traditions and physical oddments of the past. It was angry when the bridges put most of the ferryboats out of business. It loves to gaze upon the late Cleveland, early McKinley architecture in which the town still abounds. Many San Franciscans would feel seriously out of the swim if they did not know Sally Stanford, often mentioned by the press as "the town's most distinguished Madam," who holds forth in what is widely and erroneously believed to be the "Anna Held house," milk bath and all, which is a cozy meeting place for politicians and the fellows who come off the late shifts of the newspapers. At heart—and it is demonstrated in a thousand pleasant ways—San Francisco is still gas-lit.

One of the busiest and best-loved relics of its gas-lit days is the little cable cars, often almost out of sight beneath their human cargoes, which still roll up and down her steep hills. When you see the faces of the people riding the cable cars, you understand why San Franciscans love them so much. For as people mount these little fugitives from a Gay Nineties carnival, there comes over their faces a sheepish expression of not-wholly-hidden delight, and they no longer look upon their fellow-man, hanging precariously on the step, as a recalcitrant lout, but as somehow silly and lovable. Pedestrians turn and fondly smile as the crowded little cars bump past with bell busily a-clang; it's hard for some onlookers to keep themselves from walking right out in the street and patting the merry little vehicles.

If you got acquainted with the passengers on these cars, you'd find that almost every nationality was represented. More than a score of these foreign-born groups still celebrate their national feast days with dancing and banquets, speeches and parades. The largest groups are Italians, Germans, Irish, and the inhabitants of San Francisco's Chinatown—the largest this side of Asia—which has its own telephone exchange, Chamber of Commerce, and so forth.

Since San Francisco is small in area, it would be difficult for any of these groups completely to avoid daily contact with the others. The result is a sort of pint-sized "One World," an accidental but actual uniting of nations. And it was logical that this city of letters, of cultural and cosmopolitan influences, where the Opera House is just as municipally owned as the jail, should have been chosen as the scene of the first United Nations conference.

Those delegates who arrived by plane had simply to look out of the window to see that San Francisco, built on the tip of a peninsula, was an imposing regional capital, closely surrounded by scores of satellite towns and cities. But they'd also guess that Oakland, with its heavy industries and its half-million people, was of a size and consequence that made it more a full-dress rival than a mere auxiliary city. After all, those delegates who arrived by train had it demonstrated that direct transcontinental railroads end at Oakland and that further arrangements have to be made to go on across the Bay and reach the City of the Golden Gate. And delegates who were familiar with the local scene knew you can no more win friends in Oakland by referring to it as "the Brooklyn of the West," than you can by calling its big neighbor "Frisco."

Many a delegate, having taken a quick brush-up on San Francisco's past, knew that even though the Bay was first discovered as far back as 1769, nothing much happened until 1848, when California's gold was accidentally discovered. Within two years' time, California had been admitted into the Union, and San Francisco, this tag-end of nowhere, had leaped from a population of 860 into a city of more than 30,000 people, with scores of thousands of others on the way.

The harbor was lined with abandoned ships whose crews had gone off to the gold fields. The mud streets were "not passable or even jack-assable." Eggs brought up to $50 a dozen, and a fifteen-by-twenty-foot canvas tent fetched a per annum rental of $40,000. Some of those who struck it rich had all their teeth pulled out and gold ones put in. Down-and-outers were able to live on the gold dust they sifted from gambling house sweepings. Murderers, whores, pimps and thieves flooded into town. The orgies of Pompeii were all present—with improvements. Girls could be rented or bought outright, and the town was burned six times, usually by thugs for the purpose of looting. To establish some vestige of order, a Vigilance Committee was formed and its point of view generally was, "Let's give him a fair trial and hang him."

San Franciscans, heavy with gold, began to import through their great harbor the finest of the world's goods and pleasures. They demanded, and were able to pay for, the world's best talent in *chanteuse* or chef. Opulent living became an ingrained San Francisco habit.

But the Civil War diverted the Boston Clippers, the seagoing department stores which had supplied San Francisco with clocks and shoes and muslin. The town desperately needed a rail link with the East Coast, and Collis P. Huntington, "a hard and cheery old man," according to Arthur McEwen, "with no more soul than a shark," along with Mark Hopkins, Charles Crocker and Leland Stanford, pitched in and built the Central Pacific. It was a monopoly, and nature took its course.

San Francisco was furious. The railroad mercilessly gouged the whole region on its freight rates, and laid an iron hand on state politics. Reporter Ambrose Bierce detailed "the methods devised by the railroad company to punish the Demon Passenger," and the *Examiner*, objecting to the want of safety devices, declared its belief that the railroad's patrons were entitled to a degree of security "at least equal to that of a soldier on the battlefield."

Ultimately, competitive rail lines reached San Francisco, and its pain was eased. But even at the turn of the century the Bay area was still largely dependent upon the outside world for manufactured products, and traded its cereals, fruit, wool, timber and wine to get them.

In 1906 the heaving earth shook the terrified town to pieces and the ensuing fire consumed the rubble. But it was built back into place long before the great event of 1920. That year the Panama Canal, though it had been in use for some years already, was officially opened, and San Francisco moved thousands of miles closer to her East Coast sisters.

The stream of Eastern immigrants remained strong and steady, continuously bulging and bolstering San Francisco's local markets and real-estate prices. She acquired cheap hydroelectric power and, even though most of it was nearer Los Angeles, struck oil. By Pearl Harbor time, the Bay area was an important part of American industry, was making some steel and building ships, refining such quantities of petroleum that the bass out of the lower Sacramento River had long since come to have the flavor of used crank-case oil. It was fabricating important quantities of wood and paper and, drawing upon the fabulous agricultural resources of the 400-mile-long Great Central Valley, was a huge factor in processing America's food. It is a great coffee-importing center, and one of its best and largest smells is that of the roasting beans.

Not only San Francisco's water-front people but the whole town regard the Pacific as strictly *mare nostrum,* and the shipping that passes across the Embarcadero has the highest dollar value of any on the West Coast, even though at times, on a tonnage basis, some of the Southern California oil ports have taken the lead. But one of San Francisco's steadiest sources of income is that old ever-loving tourist dollar.

San Francisco has long been the secret libido of the United States tourist as a result of his belief in the city's ability to serve up sin, *bien presenté.* The Barbary Coast, which in the old days was a huge attraction to out-of-town "slummers," is now something less than a reasonable facsimile of its former iniquitous glory. Its noisiest block of night spots is called the International Settlement, is garish and briskly crummy, wanting in the rubicund dignity of the parlor houses of the old Barbary Coast.

In seeing San Francisco's sights in the months from October to

April, it's well to have a sturdy raincoat. San Francisco has no great extremes of temperature. It's usually nice and cool, but just as the summers are predictably dry, its winters are soaking wet. Also, for reasons later to be given, it's a good idea, in this city of short downtown distances, to walk whenever possible.

San Francisco's most spectacular attraction is the sight of the city itself from "The Top of the Mark," a cocktail lounge above the Mark Hopkins Hotel on Nob Hill. On a clear day a trip across either of San Francisco's great bridges—the Golden Gate Bridge, the world's longest and highest single-span suspension bridge, or the eight-and-a-quarter-mile-long San Francisco-Oakland Bay Bridge, the world's longest and costliest bridge—presents an inspiring sight.

Part of the way across the Bay Bridge you can see Treasure Island, where San Francisco held its Golden Gate International Exposition. Leland Cutler, insurance executive and San Francisco addict, who was president of the Exposition organization, laconically points out that the reason its backers did not get back the $6,500,000 they kittied in was that "the United States was tired of World's Fairs, and San Francisco and New York just didn't know it."

At the foot of Telegraph Hill, from which in the past the news of arriving vessels was flashed, lies the Montgomery Block, the artists' section, which in the spring blossoms with sidewalk shows. Here you might just possibly run across such painters as Berlandina, Dong Kingman, Matt Barnes, Bob and Charles Howard or such sculptors as Addie Kent, Puccinelli, and that cocklebur in the world of San Francisco art, Beniamino Bufano, a spiritual descendant of those early Italian artists such as Cellini and Michelangelo, who thought art should extend into public affairs. Bufano, among other things, staged a violent but unsuccessful campaign for twenty-five-cent symphony concerts. Even so, opera and symphony audiences in San Francisco resemble those of Italy, in as much as a vast percentage of the people are in humble circumstances, people who go not merely to be seen there, but to hear good music. On opening night of the Opera season, however, all bets are off and it's every Schiaparelli and Hattie Carnegie original for itself.

Besides its impressive Civic Center, where the city leads much of its cultural life, San Francisco has a couple of legitimate theaters and an enthusiastic backer in Louis R. Lurie, a former Chicago newsboy, who made a fortune in San Francisco real estate.

Many San Franciscan bibliophiles are rampant collectors of any item bearing the imprint of San Francisco's Grabhorn Press. The beauty and excellence of its hand-set and hand-bound limited editions are believed by such authorities as San Francisco's author and critic, Joseph Henry Jackson, to be unsurpassed in all the world.

From a sheer visual standpoint, Dorothy Wright Liebes' studio, where fabrics are designed and hand-woven out of everything from aluminum foil to Chinese grasses, is the most colorful spot in town. A key figure in the growing importance of the West as a fashion center, Mrs. Liebes creates fabrics not only for Eastern designers, but for technicolor sets and the *décor* of ships, airlines and hotels, as well as "the master copies" from which hundreds of thousands of Eastern mill workers make machine-woven textiles.

Just as deft with his hands as any of Mrs. Liebes' weavers was the courtly Bay-area bank clerk who came to be known as Gentleman Jim Corbett. And the same goes for Don Budge and that famed trio of distaff racquet-teers, Helen Wills, Helen Jacobs and Alice Marble. As any sports fan knows, San Francisco is the scene of the yearly East-West football classic, and the place where Joe DiMaggio first discovered the magic potency of Wheaties.

Yet gourmet San Francisco, in general, eats not merely to raise its batting average, but for pleasure. Briefly and incompletely, there are such famous restaurants as Pierre's, Jack's, Vanessi's, and Fred Solari's on Maiden Lane. There are many fine restaurants in the foreign sections, and wooden-legged Trader Vic's, though located in Oakland, is the Colony Club, with a Polynesian accent, for the whole Bay area. George Mardikian, of Omar Khayyam's, is probably the restaurateur best known to out-of-towners. But former Sergeant Georges Reymond, now executive chef of the St. Francis, must certainly be the only chef in town that ever had an Air Force general offer to forego an additional star if he could keep Georges in charge of his mess. When it comes down to the serious business of eating fresh-boiled crabs, more have probably been devoured at Fisherman's Wharf than at any other place in town.

Sooner or later, most San Francisco visitors wind up at Cliff House, which looks out over Seal Rocks, go on to the old military post called the Presidio, and Golden Gate Park. If you have your own car, a short drive will take you out into the gray-suède hills that are trimmed with green velvet and, a little to the north, to the giant redwood trees. And though the Pacific Union Club remains exclusively in town, the out-door-loving San Franciscans who belong to the Family Club have their own club farm for summer outings, and members of the Bohemian Club estivate in their 3,000-acre redwood grove. At its club-house in town, the Bohemian Club's Cartoon Room, where the writing Norrises spent many a pleasant hour, is one of the most delightful club rooms in the nation, but when summer comes, Bohemians are only too glad to escape from the fantastic crush of the city.

San Francisco is probably the most suffocatingly jam-packed of all of America's unanimously overcrowded cities. As a debarkation point for Pacific veterans, San Francisco was in much the same position as was New York in relation to those coming from Europe, except that San Francisco has only a fraction of New York's facilities for housing, feeding, and entertaining them. Beyond that, San Francisco's own population has jumped from 685,000 in 1943 to 825,000 in its most recent count. The number of residents in the metropolitan Bay area increased from 1,700,000 in 1940 to about 2,400,000 in 1944.

To meet its crushing traffic problem, San Francisco has already consolidated the street-railway system and is hastening studies on a subway that will be designed to funnel much of main-stem Market Street's traffic load underground, just as a substantial part of the city's parking problem was buried under Union Square. Beneath this block-square green can be stored, on four subterranean levels, some 1,700 automobiles.

And since thousands of Bay-area commuters increase San Francisco's daytime population by twenty per cent, even San Francisco's great and beautiful new bridges are swamped with traffic. Some idea of their traffic burden is suggested by the fact that, while the original financing plan of the Bay Bridge called for a sixty-five-cent toll, it has been possible, due to the flood of traffic, to drop the toll to a quarter, and the debt on this $77,000,000 bridge is still being paid off ahead of schedule.

But San Francisco has more luck paying off bridge bonds than suppressing crime. During the 'Thirties, the vice situation in San Francisco was splendidly stabilized by the police, to whom, it was charged, a considerable portion of the proceeds accrued. They allowed no muscling in by outside thugs. Big-time racketeers from other areas were met at the Ferry Building on arrival and given their walking papers. In 1937, the police department was investigated by private detective Edward N. Atherton. His report charged that the police department was actually being run by a bail-bond company, that the annual pay-off to the police was around a million dollars, that a number of police captains were millionaires, and that lieutenants had amassed private fortunes of hundreds of thousands of dollars. Atherton's purpose was not to clean up the town, which didn't want to be cleaned up, but merely to try to put the police department back in the hands of the people and the more mischievous members of the force into San Quentin or, if Federal charges were involved, perhaps in Bay-bound Alcatraz.

This was the cue for one of San Francisco's most colorful characters to go into action: sleek, able Jake "The Master" Ehrlich, star attorney for San Francisco's big-time underworld characters. The first case involved a policeman who, it was charged, had actually been seen receiving cash from underworld persons and whose personal fortune, it was claimed, was hardly commensurate with that of an humble and upright copper. Nevertheless, after a performance that Edward G. Robinson, who looks like Jake in a less suave and sinister way, would have to hump himself to equal, Jake cleared his man, as he did so many others of the apparently unjustly accused policemen. Ehrlich is a periodic target of San Francisco newspapermen who, when annoyed with him, purposely misspell his name, and have managed to do it as many as twenty times in one story.

San Francisco's battered old police department got another going over at the hands of Navy personnel, abetted by a few of the more fearless civilians, in San Francisco's olive-branch observances on V-J Day.

Where most of the rest of America's cities managed to shut off their liquor supply during this period of potential over-enthusiasm, San Francisco seldom did. And even after two days of rioting, when every hospital was bulging with injured celebrants and Market Street looked more like an invasion beach than a municipal thoroughfare, there was still no co-ordinated action by the civil and military police. On the third night, the *Chronicle's* Pulitzer-Prize-winning Stanton Delaplane stood in the midst of this barbaric orgy and wrote: "A looting, smashing crowd is tearing up Market Street tonight. Windows are crashing from Sixth to Third Street. The police and Shore Patrol are unable and not trying to stop it. Most of the mob is made up of sailors. . . . A good fourth of them are staggering drunk. My hands have blood on them and I don't know where it came from. . . . Four sailors kicked out the window of a leather goods shop at Fifth and Market and threw the contents into the crowd. Three sailors grabbed a girl and held her while another, staggering with liquor, stripped off her shorts. They ran away into the crowd waving them in the air. . . . One of our truck drivers saw a girl being held down and raped by a small crowd of sailors in a Mason Street doorway just off Market. A few minutes ago three sailors grabbed two passing girls and pulled them up a Fifth Street alley. . . ."

At eleven o'clock that third night, civilian and military police began joint operations. They formed a solid phalanx of men and vehicles with loudspeakers reading the Riot Act, moving slowly and inexorably down Market Street. In a short time the street was cleared and the celebration, except for one last occurrence, was over. The period was affixed to the sentence when a grand jury met and not only whitewashed all concerned—police, liquor commission and Navy—but congratulated them. With tasteful restraint, it did not congratulate the owners of thousands of dollars' worth of destroyed property, the thousand-plus hospital cases, the scores of understandably unreported rape victims, and the more than a dozen dead.

However inadequate may be San Francisco's facilities for riot prevention, it is better prepared than at any time in its history for the recurrence of earthquakes. Great numbers of its new structures incorporate "earthquake-proof" construction. It has a separate system for pulling fire-fighting water out of the Bay, once the regular system has been rattled to pieces. Its earthquake insurance rates are steadily declining. A recent policy for $1,500,000, with a $50,000-deductible clause, covering certain properties of Stanford University out in Palo Alto, carries a $13,000-a-year premium.

The Bay area will almost certainly continue its fabulous growth, but San Francisco, surrounded by water on three sides and on the other by small towns jealous of their sovereignty, has about run out of land, has pretty well reached the point where, to build something new, something old has to be torn down. Even so, the Bank of America is running up a little skyscraper, and there is also in the offing a new apparel center, to be built in the Potrero District, that will cover twenty-five acres and in which San Francisco's entire apparel industry —show rooms, design studios and factories—will be housed in cottage-type buildings, none exceeding four stories in height. The fresh-produce industry is plunking down $5,000,000 for an integrated commission district. Another project is the $25,000,000 World Trade Center, a particular convenience to Hawaiian interests since Hawaii's relationship with San Francisco is more or less like that of Alaska to Seattle. The city is also spending $20,000,000 in order to make its municipal airport the best in the country, excepting only New York's Idlewild.

But since space limitations prevent San Francisco from aspiring to become a city of much more than a million people, it's concerned more with quality than quantity. In the past, it has liked to think of itself as easygoing and fatalistic. It has long since had a great measure of tolerance thrust upon it. It has experienced more in the way both of exaltation and of terror than most of its American sister cities. There are many points from which San Francisco is vulnerable to attack. There are even more reasons for loving San Francisco and being seduced by it. And it seems likely that the very sound of its name will, for a long, long time, continue to cause an automatic quickening of interest, tinged with excitement, in the national consciousness.

7: *Chicago*

AMONG the earth's great cities, none is younger and more dynamic than Chicago, or so bluntly male. Certainly no American city is more closely associated in the world's mind with violence, energy, audacity and success, U. S. style. Few American cities have had anything vaguely resembling its growth or its growing pains.

Chicago is a thousand times more relaxed, less "mannered" than New York. New Yorkers like to think that Chicagoans make a self-conscious point of not imitating them. Generally speaking, that isn't true. Living in Chicago is a full-time job, and a less predictable one than living in more orderly New York. Chicago people sound less coldly businesslike over the phone. You have a peculiar desire to invite them all to dinner. Those you do invite will talk a lot less about arts and ideas than about some hot new line they've just installed in the store, or an exciting new industrial gadget, or about some place you can go, out on the edge of town, and have a hell of a time.

If you buy a sandwich in a drugstore, the soda jerker will probably call you "Bub" and horse around and gab as if you were lifelong neighbors. One out-of-town visitor has remarked that Chicago's ever-vigilant girls have an uncommonly roving eye. He reasons that the cool brisk wind off the lake has something to do with this. It molds their dresses to their bodies like tights and just makes them feel frisky. It is this same breeze which, in conjunction with that from the town's boosters, has given Chicago the name of "the Windy City."

To plunge feet first into vast, manifold, contemporary Chicago can be bewildering. Julian Street, distinguished author and connoisseur of, among other things, cities, has said in his travel book, *Abroad at Home:* "Chicago is stupefying. It knows no rules, and I know none by which to judge it. It stands apart from all the cities of the world, isolated by its own individuality, an Olympian freak, a fable, an allegory, an incomprehensible phenomenon, a prodigious paradox in which youth and maturity, brute strength and soaring spirit, are harmoniously confused. Call Chicago mighty, monstrous, multifarious, vital, lusty, stupendous, indomitable, intense, unnatural, aspiring, puissant, preposterous, transcendent—call it what you like—throw the dictionary at it! It's all you can do, except shoot it with statistics. And even the statistics of Chicago are not deadly, as most statistics are."

Let's see how it got that way.

By the fall of 1833, the Indians of the region had been sufficiently mauled and cuffed to gather at the village of Chicago and cede all their lands east of the Mississippi in return for the promise of a sum of money and surcease from molestation by the whites. Right there, one of the greatest, most foolproof pieces of geography on the continent was opened for colonization. Northward stretched Lake Michigan, connecting with the other truly Great Lakes, all bounded by fertile lands, except Lake Superior, and it by priceless ore. To the west lay the Mississippi, cleaving the continent and serving as the main transportation artery for fertile inland America. To the west, also, lay the oceans of plains where billions of hogs would soon spring up out of the earth. In Chicago's scheme of things, a hog was merely fifteen or twenty bushels of corn walking on four legs.

With the stage set, the play began. The plot dealt with who would seize the most of the region's wealth and turn it into money and power. The rules, unlike the Marquis of Queensberry rules for doing business today, were largely no-holds-barred. They invited the ascendancy of the most able, the most ruthless, those possessing the visceral factor in greatest plenty.

As the people flooded in, bringing with them every skill that Europe knew, the earlier settlers began amassing fortunes out of skyrocketing real-estate values, a process which, except for recurrent panics and other disasters, has continued until the present. Others were growing rich from harnessing the resources of the region, all with one interest in common: boost Chicago, grow rich on its growth. Chicago's great "greeting" mayor, Long John Wentworth, when thanked by the Prince of Wales for an elaborate entertainment, said,

"Oh, never mind, Prince. We treat everybody like this out west."

The potent individualist, the gifted, the tough, the lucky, the un-flagging, began to scramble to the top of the heap. William Ogden began stringing steel railroads across the face of the land. Heterogene-ous Chicago, which, when frustrated and worked up, usually riots, did lots of rioting during the Civil War. Yet under the fierce edi-torial leadership of Joseph Medill's *Tribune,* the town stayed more or less lined up behind Lincoln. A famous Chicago detective, Allan Pinkerton, saved Lincoln from earlier assassination, and furnished spies for the Union Army, as his firm was later to furnish labor spies and strikebreakers. Mr. Lincoln's Secretary of War said that without the invention of Cyrus McCormick's reaper and binder not enough men could have been spared from the fields to win the war. Another Chi-cagoan, who supplied the Union Army with meat and who picked up his first million in the process, was P. D. Armour.

When Mr. Lincoln actually was assassinated, still another Chicagoan got his chance. George Mortimer Pullman, who'd invented a sleeping car, managed to get Mrs. Lincoln to ride from Chicago to Springfield in it, and got so much publicity that nothing could stop him until he had his cars running on a hundred roads, just as Armour was later to do with his refrigerated cars. By this time, Potter Palmer owned most of the buildings on State Street and Marshall Field had become a prominent Chicago merchant.

All the while, depressions were following booms. The money panics were always marked by great suffering among the poor, and by bread riots. In good times, everybody was far too busy to plan for lean periods. Optimism, work and risk were the keynotes. Differences be-tween management and labor were often expressed not by mere strikes but by civil war. The industrialists of that day were less interested in listening to reason than in meeting a challenger and beating him to his knees.

Labor, frequently a disorganized mob which no one could control, was sometimes under the apparent leadership of men with just as little use for reason and an often-professed belief in dynamite.

Yet through all this strife Chicago continued to fatten and sprawl, and it grew into an increasingly rich and ugly city. Then, in 1871, it was razed by the Great Fire. But here was no opportunity to build a beautiful city. People had to have shelter, and have it fast. Chicago was broke, but its credit was good. It had a fine record as a money-maker. America believed in it. Chicago believed in itself. It was jerry-built back into place in jig time.

An architect named Daniel Burnham began to be the dominant figure in building Chicago. Since the city sat in the mud, only two feet above water level, foundations were a vastly delimiting factor. Burnham's partner, John Wellborn Root, invented the "floating foundation"—roughly, a basement full of crossed railroad rails encased in cement. Then, in 1890, Chicago, a strapping adolescent with 1,099,000 people, bid $10,000,000 for the Congress-planned Columbian Exposition, got it, and gave Burnham the job of building the famed White City on a swamp. The result, in 1893, knocked the civilized world cockeyed. It was beautiful—and in Chicago!

Let the world look alive and alter its opinion. The Chicago which had been most famous for brothels and hog meat, which Kipling had declared to be inhabited by savages, was showing signs of civilization.

Jane Addams had already won renown. She was no crackpot, but an able, energetic, endlessly good-humored woman, who was willing to work hard to alleviate the suffering of the oppressed, to quell the more damaging misconceptions of the ignorant and to put the bite on the rich to help the poor. Other good people had left their mark: Governor John P. Altgeld, who in the war between Pullman and his workers, tried to make reason and justice prevail; Carter Harrison, a long-time mayor who, though no saint, wisely worked to make Chicago a good-natured, less murderous town.

Then there had been George E. Cole, a pint-sized reformer who, after traction promoter Charles Tyson Yerkes had virtually done the city out of its eyeteeth, fixed that crooked Goliath's wagon. Dynamic Dr. Frank Billings was becoming a power in Chicago medical reform. William Rainey Harper, with the complete confidence and monumental material assistance of John D. Rockefeller, was building the University of Chicago, which, along with other colleges and universities, such as Northwestern, Loyola and industry-building Armour Institute, was to have a civilizing influence on the community.

Theodore Thomas had come to devote his life to the Chicago Symphony, and rich Charley Hutchinson to do the same for the Art Institute.

The workers for Chicago's good were as full of beans as the crooks who preyed on her. Finally, most of Chicago's aging commercial collossi, facing an imminent date with Saint Peter, began with varying zeal to shuck out a few millions here and there for good works; none, however, more than Sears, Roebuck's Julius Rosenwald has given to Jewish and, more particularly, to Negro causes.

With the growth of World War I's new industries, Chicago needed Negro workers from the South, and got them in untold thousands. It had no adequate place to house them. Racial tension broke into riots, in one of which 38 were killed, 537 wounded, and two million dollars' worth of property destroyed by fire.

Then came the periods of those three prize packages, Thompson, Capone and Insull; and each, according to his lights, abilities and uncommon energies, took the town for a "ride"—a word to which Capone and his professional associates gave a brand-new connotation in the American language. All over the world, Chicago, whose long reputation for lurid wickedness had paid off tourist- and convention-wise, became notorious for its gang wars and rackets, and was the first topic about which fascinated foreigners questioned Americans who landed on Europe's shores. But Big Bill Thompson's time finally ran out, the Revenuers jailed Capone, and the market crash in 'Twenty-nine brought down Insull's utilities empire.

The visitor's first impression of today's Chicago will depend entirely on his point of entry. Naturally, if he enters by the stockyards, the olfactory concussion is terrific. The same is true of the oil-refining areas of Whiting. Pass through Chicago's slums and you wonder if it's not about time for another thoroughgoing Chicago fire. Yet no fair-minded person could enter contemporary Chicago by boat, land at one of its southern yacht anchorages and drive northward along the lake for the length of the city, without wondering whether Chicago was not the most beautiful city on earth. He would see lovely Jackson, Burnham, Grant and Lincoln parks, wide expanses of greensward and boulevards, tens of miles of trees, the great public cultural institutions—the Museum of Science and Industry, the Field Museum of Natural History, the Art Institute, Soldier Field. Farther north is the Gold Coast, where swankiest Chicago resides.

On the left, opposite Grant Park, is the vast proscenium backdrop of the skyscrapers of the midtown business section, great buildings which rest on a newer type of foundation than that devised by Root. This is a system of caissons that have been plunged through the mud to the bedrock far below the surface, and they support buildings with more heft than Manhattan's slender shafts. Chicago, incidentally, built the world's first skyscraper, which is to say, a building that is not supported by its walls, but one in which the walls themselves are supported by a steel skeletal structure.

Here, behind the handsome façade of Michigan Avenue, is the Loop, heart of Chicago's business district, which the elevated railroad tracks encircle like a ringworm round a thumb. Within the Loop is State Street, home of Marshall Field's store and other famous mercantile establishments. Also along State Street, as well as elsewhere in the Loop, are the movie cathedrals of Balaban and Katz, and bars with brassy orchestras. Many are the *boîtes* where one may partake of that old U. S.-invented Oriental delicacy, chop suey. State Street is, in a more robust, uninhibited way, Chicago's Fifth Avenue and it shares honors with Dearborn and Randolph streets as Chicago's Broadway. Michigan Avenue, on which is to be found the world's largest hotel, the Stevens, is Chicago's Champs Élysées. Hard by the Stevens is the Blackstone which, along with the less centrally located Drake, most Chicagoans feel are their two best hotels. LaSalle Street is Chicago's Wall Street.

Surrounding the Loop is a crescent-shaped area with the points aimed at the lake, containing about twenty-five square miles of some of the worst slums in the nation. In it are packed many racial groups, but the most numerous one is Chicago's 350,000 Negroes—more, for example, than the entire population of Jersey City or Memphis or Toledo. Eighty-five per cent of Chicago lives in rented dwellings. Its present occupancy rate is around 99 per cent, an explosive figure. Particularly in the case of the Negro, there are many more people than places to put them.

Though the Negroes' problem is acute, there are many other less precisely defined ethnic islands in the mosaic that composes Chicago. The largest of these groups is Polish, 119,000 foreign-born. There are 83,000 foreign-born Germans, 66,000 Russians, the same number of Italians, 46,000 Swedes, 34,000 Czechs, 26,000 Austrians and around 15,000 each of English, Hungarians, Norwegians and Yugoslavs. Many of these folk after attaining some wealth still prefer the old neighborhoods, which in the meantime may have become shabby, in order to remain with their old friends who shared with them in the old days the high adventure of discovering America. In these communities are meeting places with a nostalgic atmosphere of the Old Country, places such as the Little Bohemia restaurant on 18th and Loomis streets.

In a city made up of so many immigrant groups, great numbers of whom could not for a long time speak English, it was natural that machine politics should flourish. In each precinct the precinct captain is of the same nationality as the neighborhood, knows the residents' troubles and their weaknesses, and knows how to enlist their allegiance. He is a neighborhood big shot, has pull with the government, helps interpret it to them and them to it, and harvest votes for the machine.

It is said that once, at a Chicago automobile show, a downstate farmer stayed till after closing time looking for the Kelly-Nash machine. Since Nash's death, it's become the Ed Kelly machine. Plainspoken Kelly says simply, "I must either run the machine or have it run me and thereby become a rubber-stamp mayor." But Chicago does not feel put upon, and on almost every social level it approves of its boss.

Kelly is not only a political boss but an engineer. He guided the progress of much of Chicago's lake-front beautification and many other successful public projects. He is believed by astute local observers to be anxious to give Chicago the best possible machine government. He is careful not to make free-wheeling Chicago a more sanctimonious town than it wants to be, and realizes that it finds bookies a convenience and likes its burlesque shows.

No longer is Chicago a notorious arena for big-time crime. In recent times some ten members of the local organized-gambling fraternity have departed this life via the shotgun route, but gang domination of the city is a thing of the past.

Under Kelly's direction, and with the complete co-operation of Chicago's businessmen, Chicago became, during the war, a servicemen's mecca. Over and above its USO activities, the city's business folk established service centers with free food and free entertainment. What's more, the city's transit system refused to accept the servicemen's dimes. Check with any serviceman, and you'll find that he liked Chicago as much as it liked him.

Chicago's public scandals still survive, but aren't what they used to be. One involving a Kelly appointee came to light when the National Education Association looked into the matter of Chicago's schools under the school-board presidency of Kelly-machine-man James B. McCahey, and McCahey-appointed Superintendent William H. Johnson. The N.E.A. charged that plums went to the "loyal," that the disloyal were punished and that grades were rigged on Johnson's say-so. It also stated that during Superintendent Johnson's tenure, the school board had adopted for use throughout the system twenty-three textbooks on which Johnson's name appeared as author or co-author. Yet the mayor has just appointed McCahey for the thirteenth time. Chicago's middle-of-the-road newspaper, the *Daily News,* famed for its international news coverage, has gone after McCahey in its editorial columns, just as the tabloid *Daily Times* has fought for municipal ownership and expansion of Chicago's inadequate, ramshackle transit system which offers nowhere near enough straps for *Daily Times* readers to hang on to.

For years surveys have failed to show why Chicago so avidly reads Colonel Robert R. McCormick's Chicago *Tribune.* Was it the funnies, which many comics addicts declare are the best in the land, was it the sound sports coverage, what? Some of the *Tribune's* competitors feel that aside from the admitted technical excellence of the *Tribune,* its "box-office" results from McCormick's deathless pugnacity, Chicago's taste for rough stuff, its lack of fastidiousness about hitting in the clinches, plus the *Tribune's* ability (1) to "sharpen the argument" to a point where the less intellectual reader can know in simple terms what the shooting's all about, and (2) its emphatic ferocity, which never leaves that reader in doubt about where the *Tribune* stands. The *Tribune* is implacably anti-New Deal, anti-British and anti-Russian. Some Chicagoans feel that the town is fascinated, if not mildly hypnotized, by the Olympian arrogance of McCormick, who tells his readers 365 days a year that the *Tribune* is "The World's Greatest Newspaper." How this can be when the Denver *Post* candidly admits *it* is "the best newspaper in the U.S.A." is hard to see. In any case, on the side of the angels or not, the *Tribune* is one of the two most powerful forces in Chicago. The other is the Kelly machine.

Riding out each morning to joust with the *Tribune*, giving tongue to the battle cry, "Read the Truth," fighting for the moral leadership of Chicago and a place by its milk bottles on the front stoop, is grandson Marshall Field's pro-New Deal Chicago *Sun*. The *Sun* pitches to the foreign-born groups that tend Chicago mills and factories. It is internationalist, seeks the abolition of slums and tries to sow the seeds of civic rectitude. It stands not so far to the left as Field's New York *PM*. The *Tribune* has nearly a million readers, and the *Sun* about one third as many.

Chicago also reads and writes a lot of books. Marshall Field and Company claims to do the biggest retail-book business in the nation. In 1930, H. L. Mencken, literary ringmaster of the 'Twenties, remarked, "With two exceptions, there is not a single novelist of the younger generation—that is, a serious novelist deserving a civilized reader's notice—who has not sprung from the Chicago palatinate." Chicago's graft and violence, its growth by tearing away, cutting away, blasting away whatever hindered it, has been realistically mirrored in its literature by James Farrell, Frank Norris, Sherwood Anderson, Theodore Dreiser, Ben Hecht and Upton Sinclair. Carl Sandburg, in his famous poem "Chicago," caught it in synthesis. And Harriet Monroe's magazine, *Poetry*, made superficially unpoetic Chicago a poet's refuge, a place where at least he could speak his piece. Further to augment Chicago's choral voice, there were Eugene Field, Edgar Lee Masters, Finley Peter Dunne's Mr. Dooley, Ernest Poole, George Ade, and that very entertaining gent, F.P.A.

But the vitality, the clash of wills, the personal anguish, the swirling economic and social currents that made Chicago pickings for the writer, was a by-product of Chicago's fundamental quest, which was in the beginning, and still remains, a quest for growth, wealth and power.

Consider that growth. In 1830 Chicago was an unincorporated village of fifty people who existed in the mud at the mouth of the Chicago River. A century later that village had grown to contain three and a third millions of people. In five of those ten decades it grew by more than half a million.

During the nineteenth century Chicago was chiefly engaged in processing the yield of rich Midwestern lands. Then, in 1906, the steel city of Gary was founded in Chicago's Indiana suburbs, and a comprehensive metal-working industry grew up around it.

Today, in the six counties that comprise Chicago's industrial area, there are 10,000 factories, whose output is second only to that of New York, and whose diversity of production is claimed to be greater than that of any other city in the world. United States census figures for ante bellum 1939 show the value of manufactures from these plants to have come to $4,250,000,000, an amount greater, according to figures of the Chicago Association of Commerce, than the output of all six industrial New England states. In the same year there were nine industries—iron and steel, machinery, butchery, printing and publishing, chemicals, petroleum refining, textiles, baking and confectionery, and furniture—each doing more than $100,000,000 worth of business annually. Iron, steel and machinery together did more than $1,000,000,000. Just as impressive are her wholesale figures, which exceeded $4,000,000,000, and her retail turnover, which was around $2,000,000,000. Her enormous Merchandise Mart, recently bought by former Ambassador Joe Kennedy, is a day-in-day-out exposition of what almost everybody has to sell to anybody else.

Chicago is by all odds the rail capital of the nation. Within her industrial area are more miles of trackage than in thirty-nine of the forty-eight states, and only sixty-seven miles less than the total railroad mileage of New York State.

She claims to have more commercial air service than any other city, and her port handles more marine traffic than passes through the Panama Canal. The lake, as a commercial source of fish, is less rewarding than in the past, but still maintains a moderate fishing industry. More to the point, it bears 34,000,000 tons of Chicago shipping. In order that she might send her barges and sewage down the Mississippi, she fell upon the Chicago River and made it run backward. When a ship has a little too much draft to travel over this thwarted intermediate waterway, she simply raises it, by means of pontoons, as gallant Hornblower did his bomb ketches, and sends it scooting on over to the Mississippi. Since its opening in 1933, the barge traffic on the Chicago Sanitary Drainage and Ship Canal to the Gulf has nearly doubled each year. In 1939, 7,000,000 tons of Chicago's water-borne traffic passed over this canal.

This, in outline, was the picture of late-prewar Brobdingnagian Chicago. Then the war came and pumped her throbbing veins full of a mixture of high life and adrenalin. She got more Federally financed plants than any other city. Among these plants was the Dodge plant for building B-29 engines, which is one of the largest factories on this planet. But there was more reason for getting these plants than Chicago's greed, boasting or political dexterity. She was big enough to handle the job straightaway without any major overhauling of her water, power, sewage or railroad systems.

What did the war do to the productivity of this brass-lunged, barrel-bellied, shirt-sleeved city? She handled, up to February, 1945, ten billion dollars' worth of prime contracts, additional fantastic amounts of food, steel and subcontracts. Her industrial production skyrocketed more than 300 per cent to a present estimated total of $14,000,000,000. Charge off $3,000,000,000 to inflation, another $1,000,000,000 to enthusiasm, and you've still got an industrial miracle. In the basic matter of steel production, she now lags behind Pittsburgh by a mere 17 per cent.

And yet, just as Chicago, by her hugeness and diversification, took the economic convulsion of war conversion in stride, so, again, is she absorbing the concomitant convulsion of reconversion. Most of Chicago's war production was the kind that is basic in peace or war. A recent survey shows that more than 75 per cent of Chicago's companies, during the war, switched customers, not products, and went on making the same old things at a faster clip for Uncle Sam instead of nephew public. An additional 18 per cent had been producing goods substantially similar to those they produce in the post-war world. Most of Chicago's wartime steel was high-alloy steel, which is tomorrow's kind. She is also in the aluminum business, just in case, and has stuck a big fat thumb in the pie of tomorrow's electronics business.

Maybe it's because of her prodigality, but no town's people have ever loved their town more than Chicago's people have during her brief history. And now, as in the past, there are a lot of people who want to see the town become great not merely as a place to cook up soap out of cow tallow but as a monument to civilization and human decency.

Some fifty local civic, religious and business groups, including everything from the Y.W.C.A. to the CIO, are working through the Mayor's Committee on Race Relations and the Chicago Conference of Home Front Unity to dispel racial tension, to try to make democracy more nearly a Chicago fact than a Chicago aspiration. These folk, under the chairmanship of Rosenwald Fund President Edwin R. Embree, have made small but solid gains. Chicago Negroes in considerable numbers now work as bus and streetcar drivers and have access to all public beaches. The job ahead, endless in its complexities and discouragements, is being faced forthrightly and acted upon with patience and dispatch.

The Chicago Plan Commission has a ten-year plan—but, as yet, only a small part of the money—for roughly a billion dollars' worth of civic improvements, conceived on such a scale as to amount to a virtual rebuilding of the city. To ease postwar unemployment and job dislocation, Chicago already had some $90,000,000 set aside, and has just voted another $50,000,000 bond issue, the sum of which fund can be applied on public works such as superhighways and extension of Chicago's new but somewhat bobtailed subway, which is at present slightly less than five miles long. This money will further provide park playgrounds for those of the city's fifty wards which haven't one already, and additional North Side lake-front beautification. Fifteen million dollars will go for airport improvements, and $5,000,000, to be matched by an equal amount from the state, will form the basis of a request for a $90,000,000 Federal loan, all of which will be used as a starter on slum clearance. Mayor Kelly thinks this should supply housing for about 50,000 people and that it will amount to a sizable drop in Chicago's housing bucket. But the real impetus to employment will come from the $1,500,000,000 which private sources are to pour into construction and remodeling projects.

Look outside Chicago for a moment at the world company it keeps. New York, almost three times its age, and Paris and London many times that, are all mature cities. Maturity implies that an organism doesn't grow much any more, that it is inclined to sit back and consolidate its gains. Chicago has just put on long pants and is still giddy with the wild surges and frustrations of adolescence. To it, growth is still natural and taken for granted, life wild and new and exciting.

Chicago's place in the new air world will be even more enormous than its present one. Should the St. Lawrence waterway project ever go through, Chicago could, after certain canal enlargements, become the nearest great deep-water port to the heart of America and siphon off titanic quantities of business from the East Coast ports. Already it is working to become a prime port of entry by air, which is to say, a first stopping point for planes from foreign countries. If, in addition, its ten-year redevelopment plan, plus a comprehensive housing plan, could be executed, and if its growth in the future resembled that of the past, then, asks the tall-dreaming Chicagoan, what is to prevent Chicago and its satellite communities, some four and a half million people in all, from becoming the greatest, most beautiful metropolitan area on earth?

It's easy enough to say, "Well, he can dream, can't he?" But in the past the wise money has never been on what Chicago could *not* do. Its motto is: I WILL.

8: *Philadelphia*

THERE are two fairly distinct Philadelphias. One is the ghost, the living legend of a great and dynamic city which, among other things, founded this free nation. Many of the physical evidences of that stately old city remain, so many indeed that, though its spunky spirit has long since withered and vanished, it can be clearly recaptured in a sensible, tactile way.

The other Philadelphia, the contemporary one, is the sprawling, and in some ways backward, city that now occupies the location of its distinguished predecessor. Too many of Philadelphia's ruling families, with their manorial ways and lethal aplomb, have, over the years, perhaps largely unconsciously, let the city down. The want of a more progressive civic spirit on the part of a majority of its citizens keeps it down and slipping further behind.

Philadelphia is a city that wears a cutaway coat and soiled, ragged underclothes. Its art galleries, museums and orchestra are in a class with the world's finest, while its day-in-and-day-out municipal services to its people are grotesquely shabby.

Where Philadelphia reflects its Golden Age, the period in which it was the pride and leader of the nation in size and puissance, it is an utterly engaging city. Sprinkled all over town are telling souvenirs, not necessarily of historical import, but things which the present-day American Pilgrim, come to look upon the birthplace of his country, will find woven into the fabric of this city which, however dilapidated, is still, to him, a holy city.

And if he is to acquaint himself with the rich flavor and texture of the Philadelphia that was great, he will need to forget his normal American haste and assume an almost archaeological point of view. He must, as it were, marinate himself in the residual traditions and oddments that still reverberate and faintly glisten with the sheen of the city's erstwhile glory. For, as much as anything else, it is these small facets that give the city its individuality.

Some of these charming facets are: the wonderful memorabilia of the old fire companies, when one's membership in them meant at least as much as one's place on the city's many soccer teams means today—or as much as, until the turn of the century, one's place on Philadelphia's famous cricket teams, which played in the frequent matches between the Gentlemen of England and the Gentlemen of Philadelphia; the little old ladies from Rittenhouse Square who have lunched one day a week at the same table in Wanamaker's Tea Room for thirty years and who, sure enough, smell of lavender; the dark old paneled offices with marble clocks; the charmingly stiff and lovely old prints; the "viewings," which mean that when somebody dies, the family receives callers who wish to look upon the remains. (It is said that one Philadelphia woman with more social ambition than position suspended the viewing of her deceased spouse at sundown long enough to change the lamented one from striped pants and cut-away coat into white tie and tails.)

The sight of old and more or less slummy row houses whose back ends are sheathed in cool, green, patient ivy; the heirlooms that can be found in most Philadelphia houses of whatever station—a brooch, a piece of furniture, perhaps an old dough table or a rocking chair made by the Pennsylvania Dutch farmers; druggists who call themselves "apothecaries," the words "legal" and "eagle" pronounced "ligal" and "igle"; the quiet erudition of many of the people and their peculiar disinclination to herd intellectually or emotionally, which is one of the reasons Philadelphia doesn't go in for riots or, on the other hand, for unified constructive action; the "busybodies," two mirrors suspended on a wrought-iron arm and so arranged that a lady in her second-story sitting room can see who is at her door or, at least as important, at her neighbor's door, without exposing herself to the caller's view.

Streets that are not merely narrow, but cozy, and some of the most rewarding old alleyways, still complete with hitching posts, any-where to be found; the fine but demure shops on Walnut and Chestnut streets; the peddlers on Market Street, and the early morning hubbub on Dock Street where the produce-mongers haggle and bustle; the violent after-dark debauchery along the notoriously tough water front; and, of course, the monstrosity called City Hall with a thirty-seven foot statue of William Penn atop it.

The recurrent rites and festivals such as the street dancing in Elfreth's Alley in June; the Flag Day celebration at the Betsy Ross House and the historical pageant in Old Swedes' Church; the annual launching of a "flower ship" on the Delaware in memory of those Philadelphians who have died at sea in the service of their country; and the elaborate Mummers' Parade on New Year's Day.

What city could possess a more beautiful nomenclature than that which has been handed down from the time when Penn's "greene Country Towne" was bursting into bloom? That early Philadelphia fixed upon such names as the Wissahickon for its most scenic creek, called its favorite river the Schuylkill—pronounced Skook'll—and a near-by stream the Brandywine. Some of the little towns, which ulti-mately became part of Philadelphia, have such pleasing names as Kensington, Chestnut Hill, Nicetown, Fern Rock and Bridesburg.

And time in Philadelphia, the visiting American soon senses, is not merely three hours different from that of Los Angeles—it's three centuries, which changes its very nature and consistency. In Phila-delphia, time is a rich thing because the past is somehow not wholly expended and gone. Nowhere, for example, except in Salt Lake City, are the men who built a city less dead than are William Penn or Ben Franklin or Stephen Girard or Cyrus Curtis in Philadelphia. Every-where the visitor goes, there they are, affecting his experiences of the moment, altering the sights he sees, the opinions he hears, and the customs he encounters. And there are few Americans with soul so ossified that they can walk through the old buildings on Independence Square without sensing in a living way the men and events that here struck so powerful a blow for freedom and human dignity that it still rings and roars in every tyrant's ears.

But by the time these events occurred, Philadelphia was already approximately as old as Denver and Seattle are today. Nor does that include the period when the Swedes and the Dutch were cuffing each other about in their efforts to possess and hold this region.

Philadelphia first came more or less officially into being with the arrival of William Penn and his Quakers in 1682. The Penns had been given a grant in the New World by Charles II, in settlement of a debt of 16,000 pounds. Charles insisted on calling the colony Pennsylvania, in spite of the protests of the Penns, who felt that this involved them in personal vainglory.

During the first year of the colony's existence, eighty houses were built in William Penn's tiny City of Brotherly Love, and by the end of the second year there were six hundred. Meanwhile Penn changed street names from those of famous persons to such botanical designations as Poplar, Mulberry, Cherry, Vine—Chestnut, Walnut, Spruce and Pine.

William Penn was a holy man, a lofty man, and, moreover, a very decent man, but at the same time a man who liked to make the things he undertook succeed. Essentially he was an able promoter, administrator and politician, and these abilities demeaned him in no way at all. Certainly he was one of the few frontier colonists who did not make a regular practice of victimizing the Indians. In fact, Penn's oral agreement with the Indians was said by Voltaire to be the only Indian treaty that was "never signed and never broken."

Before long the Quaker City had developed a lively trade with the Caribbean islands in tobacco, grain, horses, meat, lumber and wool, and this, in turn, engendered a local shipbuilding industry. By 1723, when, as the more possessive Philadelphia historians have it, Benjamin Franklin was born in Philadelphia at the age of seventeen, he saw, as he gaped and gnawed those most publicized of buns, a colorful, prosperous scene. The people were dressed well, and were able to refresh themselves with West Indian turtle and good Madeira.

Although Franklin got off to a slow start, due to a wild goose chase to England, he would in good time prove to be, both to his adopted city and his country, just as handy as a pocket in a shirt. Eventually he fell out with Thomas Penn, who had inherited the proprietorship of the British colony of Pennsylvania. Penn considered Franklin a dangerous radical who was putting ideas of freedom "into the heads of the unthinking multitude." It is certainly true that he was putting his Poor Richard quips and adages on almost every Philadelphia tongue.

By now, Philadelphia was filling up with non-Quakers, great numbers of Scotch-Irish and Germans, and Franklin, with his agnostic sentiments, was something of a non-Quaker rallying point.

When the British passed the Stamp Act in 1765, Philadelphians were furious and resolved to boycott the mother country. They raised such a rumpus that the Stamp Act was eventually repealed, only to be replaced by the Townshend Act, whose tax on tea resulted in the Boston Tea Party. Then in May, 1774, Paul Revere rode into town bringing the news that England had closed the port of Boston.

The colonial hornets' nest began to stir in earnest. On September 5, the original Continental Congress assembled in Philadelphia's Carpenters' Hall. Washington, Patrick Henry, the Adamses—almost everybody who counted—were there. But it was not until the Second Continental Congress met, after the British troops had tied into the Minute Men at Lexington, that the decision was reached for the colonials to break off from England and fight for their freedom.

Though Washington and particularly Franklin both possessed clear prose styles, Thomas Jefferson was asked to put the Declaration into words. The Congress accepted the draft in Independence Hall, July 4, 1776.

As the *de facto* capital of this brand-new country, Philadelphia (pop. 35,000) got beehive busy, recruiting men, building guns, naval vessels and all sorts of military materiel. Robert Morris and Ben Franklin looked after finance and procurement, the latter junketing to France with the success that attended most of his ventures. Indeed, everybody was taking a big dish in the war except the Quakers, who were morally opposed to any kind of war for any kind of reason. Then General Sir William Howe defeated Washington at the Brandywine and, accompanied by 18,000 soldiers, moved into Philadelphia, where the British remained comfortably ensconced throughout the winter, enjoying dalliance with Tory belles while Washington's ragged army froze and suffered at near-by Valley Forge.

Once the British evacuated the city in 1778, things began to move back on a passably even keel. The town kept on growing. The Bank of North America, serving as the national depository, opened in 1782. Five years later, the first American chamber of commerce, which was called the Pennsylvania Society for the Encouragement of Manufacturers and Useful Arts, came into being. Then the following year, at Independence Hall, one of the most important documents in the history of the world was adopted: the Constitution of the United States.

Philadelphia had been the seat of national government from 1775 to 1789, save for a brief period when it was in York, Pennsylvania. The government was then moved to New York, but it came back to Philadelphia in 1790 and remained there until 1800, which meant that George Washington, by no means the least colorful of presidents, gave the old town something to look at when he went abroad on the streets in his coach of Gallic origin, which was ornamented with flowers and cupids against a background of Jersey cream.

In 1793 a plague of yellow fever just about wiped out the town, scaring off great numbers that it didn't kill. But the town weathered this disaster and in the War of 1812 Philadelphians did not want for excitement since there was considerable fighting around the mouth of the Delaware River, practically in their own backyard.

By the time the 1820s rolled around, the Erie Canal had been cut to the west and was funneling the riches of the Great Lakes region into New York, which now took the lead among American cities in size and wealth. Baltimore, to the south, also moved ahead of Philadelphia for a time. The Quaker City's doldrums persisted and reached a new low when Andy Jackson fastened his teeth into Nicholas Biddle and took away from his Bank of the United States its enormously lucrative privilege of lending and acquiring the interest on the nation's money.

Near 1850 trade-hungry Philadelphians began organizing what would ultimately become the financially and politically powerful Pennsylvania Railroad, a company which still has a kind of special meaning to most Philadelphians, and along whose "Main Line" (to the West) some of the city's richest outlying suburbs have come to be built.

In World War I both the Navy Yard and the Frankford Arsenal

poured forth a torrent of munitions, though on April 9, 1917, there was a hideous explosion at the Eddystone Ammunition Works near Chester, killing more than a hundred persons and injuring or maiming more than three hundred others. In 1926, celebrating the one hundred and fiftieth anniversary of American Independence, the city held a Sesquicentennial Exposition, which was something of a fizzle, and in 1936 so far forgot its traditional Republicanism as to vote for Franklin Roosevelt.

During the recent war, Philadelphia, like many another city, was too busy with her war effort to do much about putting her own house in order, yet neither had she done much in the years that preceded the war.

Today, Philadelphia, which contains about three million souls in her metropolitan area, is far behind both New York and Chicago in size and commerce, and is being fast overtaken by Los Angeles.

Whether or not her more vital, enterprising, daring and progressive people have, through the centuries, been lured away by the possibilities of adventure and riches to be found on the frontier, there appears in modern times to have been insufficient regenerative energy to meet and overcome the civic dry-rot that has been making unswerving headway upon the city. Most forward-looking steps are taken in Philadelphia, if at all, only when they have become history in other American cities. As one venerable Philadelphian put it, "We are a taller race and a fairer race than the Chinese, but, alas, not so progressive."

A part of Philadelphia's lethargy springs from its age-old political corruption, and the acquiescence of many of its most powerful and respectable burghers, who too often have endorsed—tacitly at least—the city's machine politicians. These machine politicians have, in turn, maintained their organizations by permitting their lieutenants to forage freely for petty graft. There are few more extravagant trinkets a city can purchase than subways. Two of Philadelphia's expensive holes in the ground never have and, in all likelihood, never will be used. Yet virtually all Philadelphia's transit facilities—the port, the airports, and the streets—are in want of modernization.

Back in the days when the Vare boys controlled the city, they made a fortune by turning Philadelphia's garbage into pork. Today Philadelphia's garbage collection efforts are notoriously feeble and insufficient. Philadelphia house flies carry with them not only the bacteria they pick up from rotting garbage, but that which they encounter in the city's thousands of outdoor toilets. The city's filtered and chemically treated drinking water, which comes from two of the nation's filthiest rivers, the Schuylkill and the Delaware, usually tastes and often smells vile. The rivers themselves are polluted and reeking with industrial wastes and untreated sewage. From the standpoint of police protection, there are some parts of the city, even better-class residential districts, where it is unsafe to go abroad on the streets at night. None of these things are new and casual oversights, but are old, neglected running sores. And most of them tend to make day-to-day living in Philadelphia proper an uphill, disagreeable job.

The people who own the city have abandoned it and gone to the suburbs, beyond the reach of the municipal real-estate-tax collector. This is true of many large cities, of course, but it has happened in Philadelphia to a greater extent than in most of the others. So seriously did the exodus of wealth cut into municipal revenues that a few years ago the city enacted a wage tax—now one per cent with no exemptions—applicable to everyone who earns his living in Philadelphia proper, whether his home is there or not. This evoked a loud squawk from suburbanites at first, but the tax has not been upset in the courts and is now firmly embedded in the municipal economy.

The flight of wealth has been tough on the city itself, but it has resulted in what many well-traveled Americans regard as this country's most beautiful suburbs. To the west and north of the city proper stretches an enchanting countryside of gentle hills and heavily wooded valleys through which course dozens of clear, rocky little streams. In this naturally lovely setting, the Philadelphians who could afford it have built suburban towns and estate districts of surpassing beauty and good taste. The stone houses of colonial and English design are as attractive architecturally as any in America. Millions of dollars have been spent on fine shrubbery and gardens, and in May and early June the whole Philadelphia suburban district becomes a fairyland of bloom. The suburbs have their own water supply and the product is excellent. The suburban police systems are first-class, and other civic services are as good as they are bad in Philadelphia proper. Living in these areas—and a pleasant pattern of living it is—is made easy by fast commuters' lines which radiate from the city like the spokes of a wheel. Many of the finest Philadelphia suburbs are within twenty minutes of the heart of the city.

At first only those with comfortable incomes moved out of Philadelphia. Now the middle-class hegira is under way, and the laboring folk are beginning to move out, since the city is least habitable for the poor. For while huge Fairmount Park is one of the nation's finest, recreation areas in the poorer sections are very scarce indeed.

Philadelphia is the only city on earth its size that co-exists within a hundred-mile radius of a larger city, and there is a constant tendency on the part of New York, the capital of the world, to race Philadelphia's heart out and drain off its ablest younger citizens.

Recently certain local groups have polled the city on what its people thought was wrong. The obvious answers were forthcoming. And on the strength of dire necessity, Philadelphians have voted to lay out $78,000,000, with which to make some kind of beginning on such projects as potable water, a new sewage-treatment-and-disposal system, the removal of 25,000,000 tons of filth and sludge from the Schuylkill, the development of a more fluent traffic system, a larger and better-equipped police force, port improvements, etc. In conjunction with its favorite railroad, the city will soon remove that famous old nuisance, "the Chinese Wall," a stone and earth embankment over which trains have so long run to Broad Street Station in the heart of the city. Furthermore, since earlier city administrations have usually worked at cross purposes with those who had preceded them, Philadelphia now has a City Planning Commission and hopes that its energies can be orchestrated in such a way as to make some kind of long-term sense.

When you turn your attention to the plus side of Philadelphia's ledger, you find that, however much her position among the cities has retrogressed, she still makes and sells a lot of goods.

She has certain natural advantages such as an extremely heavily populated market area—a third of all Americans live no farther than an overnight train ride from Philadelphia—and her port, which is second only to that of New York in export and import tonnage. She has a really splendid diversity of enterprises, a five-billion-dollar banking structure, a fairly good record where strikes are concerned, and is surrounded by a region that is rich both agriculturally and in mineral resources.

Philadelphia makes a little bit of everything and a lot of a great many things, amounting to $2,250,000,000 worth a year. Her biggest business, some of which has been lost to the South, is textiles: hosiery, rugs, cloth and clothing. She does a large business in steel and the countless products she fashions from it: bearings, gears, gadgets, locks, tin cans and, in impressive degree, ships. The Delaware is the American Clyde, along which can be found not only such great private shipbuilders as Cramp's and Sun Ship, but the mammoth Philadelphia Navy Yard, which during the last war employed 70,000 people. Philadelphia also makes considerable railroad rolling stock.

One of the impressive things about Philadelphia's vast manufacturing establishment is the great number of well-known products which are made there—products whose names are almost household words. The roster includes such items as *The Saturday Evening Post*, Stetson hats, Whitman's candies, Disston, Plumb and Yankee tools, Fels-Naptha soap, Exide batteries, Hires root beer, Lester pianos, Philco and RCA-Victor radios and phonographs, Phillies cigars, Pioneer suspenders and belts, Baldwin locomotives, Budd stainless-steel trains, SKF bearings, Burpee seeds, Scot tissue, Campbell soups, Esterbrook pens and pencils, Lee tires and Autocar trucks. Some of these are manufactured in outlying industrial towns such as Chester, Ardmore and Conshohocken, and in Camden, New Jersey, which lies just across the Delaware River—all usually considered a part of the greater Philadelphia industrial district. The reservoir of industrial skills which has been built up in Philadelphia over the years is perhaps more extensive and diverse than anywhere else in the world.

Printing is important to Philadelphia, which does most of the nation's medical publishing and houses the vast Curtis magazine group, that prints more than a million magazines a day right on Independence

Square; the Cuneo Press, a printing establishment which turns out magazines on contract for other publishers; the *Farm Journal* and other publications. In the field of daily journalism, the *Record*, which campaigns most energetically against the city's sluggish ways, prints something like 270,000 papers, the *Daily News* 143,000, the *Bulletin* more than 700,000, and the *Inquirer* about 579,000.

Food processing is another key Philadelphia enterprise, and a lot of the things the city sells are things that it made famous, such as its exceptionally good ice cream, Philadelphia cream cheese, its hearty tripe soup called Philadelphia pepper pot, and finally that nourishing mélange of corn meal and pig squeal, scrapple. It also produces the toddy makings that precede the soup and the cigars that come after the ice cream.

From the standpoint of respectable cultural institutions, Philadelphia has long had a strong position. It is a try-out town for Broadway theater companies, and many of them come back after successful New York runs to entertain Philadelphians. The city's theater-going citizens can see most of the good shows, eventually, without going to New York. The Philadelphia Orchestra, lately directed by Leopold Stokowski and presently by Eugene Ormandy, is respected all over the world. During the summer, the orchestra plays a regular schedule to enormous audiences at Robin Hood Dell, the lovely outdoor amphitheater.

The Pennsylvania Academy of the Fine Arts and the Curtis Institute of Music are in mid-city, while the Barnes Foundation Art Museum is out in Merion. Many of the city's other cultural institutions are built around the somewhat breath-taking Benjamin Franklin Parkway. There you will find the Rodin Museum, the Academy of Natural Sciences, including a free natural-history museum, the Free Library of Philadelphia, the Philadelphia Museum of Art, said to be second only to the Metropolitan in New York, and the Franklin Memorial, which contains both the Franklin Institute, believed to be the finest scientific collection in the world, and the Fels Planetarium. Just west of the Schuylkill River is the nation's oldest zoo, while the Aquarium is on the east bank. If there's any historical point you need settled, the Historical Society of Pennsylvania knows all the answers and has many interesting exhibits of pictures, furniture, manuscripts and relics. But you can see the Philadelphia story unfold in sequence at the little Atwater Kent Museum not far from Independence Square.

Independence Square, probably the most hallowed ground that Americans know, contains, besides Independence Hall, the lovely little building called Congress Hall, where that body met in its infancy. Here, too, are the Old City Hall and the meeting house of the American Philosophical Society, which still meets just as regularly as it did when Franklin founded it as a place where those with an interest in discourse and learning might meet to the mutual pleasure and enlightenment of all.

A part of the face-lifting Philadelphia has planned is a new and stately Mall, by which Independence Square can be approached from the Delaware River Bridge, several blocks to the north. Yet it would also be nice if the Tom Thumb Sandwich Shop at Seventh and Market streets would hang out a sign saying: "Here Thomas Jefferson wrote the Declaration of Independence."

Philadelphia has a Quaker-born tradition of good schools. It was the Quakers who built such excellent schools as Friends' Select, Penn Charter and Germantown Friends.

Among fine non-Quaker schools are Germantown Academy and Episcopal Academy; and, for girls, Baldwin, Shipley, and Stevens. A unique school and junior college for the free education of orphan boys is Girard College. The University of Pennsylvania is one of the institutions Franklin helped to found, and Philadelphians feel that the University's medical school is the best in the world and ask why, if it weren't, the Mayos would send their sons there. Though there are no doubt others who, knowing that Jefferson and Hahnemann Medical Colleges have tutored some of the most distinguished men in medicine, might take a divergent view. Philadelphia is also the home of such other famous schools as Bryn Mawr, Temple University, Villanova, and many others.

Nor, in Philadelphia, are the students apt to be caught up in the distracting glitter of night life, since, generally speaking, there isn't much. Philadelphians love to entertain in their homes or clubs. They also like to go on bird walks along the Wissahickon. It is socially necessary to be invited to the Assemblies, which started back in the days when the British held the city. It is a high distinction to belong to the First City Troop of Light Horse, just as it is *de rigueur* to belong to the Philadelphia, the Rittenhouse or the Union League club. But if you like to have your social distinction and eat it too, you'd be very lucky to be allowed to join one of the famous old eating clubs, such as the Green Tree or The Fish House, where the members do the cooking and where George Washington loved to dine.

All these things, along with the city's Job-like assortment of maladies, compose the complex blend that is Philadelphia. But, as Struthers Burt says at the end of his book, *Philadelphia, Holy Experiment*, "Run away if they may have to; stay away as long as they will; upbraid the city often, as is the habit of Philadelphians; let the native son, or daughter, come back for a visit, or for good, and they find themselves suddenly and strangely happy and content. As they step once more into the narrow, crowded streets, and smell the soft, sooty air, and see the faces of the people who pass, they are suddenly happy.

"There must be some sort of magic, mustn't there?"

There is a kind of magic about Philadelphia, and much that is amusing. Where but in Philadelphia would there be a family, whose ancestor was demoted in the Revolutionary Army, which still keeps Washington's portrait face to the wall? Where else would a royal guest be troubled by forgetting whether he had eaten biddle, been entertained by Scrapple, or vice versa? From what other city might one of its daughters, on being presented at court, reply to the queen's question as to where she lived: "On the Main Line"?

But Philadelphia's magic is framed in so much backwardness and frustration that the modern world won't pause to savor it. It is true that in this manifold and mellow, this soiled and sick old city, the air is burdened not only with evil smells but with the evanescent echoes of great dreams and great deeds. Here at twilight the ghosts of Washington and Franklin can most easily be conjured up. Yet even its glorious yesterdays do not mitigate its remarkable delinquencies today.

After making a study of Philadelphia, Lincoln Steffens said the city was "corrupt and contented." It seems likely that, if he were still alive and could look upon the self-imposed *Götterdämmerung* of what was once America's finest city, he'd find little reason for altering his estimate.

9: *Detroit*

Y OU CAN slip up on Detroit in the dead of night, consider it from any standpoint, and it's still: hell on wheels.

When this puissant, dynamic city rares back to pass a miracle, the nation knows it can expect a stud miracle. Detroit is the town that focused and machined our native gadget-mindedness into the industrial fluency with which we have stampeded history. In Detroit the industrial revolution attained not merely new magnitudes but new dimensions. Here many of the assets and liabilities of the machine age have been fantastically exaggerated. And it's perfectly natural that this high-compression town with the skyrocket destiny should now and again be ridden by the scarlet ghost of internal combustion.

For forty years it's been a feast-and-famine, gold-rush town. It still is. It is raw and brassy, a municipal orgy of production, a stainless steel cornucopia that not only pours forth abundance, but emits raucous klaxon toots.

Detroit has an excellent school system, but many of the men who brought Detroit to its dominant position never got out of the grammar grades and still wear the service stripes of toil proudly on their hands. Yet at the job of performing world-changing magic, these scarred and callused hands have far outdone either those of Merlin or Houdini.

The lonely dean of this school of shop learning was, back in the pre-self-starter days of the Model *T*, probably responsible for more broken arms than all the boy-climbed trees in history. By the thousands Mr. Ford put otherwise dignified burghers into Mother Hubbards called dusters, and with cold patching filled their pockets. Certainly nothing has ever delighted or killed, bankrupted or enriched, so many of us as has the automobile—plus its less classy kinfolks, the truck and the tractor. But just as much a part of our national motorization was the fiscal means by which we indentured ourselves in order to possess and jockey this tin Pegasus. For the installment plan, no matter how you figure it, was one of the more important founding fathers of twentieth century Detroit.

Between Detroit and her big American sister cities, there is a profound difference. New York and Los Angeles have the warm and exciting human quality—weakness if you prefer—of glorifying, overemphasizing and loving, the individual. Detroit, since the passing of those earlier days when her streets were rank with the acrid musk of individual automotive lions, has been engrossed in split-second manipulation both of men and materials in the mass. Detroit is a team-town, and its teams are the phalanxes of men incident to its appalling production.

Detroit's critics say that while Chicagoans adore their own great, powerful, mangy bear of a city, hundreds of thousands of Detroit's people look upon their town merely as a carnival concession where one tests one's strength with a sledge hammer in the hope of ringing the bell and winning the golden cheroot.

Detroit was once a quiet city with a subtle Gallic flavor. The graceful days of old Detroit are still lovingly remembered in the downtown Detroit Club, where arteries may harden in dignity and peace, and in the even more blue-blooded Yondotega Club.

The Detroit Athletic Club, the handsome hang-out of the top automobile men, is the seat of much of the town's muscle and drive. Here the hard, metallic dreams bounce across the dining tables, articulated in Detroitese, which is a language with a high content of short, blunt, Anglo-Saxon punch words. These are the men who direct the endlessly complicated campaigns to produce, promote and distribute the new models.

It is easy to forget that Detroit is a great port, with seven of the fifteen largest cities in the United States and Canada within a steaming range of 750 miles. The Michigan Customs District, of which Detroit is the principal port, is surpassed only by the New York Customs District in the value of its exports. Detroit also contains the leading stove-manufacturing plant in the world, the leading add-ing-machine, pharmaceutical, electric-refrigeration plants, and the leading copper and brass-rolling mills. It is first in the production of salt, paints and varnishes, vacuum cleaners, twist drills and other products. Nevertheless, as a result of the astounding size of its automotive business, Detroit is still, essentially, a one-industry town. Its prime function, before which every other consideration fades into unimportance, is the gushing creation of motor vehicles.

To gain some idea of the Gargantuan proportions of Detroit's prewar automotive industry, consider these facts: It devoured three quarters of all American rubber imports, 70 per cent of all plate glass manufactured, 57 per cent of all malleable iron, 40 per cent of the mohair and lead, 33⅓ per cent of the nickel, 20 per cent of the American steel output, 15 per cent of all aluminum and almost as much of the nation's cast iron, tin, zinc, hardwood lumber and cotton.

But nothing can grow to such titanic proportions without engendering all sorts of corollary growths and creating innumerable tributary dislocations. And, as the motor firms grew into corporate principalities and empires, the organization of its workers mushroomed the UAW-CIO into the world's largest union.

This union became a thing of such formidable might and power, so unwieldy in size and, like every other section of society, including the automobile companies, so riddled with factions, that even its own properly constituted leaders could maintain little more than approximate control over it. So, as in most places where power and money change hands in stupendous hunks, Detroit became, and is, a battleground where men struggle to control the machine and the unions, to fend off unemployment, to try to integrate production and consumption, and to assimilate the minorities into some reasonably equitable scheme.

But in any battle the lay of the land is a vital factor. Let us, for the moment, sheathe our knucks and examine a few of the physical and cultural attributes of this municipal arena.

The heart of downtown Detroit was laid out in compliance with the plan which the French engineer, Pierre L'Enfant, had previously devised for Washington, D. C., and is a very fetching place. But, just as in Washington, the visitor who hasn't spent fifty cents for a street guide will in all probability not get where he's going if it's more than a block off the main stem which, in Detroit, is Woodward Avenue. This spacious thoroughfare was named for one of Detroit's earlier and most honored citizens, Judge Augustus Brevoort Woodward, who used to pal around with Thomas Jefferson. Woodward Avenue cuts squarely through the solid half-circle of Grand Circus, Detroit's main downtown park.

Brief Washington Boulevard and Madison Avenue also wing out from Grand Circus and are made both more handsome and utilitarian by reason of carefully planted and tended esplanades. Due to their novel design, they permit motorists wishing to make left turns to do so with ease just short of the intersections. Grand Boulevard describes a croquet wicket encompassing the downtown area, with its prongs touching the Detroit River. Within this area are the mammoth Hudson's department store and many of the great hotels, such as the Book-Cadillac and the Statler. Then, as is the case with so many of our cities, there is a horseshoe-shaped belt of slums with its points coming right up to the river. Farther out are the great automotive plants. Jefferson Avenue is Detroit's Riverside Drive.

Detroit's government is non-partisan, which would suggest all sorts of tranquil civic discussions of this or that town problem in the light of sweet reason and with no party pressures. In practice, Detroit's politics are a relentless fight to determine whether the UAW-CIO or the coalition of its opponents will run the town. Every other consideration is secondary. In the 1945 mayoralty election, bouncy, glad-handing young Dick Frankensteen, then a vice-president of the UAW, lost to Detroit's perennial mayor, E. J. Jeffries, after polling the most votes against a field of eight in the primary.

Jeffries usually gets the backing of all the Detroit papers, the *News,* the Hearst-owned *Times,* and the Knight-owned *Free Press,* which won the Pulitzer Prize in 1944 for the exposure of graft in the Michigan legislature. Nor have the Pulitzer folk failed to tie a blue ribbon on the good writing arm of Malcolm W. Bingay, editorial director of the *Free Press,* who is also a loving, book-length Boswell to his Johnsonianly blustery city. Moreover, Detroit is the home of the newspaper poet, Edgar A. Guest, "the voice of the common man," perhaps Detroit's best loved citizen. Though having filled his niche with modesty and industry, this durable journalist has probably been the target of more snide cracks from the nation's Grade 8 cognoscenti than any other journeyman versifier alive.

Across the Detroit River in the most implausible of directions, which is to say to the south, lies Windsor in Ontario, "the sun parlor of Canada." And, though the Canadian border with its tariff restrictions chops off half of what Detroit's trade area might be, Windsor, as part of a foreign country, amounts to an important condiment in Detroit's potpourri of tourist attractions. In a few minutes you can reach Windsor from downtown Detroit by tunnel or bridge. It's almost as simple as going from Manhattan to Brooklyn. No passport is required—just evidence of your American citizenship, and, if you drive, your motor registration card. If you stay as long as forty-eight hours, you can bring back a hundred dollars' worth of stuff duty free.

You may as well have some notion of Detroit's tourist attractions, because Detroit has serious designs on, and a pretty good argument for getting, your vacation dollar. It's simple: when you buy a new car, why not trade in your old one to your home dealer, but take delivery on the new one F.O.B. Detroit? The theory is that what you save on your car's transportation will cover the cost of your own.

A good way to begin a rubber-necking tour would be to get a bird's-eye view of Detroit and Canada from the top of the forty-seven-story Penobscot Building. One of the things you'll notice is that Detroit is built on land as flat as a windowpane. If you are interested in going out to the great auto plants, any or all of them will make you a welcome visitor. And, if you tour the Ford empire at Dearborn, nine miles from Detroit, you'll probably want to have lunch at Dearborn Inn, see the Ford Rotunda, Greenfield Village and the Edison Institute Museum. Mr. Ford's transported and restored Greenfield Village is an engaging sample of the quiet, old-time, horsy world, complete with chestnut-shaded smithy.

Back in Detroit, the General Motors Building is billed as the largest office building of its kind in the world, and, before long, the proposed General Motors $25,000,000 Technical Center, which is, among other things, to be a kind of airport for C. F. Kettering's imagination, will be a must on every tourist's list. For the art lovers, there is the Art Center, which contains the Detroit Institute of Arts, the Public Library and the Horace H. Rackham Education Memorial. Over in Grosse Pointe at the Alger House there is one of the finest collections of Renaissance art in this country. At the Shrine of the Little Flower you will, with whatever emotions, find Father Coughlin still at large. Offshore, in the Detroit River, is Belle Isle, the city's beautiful thousand-acre park offering all sorts of recreation. Yet a real baseball fan might prefer just to chuck the whole thing and go out to Briggs Stadium and watch the Tigers do their stuff.

But even though Detroit has found another Ty Cobb in that top-notch American, Hank Greenberg, many Detroiters are troubled and worried nowadays and fall a prey to the rash of cultists and Voodoo quacks who are flourishing here, as in other of our urban areas. For in Detroit, to a greater extent than most cities, there have been many displaced persons, both black and white, people accustomed to the quiet ways of hamlet or farm, association with old friends, the sense of continuity that stabilizes the habits and emotions of any society dominated by agriculture. In Detroit they have found high pay, high pressure, loneliness, confusion and insecurity. All day long at high speed, over and over, they perform the same benumbing, hypnotizing operation on a production line or an automatic machine. And just about the time they start seeking emotional release by dwelling in memory on the pleasant valleys and green hills of home, off goes the end of a finger in a drill press.

To whom, under such circumstances, might not a wildcat strike appeal? Or, when a few other factors are added, such as a drastic insufficiency of housing, you may get a race riot, such as that which occurred in Detroit in 1943. The town was full of newly arrived Negroes, heady with the ammoniac flavor of increased freedom and wages. It was also full of poor-white Southerners, which Detroit pleases to call hill-billies. Mayor Jeffries was running for re-election. He appointed as police commissioner, John Witherspoon, a splendid lawyer and tax expert. Witherspoon received orders to hold the lid on until the election was over. He passed the word to the cops to take whatever back-talk was handed out to them. Under no condition were they to let go with their shillelaghs. The poolroom boys, the barflies and hoodlums caught on fast. The cops were on the run.

Then on a hot summer night two rumors began to flash over the town: (1) that a white woman had been raped by a Negro, and (2) that a Negro woman and her baby had been pushed into the river by a white man. The riot started.

After more bumbling than seems to have been necessary, the troops were summoned, and at the sight of this show of authority, Woodward Avenue, the scene of most of the fighting, emptied. But by then thirty-odd human beings lay dead. And this disaster was especially saddening to old-line Detroiters, who had proudly thought of their town—the northern terminus of the Underground Railroad in slavery days—as a proved friend-in-need to the Negro.

Though Detroit's quarter-million Negroes compose the largest minority in the 2,500,000 people who inhabit her metropolitan area, there are many others. Some 100,000 Canadians have moved to Detroit, as have roughly 70,000 Poles, 30,000 Germans, 25,000 each of English, Scots and Italians, and some 20,000 Russians.

Oddly enough, Detroit has very few French citizens, despite the fact that it was they who founded the town. The King of France had taken a shine to a beaver hat, and this, in turn, created first a fad, and then a demand for beaver skins. The quest for pelts brought French *voyageurs* to the northern areas of the new world, and, subsequently, to *D'etroit*. The word meant "narrows" and was what the French called the strait which flowed between—not to mention such relatively small potatoes as Lake St. Clair—lakes Huron and Erie. It was the American Dardanelles, the strategic key to this whole fur-rich region. So in 1701 the man with the sixteen-cylinder name, Sieur Antoine de la Mothe Cadillac, in haste to beat the British there, built Fort Pontchartrain on the strait, and, on the fifth of June, Detroit came into existence.

The British finally chased the French off in 1760, and, in due time, we the British. There were the usual Indian massacres, fires and epidemics. Though the town got some trade from the pioneers heading west, until the railroad age began, the iron horse for a long time shied off from out-of-the-way Detroit. But the Michigan timber business got booming, and the famed mineral riches of the lakes began to come to light. Meanwhile, Detroit was becoming a handsome town, and was not without cultural pretensions.

Then, just before the nineteenth century ran out, a new fad hit the East Coast. It was the importation and sportive use of the new European wonder, the automobile. While commenting on the dazzling scene in Newport at this period, the *New York Times* remarked, "Nothing that was ever introduced here has so caught the popular fancy as the automobile."

By 1894 a Detroit man, Charles B. King, was actually building these improbable contraptions. One of his first sales was to a Cincinnati circus. The car was to be used for parade purposes. But because Cincinnati is a hilly town, it was arranged to have an elephant next in the line of march, just in case.

R. E. Olds was one of the next big names to enter the automotive scene. He finally raised $10,000 and in 1897 organized the Olds Motor Vehicle Company at Lansing, but a little later, when he was given further backing by a Detroit capitalist, S. L. Smith, Olds moved into Detroit. Then he had a significant accident. The company had a fire which burned all but one of its varieties of models. Consequently Olds leveled down on the production of that one—and the first faint whisperings of mass production had come into being.

Of profound importance to Detroit's future was the fact that, at this time, the town was one of the principal carriage-producing centers in the nation, and was also building engines for boats.

But one of the most telling decisions in automotive history had been made when the sixteen-year-old Henry Ford decided his hand did not fit a plow handle. His father insisted that it did. But nature had not equipped Henry Ford with a yielding disposition. He took to the tall and uncut, and wound up in Detroit, where he got a job in a machine shop by day, and mended clocks at night to earn his keep. Finally, after considerable trial and error, he completed his famous 999, installed Barney Oldfield at the wheel, and made a clean sweep of the race tracks. This publicity attracted financial backing, and in 1903 the Ford Motor Company was born. It was capitalized at $100,000, but it had only about a fourth that much actual cash.

Ford soon determined to make the automobile a poor man's necessity instead of a rich man's luxury. The next thing anybody knew, he
had pieces of tin running a human gauntlet, and by the time they
reached the end of it, they deserved the exalted name of Lizzie, would
run like a spotted-bottomed ape—and with about as much grace.

To move the work to the man, at waist level, was a revolutionary
leap into the arms of efficiency. Ford drove down the cost of his car
from $950 to $365, and wherever this vehicular Ichabod Crane rolled
down the road, it left in its wake good-roads boosters, garages, and
filling stations which took over from the hardware and drugstores the
job of selling gasoline. It liberated the farmer from the isolation of the
farm, and wowed us all with a whole special literature of corny jokes.

Then in January, 1914, Mr. Ford caused great numbers of the
civilized world to conclude he was a little dotty. When he could get
all the labor he wanted for $2.50 per day or less, and when an existent
labor surplus invited employers to drive wages down, he announced
he would pay his workers a minimum of $5.00 a day. Conservative
business elements cried out that Ford's eleemosynary zeal was a menace to the capitalistic system. Nevertheless, in 1919, Mr. Ford bought
out all his stockholders, and, little more than twenty years after his
company's founding, he was worth a billion dollars.

Meanwhile, other dynamic names, such as John and Horace Dodge,
the Fisher brothers, the Chevrolets, had burst blazing onto the Detroit
firmament—all names that have become deeply rooted in American
diction and life. One of the flashiest speculators in the automobile
business, W. C. Durant, has almost been forgotten. He first picked up
the company of David Dunbar Buick. Then he acquired Cadillac,
Oakland, Oldsmobile and, in 1908, came within an inch of getting
Ford. He would have, at a price of $8,000,000, except that Ford
wouldn't accept Durant's securities in payment. But Durant was, alas,
more adept in obtaining automotive white elephants and in suffering
patent disasters. Soon hard times knocked the whole front out of
Durant's door. He went borrowing in Wall Street, and, in the end, the
bankers took over his company. From Durant's fallen empire has risen
General Motors, which is today so huge that the effects of its policies
are almost geologic.

Then Walter Chrysler, late of Baldwin Locomotive, Buick and Willys-Overland, formed his own company, which absorbed Maxwell and built automobiles around the new motor that Fred Zeder had devised. A little later, without the expenditure of a nickel in cash, Chrysler acquired the then languishing Dodge interests. And, in the automobile world, the term "Big Three" came into being.

By 1929 the automobile industry was a thing of majesty and glory. It was making more than 5,000,000 cars a year and was reputed to be, in its combined manifestations, dragging down every fifth consumer dollar, aside from such funds as went for rent and insurance. Then the great depression of the 1930s sank its teeth into brittle, one-industry Detroit with especial savagery. Banks busted. School marms had to be paid in scrip. There was vast unemployment, and the sit-down strikes spread over town.

Sentiment and talk grew radical. If this was the best the companies could do, some of the hard-pressed workers were saying, maybe there had better be a change of ownership by whatever means necessary. The fuse was burning short in Detroit.

As early as 1935, the UAW had received its first charter, and the fight to organize the automobile companies had begun. Detroit became a kind of city-wide Donnybrook. The union leveled down on one company at a time and brought it to its knees. The fight was just as furious inside the great labor lodge. The UAW walked out of the AFL and joined Lewis' CIO. Then in 1939, the bucking, pitching UAW did a fast sunfish; Homer Martin lost his seat in the saddle, and R. J. Thomas grabbed the presidential reins. Not until 1941 did the UAW bring Henry Ford, clasping the moist hand of Harry Bennett, up to the lick log. Now the town was as tightly organized as a cow hand's footwear, and wages had virtually doubled.

Meanwhile Adolf Hitler had begun his tragic monkeyshines. Mr. Roosevelt asked Detroit to get rolling; the spent, bullfrog voice of Wendell Willkie cried out for "production, production, production!" We saw the blue-blazing competitive instincts of the automotive industry yield before the national emergency when they pooled their precious trade secrets in the automotive council for war. We saw General Motors develop the Allison aircraft motor while Packard put the Rolls-Royce Merlin into quantity production, and Buick energized our bombers with the great Wright radials. We saw Willow Run materialize and perform its vast function. We saw the endless essential engines of destruction, the trucks, the half tracks, the tanks, the jeeps, inundate our enemies. Though in this connection money meant little, Detroit's motor industry, to employ the dollar as a means of measurement, put out twenty-eight billion dollars' worth of good girding for the loins of G.I. Joe.

By war's end new names were coming into prominence in Detroit, names such as those of young Henry Ford II, new titular head of the Dearborn empire, and pugnacious, redheaded Walter P. Reuther, the UAW vice-president in command of the General Motors front. So, too, had Mr. Henry Kaiser dipped a toe into the chilly Detroit waters and gained access to Willow Run for the purpose of building automobiles.

But with Ford willing to go to almost any length to avert a strike and, significantly, not being answerable to stockholders, and with Chrysler lying low, Detroit knew that everything depended on the General Motors strike. Reuther was yelling his head off that he could prove that G.M. could grant a 30 per cent wage raise without upping prices. This claim cast Reuther in the dual role of the John Brown of the UAW and the St. George of the nation's inflation-conscious consumers.

After a strike that to many an impartial observer seemed unduly and, from almost any standpoint, uneconomically drawn out, Reuther won a compromise eighteen-and-a-half-cent increase for the G.M. workers. Now, for the first time in public, Reuther turned his sharp, bright eyes on the job of earnest, limited R. J. Thomas, the UAW's president.

Finally, Reuther, by a close vote, was elected the new UAW president. But since he is surrounded by a group of exuberantly anti-Reuther secondary officials, the outcome of the dog fight for the actual control of the union is yet to be determined.

Incidentally, it sometimes happens that after Detroit has had one of its labor-management brawls, it holds some sort of big public shindig such as its week-long Golden Jubilee celebration built around the story of the automobile industry. In pulling that off, the lions of automobile management lay down with the lambs of CIO and AFL. Not only do Detroiters, just like other people, enjoy a frolic now and then, but a city-wide get-together, after one of these labor-management Armageddons, acts as a kind of catharsis, tending to clear the atmosphere of remembered insults, slander, and assorted blasphemies.

In older and simpler times, the traditional key to prosperity in Detroit lay almost solely in whether there was or was not a strong market for automobiles, and it is still a thing she's got to have. Never before has she had a better one; never before has she been subsidized to create other types of goods while at the same time the public was busily reducing its on-hand supply of automobiles to creaking, exhausted jalopies. The talk around Detroit is that the industry should have no trouble in selling 25,000,000 cars in the five years following the war.

Another question that concerns Detroit is that of decentralization of the automotive industry. It is a process that has been going on for years, ever since the first automobile company built a plant in a foreign country, so that its methods and designs might leap that country's tariff barriers. Again, within the United States, the automobile-parts manufacturing industry, which employs 400,000 people, is scattered over thirty states. Yet it's worth noting that 80 per cent of the volume of the parts business originates within three hundred miles of Detroit.

Finally, the building of every regional assembly plant has been a further step toward decentralization, and the function of these plants is slated to become even more extensive in the future. Decentralization, through the establishment of more regional assembly plants, would certainly suggest that heavier parts will in many cases be manufactured most economically, not in Detroit, but near these regional plants. However, Detroiters like to think of this trend not as decentralization but as "out-of-town expansion."

Detroit has already proved her ability to produce more motor vehicles than the nation can consume. The problem of increasing the standard of living of the rest of the world becomes, therefore, less a question of neighborly solicitude for Europe, Asia, and South America than a necessary means of preserving, for Detroit, the joyful old custom of three hots a day. She is not merely the automotive capital of the nation but of the world, and with her inevitable future need for broader markets, she has, perhaps, the greatest stake in lowered tariffs and free world trade of any American city.

In addition to the chronic job of adjusting herself to the rise of trade-unionism, Detroit's real problems, like those of this totally un-isolated nation, are world problems. As a city she is in direct competition with every automobile manufacturing and/or assembling plant that lies beyond her bailiwick, American-owned or otherwise. And in labor, management and machines, in technology, skill and drive, Detroit always has been, is, and is likely for a long time to remain, six jumps ahead of them all.

Should the future open up to her the St. Lawrence waterway, cut a few express-ways through the barriers of international trade, grant her a moderately prosperous world economy and an orderly working arrangement between management and labor, the earth will tremble as this she-giant rises from her hands and knees and begins to move mountains, three ranges at a time.

10: *Portland, Maine*

PORTLAND, "down East" in Maine, is, if something less than a sprightly town, one with a natural setting so beautiful that any city might envy it and a record for resurgence in the face of disaster that almost no American city can top.

It's a town where "newfangled" is a word of particular opprobrium, where eggs are not "poached" but "dropped," and where a Democrat in public office is as out of place as a tomato in a New England clam chowder. It's a town where many a shirt is red plaid and woolly, where ice is still sawed during the long winter for consumption during the brief but lovely summer. It's a town where, every winter, the severity of the cold causes the streets and roads to pop open with "frost heaves." Yet to the people in northern Maine's potato-growing Aroostook County, life in Portland, where the temperature hardly ever drops beyond twenty below, seems a pretty soft snap.

Although Portland is the largest city in Maine, it has only about 75,000 citizens within its corporate limits, and about as many more in its metropolitan district. It is built on a peninsula that extrudes, like a leg bent at the knee and cut off at the shank, into bewitching Casco Bay which, counting the tiniest, contains an island for each day in the year.

Most of the city proper lies between the parentheses of handsome Eastern and Western Promenades, which are boulevards on the heights at either end of this sway-backed peninsula. Yet for all the beauty of the outer bay, Portland's Back Bay is, at low tide, merely a naked mud flat which, like all its brothers, caresses neither the eye nor the nose. Oddly enough, one of the pleasantest residential sections in the city is in the Woodfords area on Baxter Boulevard which circles Back Bay.

Architecturally, you can more or less name it and take it in Portland.

Unlike little southern New England coastal towns, which are pretty uniformly Cape Cod, salt-box and Greek Revival houses nestling around a central green and seeming to fit their setting perfectly, Portland is a hodgepodge of mansard roofs and widow's walks, of Victorian brownstone and Georgian red brick, plus a generous dash of *fin de siècle* mongrel. Yet in summer, when the rain has washed the soot off the houses, when the grass turns green and the city's hundreds of tall old elms spread over and tend to blend these disparities, Portland can, once you get the hang of it, seem a very likable old town.

Coming to Portland from more central parts of the nation is somewhat like reading a volume of Proust immediately after having left a newsreel theater. It takes a little while to attune yourself to a special point of view that has a great deal to do with complete unhurriedness and a certain quiet disillusionment. Impatience and the long Maine winters just don't go together. Most everything here seems to follow long-established cycles. For example, many an old Portland family has long since sold its town house. It spends the summer at its beach house, and as the first cold winds drive the tourists away, these old families close their beach cottages and move into the Eastland Hotel, the homey old Lafayette, or one or two others.

During the winter these elderly people, having secured a moderate off-season rate, have a quietly gay old time playing cards, reminiscing, and expressing themselves freely on the actions of the government. They know there will be no upsetting editorial opinions in either the morning or evening Gannett papers, which take for granted that you, their reader, have the good sense to be a thoroughly conservative, rock-ribbed Republican. These folk are, moreover, positive that, whether it's on the menu or not, they can always have chopped corned-beef hash or fish cakes for breakfast, a lobster or a chowder when they feel like it, or a good baked Maine potato. Finally, they know that, unless the heavens fall, there'll be baked beans and brown bread just as surely as Saturday night rolls around. To be snowbound under these circumstances strikes Portlanders as a great improvement over the John Greenleaf Whittier arrangement.

To while away the winter, they can also browse in the extraordinary number of bookstores that dot this small city. In some of these shops can be found copies of the old books, long out of print, that go to compose the voluminous literature of Portland that has accrued during its long life. The story of Portland goes back more than three hundred years.

The very first settlers in the vicinity were one Christopher Levett and party, a group which holed up on an island in Casco Bay in 1623. But after experiencing one Maine winter, Mr. Levett recalled urgent business in England, leaving his company to guard this new possession. That was the last Maine saw of Mr. Levett, and his company vanished into the roomy confines of unrecorded history.

The next settler, Walter Bagnall, who had been run out of Massachusetts by the scandalized Puritans, was so canny a Yankee trader and so fond of "making merrie" with Indian maidens that an Indian chief, instead of bothering to run him out of Maine, simply knocked his brains out.

Four years later, in 1632, an uncommonly truculent fellow, Mr. George Cleeve, came upon the scene and for almost twenty years kept things in so litigatious an uproar that few of his incoming neighbors knew for certain which end was up or what belonged to whom. Finally, in the 1650s, the Maine colonists decided, "What's the use?" and submitted to the jurisdiction of the more stable Massachusetts government.

By 1675 there were in excess of four hundred people living on "The Neck," the protuberance that would one day be called Portland. But that year, the Indians, carrying out a local operation in the King Philip's War, swept down on the settlement and killed all those whose boats and heels were insufficiently swift. Before long, however, the townfolk ventured back. But they neglected to maintain adequate defense and, in 1690, the Indians, under the tutelage of the French, once more attacked the town, this time butchering the entire population, with the exception of five persons who were carried off to Canada as souvenirs.

Again the peninsula was devoid of white people, and remained more or less abandoned until 1716, when a fort was established by Major Samuel Moody. Others followed, and before long things were humming. To discourage the presence of red men, a bounty of a hundred pounds was offered for the scalp of any Indian male over twelve years of age—pickings so rich that even the Reverend Mr. Thomas Smith found it meet to participate in this gory but lucrative hunting. Out of its splendid harbor the town exported fish, furs and lumber to West Indies ports, and brought back sugar, molasses and rum. This last item, after being duly spiced and buttered, was employed to make the Maine winters more nearly resemble those of the West Indies. Ship- and boat-building were coming along at a brisk clip. And the locality was doing a lively business in purveying its finest white pine as masts to His Majesty's Navy.

At first nobody gave much thought to the possibility that these masts might boomerang and bring the wrath of the Royal Navy down on the town. But when England began such petulant shenanigans as passing the Stamp Act and later closing the port of Boston, the colonists on Casco Bay refused to sell the English any more masts. This so annoyed British Captain Henry Mowatt that, in October, 1775, he returned with a war fleet, demanded the town's piddling armament be handed over, and, when this was refused, cracked down with cannon balls, grape and bombs. This bombardment continued until Captain Mowatt saw fit to send landing parties ashore to burn what remained of the town.

Thousands were homeless and sheltered only by tents. On every hand, people said the old town was done for. During the Revolution, British ships roamed at will in the harbor, but, militarily, ignored the town. Finally, it was rebuilt, and on July 4, 1786, the peninsula, which had had several names in the past, but had most recently been considered a part of Falmouth, took the name of Portland.

By 1800, Portland contained about four thousand people, had a newspaper, a bank capitalized at $100,000, and was doing a brisk business with her recently punitive kindred in England. Then Portland's own Commodore Edward Preble subdued the Barbary Coast pirates, and it was even safe to ship into the Mediterranean. Later, in the War of 1812, Portlanders did their spot of highly profitable privateering.

Meanwhile, as the back lands began to be cleared, new enterprises sprang up. But, more exciting, in 1820, Maine was separated from

Massachusetts and became a state in its own right, of which Portland was declared the capital for several years.

Between this time and the Civil War, Portland was busily arranging better transportation facilities such as railroads and coast-wise steamboat service. In this same period, with what emotions you can imagine, she experienced the arrival of her first transatlantic steamer.

Portland felt so strongly about the Civil War that she sent 20 per cent of her population, then 25,000, to the conflict. What's more, she got herself raided by Rebel 'Skeeter Fleeters, but this time Portland lost only a revenue cutter, and, in the end, not without effective intrepidity on the part of the townfolk, followed and captured the raiders.

But Portland was, alas, not finished with disasters. On July 4, 1866, a celebrant tossed a firecracker in the wood shavings around a boat yard. There was a high wind and, fifteen hours later, much of Portland was gone with it. The remains reminded the town's distinguished son, Henry Wadsworth Longfellow, always a ready man when a quote was needed, of Pompeii. Once more Portland moved into the tents—which by now it probably kept handy.

Yet after an extremely busy and productive interlude of more than a quarter of a century, Portland was, by 1900, the outstanding city of northern New England and one of the most prosperous in the country. But the combination of factors that made it so resplendent began to shift into a state of slowly increasing imbalance. The annexation of the adjoining town of Deering maintained Portland's population growth, which had begun to fall off in the 'Nineties. But despite this artificially enlarged new population, there was a gradual drop in earned income per capita up until the time of the first World War, after which both business and population levels began to fall off. In 1923, the Portland income began to dip below the national average, and to respond less in such peak years as 1923 and 1924. A precipitate slump in Portland's maritime activities began in 1924, when a change in Canadian trading policies shifted the bulk of Montreal's winter shipping from Portland to St. John and Halifax.

Between the years 1919 and 1939 the number of manufacturing establishments had shrunk to approximately one half. The loss of employment was nearly 40 per cent. And according to the rule of thumb that one wealth-producing worker can, in a healthy community, support no more than three workers in the service industries, Portland had dropped beyond the danger mark. Per-capita wealth, which had been going down since 1923, hit an all-time low in 1939, contrary to both state and national trends.

In 1940 the Greater Portland Research Council, from whose reports the foregoing post-1900 facts have been taken, bluntly declared, "We have a shrinking over-all economy based on either New England or national standards. . . . Such a situation discourages new enterprise. It makes the position of enterprising enterprise more difficult. . . . Our [brightest young people and our] skilled labor drifts away. The entire situation deteriorates gradually, perhaps almost imperceptibly, but definitely."

Today's visitor to Portland needs no charts and graphs to learn that for many years Portland's economy has been withering. For while nobody likes to paint up and clean up better than a New Englander, a great many of the houses in Portland proper appear not to have been painted in years. There is an extremely large number of old frame multifamily fire traps, one of which every now and then goes up in flames and incinerates varying numbers of its inhabitants. Portions of this peninsula are blighted or near blighted, and the recreational facilities within the city are woefully deficient.

Portland's water front and the adjacent areas, being the oldest part of the city, are spectacularly dilapidated. Portland has been fighting for a $15,000,000 appropriation from the Maine legislature to rebuild its harbor installations. But the fiercely anti-city-slicker legislature can't be budged. In matters of taxation and state finance, there is a never-ending, three-way battle among the agricultural, fishing and industrial factions. Portland, however, managed to raise between two and three millions from its Port Authority to do a little patching.

Too, since the taxes Portland pays the state are based on property assessment, Portland has seen fit to lower its assessments to 60 per cent of actual value in order to diminish its contributions to the state. This policy, along with the actual decline in value of much of its property, has forced up Portland's city-tax rate to slightly more than fifty dollars on the thousand, a figure that is anything but enticing to prospective builders and businesses. To keep that rate from attaining an even higher figure for 1946, Portland's City Council took the decision to venture, on a small scale, into deficit financing.

An important factor in Portland's dilemma is that she is largely blocked off from New England by Boston and Boston's port, and from Canada by tariff walls. Thus pocketed, she pretty much has to live off her own scant natural resources. This situation, some less bouncy Portlanders feel, is just downright unfortunate and might as well be accepted. But Portland's more determined younger citizens, such as Ed Kessler of the Chamber of Commerce and Portland's attractive Mrs. Helen C. Frost, who heads the Council of its city-manager government, take the view that Portland has in the past successfully climbed many a steeper road, and that if this one appears to be somewhat uphill, nothing can be gained by delay in beginning the ascent.

Yet to appreciate the steps that are being taken, it is necessary to consider what happened in Portland during the war.

World War II boomed Portland deliriously. Early in the struggle, before America was involved, the British government ordered thirty freighters from the Todd-Bath Iron Works. The yard to produce these vessels was built in Portland. This kind of order for so small a city was not mere big business, but gigantic business. Then came Pearl Harbor, and the United States Maritime Commission built a mate to the Todd-Bath yard to produce for our own requirements, as did the Todd plant, once the British order was filled. Liberty ships were turned out in quantity.

By this time Portland was swelled to bursting with 30,000 new people. Most of them were housed in barracks, but a substantial number were ensconced in new permanent construction and many of these folk planned to live in Portland after the war. To assimilate these new citizens and to prepare for Portland's peacetime economy, more enterprises had to be devised. Lawrence C. Plowman organized fifty public-spirited Portland citizens into a body known as Industries, Inc. They put up $100,000 to purchase a million square feet of industrial site on Back Bay, on which they offered to build and sell plants to fit the requirements of any and all takers who looked as if they could make a go of it in Portland.

A similar project was undertaken by another group, which calls itself the Greater Portland Development Commission. After the war was over and ship contracts were canceled, the Commission sent a representative to Washington and offered the Federal government a dollar for the Maritime Commission's vast West Yard in South Portland, complete with ways and docks, outfitting piers, its many huge metal buildings, and sixty-six acres of Portland water front.

The Federal government smiled, said now it knew the deal was on the level since none but genuine Down-Easterners would ever have dreamed of offering so little for so much. In the end, it agreed to sell what cost in excess of $5,000,000 for $224,000, the original cost of the land. It was further arranged for this sum to be painlessly financed, and the deal was closed.

To date, the Development Commission has lined up a shoe factory, a wool-washing plant, a hardwood-appliance factory, a boat yard for construction and repair of small boats, and several other concerns to occupy these buildings. Over in the Broadway Plate Yard, also in South Portland, where the wartime shipbuilders stored their plates, the Commission organized an integrated lumber-finishing and shipping center, to be used co-operatively by the big lumber companies of the north. A part of this group of wood-working industries will be composed of a wood-flour plant and another for the production of prefabricated housing.

There are also other bright aspects of Portland's economic position. And economics, no matter how you slice it, is, at this time, the crux of the Portland story.

For example, it is considered a virtual certainty that Portland, which became increasingly important to the Navy during the war, will have its income increased by becoming a permanent naval base, the North Atlantic anchor of our sea defense line.

And it is certainly of more than local interest that Maine's lobster crop, which had for years been going literally and figuratively to pot, is back on the increase and setting new production records. This is believed to be the result of Maine's new double-action, neither too young nor too old, lobster-taking law, plus its efforts at reseeding with hatchery-raised infants.

Something else that's relatively new under Maine's soft, yellow-white sun is its shrimp industry. Only in comparatively recent years has it been learned that there was a yearly run in Maine waters of these small preludes to the dollar dinner.

In the general fishing picture, Portland, next only to Boston and Gloucester, is right in there landing nearly 40,000,000 pounds per year of lobsters, scallops, clams, cod, haddock, mackerel and the like.

And Portland is particularly adept at canning things. As a matter of fact, commercial canning in America is said to have started in Portland, just as did the making of chewing gum. Portland cans sardines, corn and beans in quantity. But one of its principal fortes, and one where it has an inside track, is in the making of paper and paper products. For Portland is not only very close to the pulp supplies of northern Maine, but lies closer, on the great circle route, to the pulp supplies of Scandinavia than any other United States Atlantic port. And, at times, this Scandinavian pulp is cheaper laid down in Portland than the home-grown variety.

Yet where lightly-industrialized Portland really earns most of its living is by wholesaling to its thinly-populated interior regions, and retailing to its own environs. However, if Portland's wholesalers had to depend only on the purchases of Maine's regular inhabitants and the little country stores, Portland would be a smaller and poorer town.

But as New York's summer suit begins to stick to its body and the corrugated heat waves from Manhattan's buildings are heavy enough for a monkey to climb, thousands of New Yorkers and the inhabitants of other sweltering Eastern cities begin to think of the coolness, the natural grandeur and the repose of Maine woods and lakes and streams. The highways, trains and planes begin funneling in these overhet Pilgrims—from Maine's point of view, $100,000,000 worth, a figure which, each year, until the next depression, will probably be substantially exceeded, due to the uncommon plenitude of money, tires, sleeping-car accommodations, and the relaxation of Canada's restrictions on the export of money. For Canadians are crazy about Maine and have proved it by becoming Portland's largest group of foreign-born citizens. The seaways also bring many visitors, since, according to no less a yachtsman than Mr. Harrison Smith, there are no more enchanting summer cruising grounds than the isle-dotted waters of Casco and Penobscot bays. Yet it's worth noting that the water in these bays is far too cold to invite the corporal immersion of sissies.

Maine's summer visitors do not necessarily all come to Portland, except perhaps to spend the night and pass on to the northland. If they are going to the hundreds of summer camps in southern Maine, they may never reach Portland. Nevertheless, so far as Portland's jobbers and wholesalers are concerned, their year-round clientele of 800,000 in the state of Maine has been increased by 1,000,000 vacationers, who are ready to yield to the little special extravagances one allows oneself when on a holiday.

Should you visit Portland, you will find that her retail shopping district on Congress Street is very inviting and that her people, though independent and allergic to being pushed around, are neighborly and unpretentious. You will admire the architectural beauty of her extraordinarily handsome City Hall, which has it all over most city halls. Inside, perhaps to your astonishment, you'll find a beautiful auditorium which seats three thousand people. In the background of the stage is a huge organ on which in the summer the city gives weekly concerts. This organ, like Portland's splendid Boys' Club, is one of the philanthropies of Cyrus H. K. Curtis, who got his start in publishing as a boy printer in Portland.

You'd no doubt want to visit the Longfellow homes, both the one in which the poet was born, near the water front, and the newer building where he spent his boyhood. On any really clear day you can stand on the Western Promenade and see the Presidential Range of the White Mountains eighty miles away. But the best view of Portland's sea approaches can be had from Fort Allen Park on the eastern end, a spot that is guarded not only by numerous near-by forts but by a dredged-up cannon from the battleship *Maine*. On Sunday you can attend such hallowed old churches as the First Parish Unitarian Church with its doored-pews, one of whose early ministers was later hanged, by the Salemites, for the alleged practice of witchcraft. It was at Portland's Williston Congregational Church that, in 1881, the world-wide Young People's Christian Endeavor movement was born.

Art lovers will find many Maine paintings in the Lorenzo de Medici Sweat Memorial Museum. But if you've got the antique bug and like to prowl in junk shops, you might keep an eye peeled for a random piece of fine old Portland glass. Mrs. Abraham Lincoln's set cost $45,000, brand new.

You'll almost certainly want to see the old Maine lighthouses, particularly the much-painted, very famous old Portland Head Light on Cape Elizabeth. One of Portland's most interesting landmarks is the Observatory on Munjoy Hill, a high old wooden tower from which, in the early days, the first news of incoming ships was announced by flying the house flag of the owners. It was from the top of this tower that Captain Lemuel Moody watched the first between the *U.S. Brig Enterprise* and *H.M. Brig Boxer* as they slugged it out off Portland's shores during the War of 1812. During the battle Captain Moody busily roared a blow-by-blow description to the throngs at the base of the tower. Though the *Enterprise* brought the *Boxer* into camp, both captains were killed and were buried, each wrapped in his country's flag, in Portland's Eastern Cemetery.

If you find your curiosity being piqued by the use of the phrase "down East" for an area that is so definitely up north and ask Portlanders about its origin, you'll probably be told that it's a term the sea captains coined in sailing days, since, in sailing from New York, Philadelphia, Baltimore or Boston, the course was easterly and usually downwind.

If the thought of digging for buried treasure seems engaging, you can add your spadework to that of many predecessors on Jewell Island in Casco Bay where Captain Kidd is reputed to have buried a pretty penny. These islands are inhabited not only by Miss Edna St. Vincent Millay and other summer folk, but by a year-round population of almost pure English stock, whose insularity and intimacy with the sea make them, according to expert testimony, an especially mystic and imaginative people. They are also known for their remarkable sense of humor.

The summer visitor with a taste for aquatic sports finds himself in the happy hunting ground. Most any kind of boat, from a canoe to a cabin cruiser, can be rented at reasonable rates. You can cruise by small steamer in Casco Bay or take a swan-boat ride on the lake in Deering Oaks for a nickel. Portland already has the plans drawn for a recreational area, containing beaches, yacht harbor, swimming pool, et cetera, which, if it ever gets built, will greatly ornament the eastern end of the peninsula and brighten Portland life in general.

If you hanker for a New England farm, you can pick one up in the neighborhood of Portland for almost any price. There are a surprising number right in the city limits. But unless you are exceptionally skillful and rugged, don't expect it to make money. The best excuse for buying one is that you just happen to love being in Maine, which is understandable since Robert P. Tristam Coffin's state, "bitter as the sea and pungent with the fir and bayberry," has, though expressed in wholly different and even contradictory terms, many of the haunting and gripping qualities of the South. But, on the business side, you'll note that such south-Maine farmers as Mr. Kenneth Roberts and Mr. Ben Ames Williams find it expedient to carry on certain profit-bearing side lines. For the crisp air gives Maine's chicken-hungry foxes so sharp an appetite that they come right up to the towns and cities. In the past year alone Mr. Linwood C. Morrill and his son Irvin caught forty-seven within a fifteen-mile-radius of Portland. However, it's been several years since a moose has been seen in the city limits, and it is generally necessary, in order to bag big game, to take a run up to the north woods.

Even so, deer and moose are a very real traffic hazard in many parts of the state. If you run into one of these animals and kill it on the highway out of season, you must report your accident to the game warden, who claims the carcass and delivers it to one of the state institutions for food. You may then present a bill for damages to the state legislature, and if your claim is fair and just, the state in due course will pay the repair bill on your car.

But unless you come for the hunting or the winter sports, your visit will most probably occur in the summer, when Portland is busy and bustling, when the lobster pots that were mended in winter are out in the ocean, perfumed and beckoning their crusty quarry.

Truck gardens are nursed along as fast as they will go, and the so-long-barn-pent cows, gorged on summer grasses, are giving freshets of milk. The trailer-borne section of Portland's Children's Theater is pumping up its tires and shaking out its wigs in preparation for the performances it will give in the city's parks. Congress Street is packed with milling, sport-shirted male vacationers and their slack-sacked ladies. To avoid this crush, the old families have long since gone out to their beach houses on Cape Elizabeth, there to watch the waves shatter themselves on the rocks, while at the summer camps, perhaps on near-by Sebago Lake with its landlocked salmon, with its trees and wild flowers, with its nights pierced by stars and the plink of guitars, many a young city-dwelling factory or office worker finds that life becomes almost unbearably packed with spring and romance. And by the thousands, via bright penny postcards, they give that age-old vacationer's cry of ecstasy: "Having wonderful time. Sleeping under blankets. Wish you were here."

11: *San Antonio*

S AN ANTONIO is a tough town. It is also a gay, captivating, easy-going town. From one point of view, it is the quintessence of Texas. From another and just as valid viewpoint, it is a Mexican city occupied by its conquerors, the Texans, and by the United States Army. Nor is this the first time it has been conquered. Over it, the shadow of the Spanish spur with its murderous rowel still lies like an ageless spider.

It has a brutal, bloody past in which its people held their houses and hearts together with rawhide, wore it for britches and wore it for skin. Here have been packed in tight proximity the soldier and civilian, the Catholic and the fundamentalist Protestant, the millionaire and the peon. Though the town is crowded with churches and old missions, it has never been a hotbed of moral restraint. For over two hundred years it has drunk freely, gambled, loved and fought in the soft moonlight.

Like all great ports of entry, where differing civilizations meet head on, as they do in Shanghai and Marseille, San Antonio is cosmopolitan and manifold. Yet its beauty, its vices, everything it is, is fundamentally indigenous, home-grown, durable, real.

San Antonio's stock-in-trade is cows, the yield of rich land and hot weather, oil, soldiers, cheap labor, fun-and-forgetfulness, historic beauty, climate, geography, chile con carne, Mexican handicraft, and its own indelible character and individuality.

San Antonio lies at the northernmost part of the great Texas ranching region known as the Brush Country, where the Kings and the Klebergs and the Kenedys have, through the years, punched their hundreds of thousands of heifers. Nearer at hand are the fertile black farming lands. And then, of course, there are oil fields dotted around at such places as tiny Victoria with its more than a score of local millionaires. Down on the border is the Rio Grande Valley, which grows fruit and vegetables with dazzling fecundity when irrigated with water from the river and tended by the gifted hands of Mexican workers. Much of this spate of Valley produce is marketed in San Antonio. Because of its geographical position, San Antonio is also the market to which most Mexican buyers come for American goods. And the bilingual San Antonio wholesalers speak their customers' language in more ways than one. To many citizens of Mexico, San Antonio represents the United States in general.

The cheapness of Mexican labor has made San Antonio the capital of the pecan industry in America. Here, thousands of people have breathlessly shelled pecans in a race with starvation. The abundance and cheapness of Mexican labor have also made it possible for moderately well-to-do Texans to live comfortably, almost luxuriously, on very little money.

And while the devil himself would have to carry a palm-leaf fan during the heat of the day in San Antonio in the summertime, its winter weather is sparklingly glorious, its skies picture-post-card blue, its sunshine soft and golden, remedial to the ailing, intoxicating to the fit.

Its military population, in war or peace, is one of the biggest in the nation and, in spite of the aforementioned climate, one of the most disgruntled. During those earlier days of speculation as to where the Second Front would be opened, Green Peyton, biographer of the city, quipped: "San Antonio *is* the Second Front." And the reason there was not more discord between the Army and San Antonio was because San Antonio is indifferent to the whole thing. It was the citizen-soldier who felt belligerent. He had been uprooted from home, rammed into an itchy uniform, and was being schooled, through various kinds of discomfort, to offer his life for the nation. To him it was a momentous and world-shaking experience. Yet San Antonio took him entirely for granted, and he hated the place as much as Navy men hated Norfolk.

In the case of San Antonio, there was a reason for this. In the first place, San Antonio's way of life was probably changed less by the war than was that of any other American city. For well over two hundred years San Antonio has been a military post. When Spain ran the town, it was garrisoned by the combings of Mexico City's jails. If the Viceroy ever got around to sending them any pay, somebody stole it en route. The sole means of subsistence for the military was by stealing from the civil population or shaking it down in one way or another. And right there San Antonio decided that while it is a meritorious thing to be well represented on the firing line, it is nevertheless meet, when surrounded by vast numbers of the momentarily inactive military, to bolt the windows at night and keep your daughters sleeping in an upstairs bedroom.

In hewing to this point of view, San Antonio has often been tactless in the extreme. During the first year of the war, when the townfolk finally wangled a military curfew, one newspaper carried a banner head crying:

PROSTITUTES AND SOLDIERS MUST BE OFF STREETS BY
ELEVEN O'CLOCK

Landlords, in advertising their dwellings for rent, usually added, "Army personnel need not apply." They knew the psychology of young men at a way station to the war—that civilian values cease to be important and that antique furniture and Oriental rugs are civilian values.

There was, however, one group who got a very different reception. San Antonio, with three big airfields, was funneling into town as air cadets some of the most tempting matrimonial catches in America, college-bred boys from some of the best-heeled families in the land. The sharp-eyed San Antonio mamas, strategically located not only geographically but emotionally—for what is more natural than that a man and a maid be joined together before he wing off into the wild blue yonder?—were poised and ready. And friends, they did mortally make hay. San Antonio's nickname of "Mother-in-law of the Army" came to have a deeper and more aggressive meaning than ever before.

But while young citizen-soldiers hated San Antonio, old regulars love it and love to retire there. More, in fact, have done so than in any

other American city besides Washington, D. C. By retirement time
the old soldier has come to like San Antonio's professional attitude
toward the military. Too, here, as often as not, are many old friends
and fellow campaigners, to share in youthful memories of drinking
and wenching and painting the town. What's more, if these veterans
get sick, they can go to a military hospital very cheaply and, if worse
comes to worst, die almost free of charge.

More numerous in San Antonio than the military, and packed in
still tighter, are its earlier proprietors, the Mexicans, who live on the
West Side of town midst all of the color and folkways of any Mexican town beyond the border. Here nobody hurries, and April Fool's
Day doesn't show up until December 28, which is called: *Día de Ino-
centes*. Bookstores specialize in "love cards," a sort of Valentine with
no seasonal significance, and the principal cures are herbs and charms.
A nativity play called *Los Pastores* is performed every Christmas and
in it the Christ Child is offered tamales. On January 17, all the domestic
animals and pets, from parakeets to burros, are dolled up and taken
to the churches for a special blessing. There are peddlers and shop-
keepers selling fancy, hand-worked leather goods, a penny's worth of
tortilla, baskets, shawls, corn shucks for rolling tamales and cigarettes,
glazed sweet potato candy, silver and turquoise jewelry, cheap shoes
(San Antonio is a famous dumping ground for outsize shoes since
Mexican women have tiny feet and a great many of them have not
the affluence that would permit them to be choosy about fit and
style), pottery, gaudy funeral wreaths of artificial flowers, *serapes*,
sombreros—everything that grows out of Mexican handicraft or
Mexican life.

Here San Antonio is both its most colorful and its most grimy. Here
is the fountainhead of many of the town's troubles—troubles emanat-
ing from ignorance, impetuosity, but chiefly from poverty. In 1934
pecan shellers earned as little as $1.56 a week. Sweatshops where half
of America's infant wear is made paid commensurate wages. As late as
1942 roughly nine-tenths of San Antonio's families paying $3.50 and
less per month for housing were Mexican. And in these hovels, thousands of which had neither water nor sewers, the death rate from
infant diarrhea was kept at appalling heights. It was this section which

was primarily, almost wholly, responsible for the fact that San Antonio had, and still has, the highest tuberculosis death rate of any large city in the United States. Here, too, flourished rats that carry the fleas that send San Antonio's yearly number of typhus cases skyrocketing. San Antonio, which has always been a great little place for syphilis, stabbings and safe crackings, as well as political skulduggery, could trace most of its troubles to its picturesquely starving West Side.

But these days things are looking up for San Antonio's Mexican population. Over twenty-five hundred families live, proud and beaming, in new, flower-decked low-cost dwellings constructed by the San Antonio Housing Authority. The Federal Wage and Hour Law vastly brightened the whole economic complexion of life on the West Side. San Antonio is already busy with DDT-loaded flit guns which were the salvation of lousy, typhus-ridden Naples. Moreover, North and South Side San Antonio have finally realized that the preservation of its own skin is dependent upon health conditions in the Mexican quarter.

But in the truly cosmopolitan hodgepodge that is San Antonio, not all "foreigners" are Mexicans by any means. In the Italian colony, people still play *boccie* and celebrate Columbus Day. The Belgians maintain their own church, with services conducted in Flemish. Four-fifths of the Chinese population in Texas live in San Antonio, many of whom speak Spanish with a Chinese accent and English with a Spanish accent. There are 40,000 persons in San Antonio who are either German or of German descent. Since 1845 this group has influenced San Antonio's music, law and medicine. Nine per cent of San Antonio is Negro.

Workaday and white-collar San Antonio lives on the South Side of town, the silk-stocking folk on the North Side. These people live graciously, entertain often and well.

San Antonio's biggest annual party is the *Fiesta de San Jacinto* with its "Battle of Flowers" parade. This fête is held every spring in commemoration of the day cagey old Sam Houston outfoxed Santa Anna and won Texas' independence from Mexico. The streets are full of flower-decked floats and bands and fun. It is fun because San Antonio, which loves a party and a parade and anything involving people on horseback, has its heart in it. There are many tributary social affairs with upper-crust San Antonians, who'd as soon shoot you a game of polo as look at you, crowning queens and giving balls.

"Society" is still the biggest local news in the San Antonio papers, and the town's attitude regarding the importance of it in the general scheme of things is pretty much pre-World War I Newport. The dominant faction in this social scene is the cow aristocracy. Which is as it should be, because this is their town. They and their daddies and granddaddies built it, supported it, shaped it in their own rugged image. They licked the Indians and the coyotes, the rattlesnakes, the notoriously recalcitrant old longhorns, Mexico, and—at intervals—each other. These cowmen had to be tough to survive, and San Antonio had to be tough to hold them. A general with enough stars may be accepted socially almost as their equal. But, although there's about $100,000,000 a year coming in from oil within San Antonio's sphere of influence, oil money, as compared to cow money, is worth, socially speaking, about four bits on the dollar.

One of the newest enterprises of San Antonio's bon ton is the launching of a five-day opera festival. Where, in the past, the town has supported its own very good symphony orchestra, it has now also begun the importation of Metropolitan stars, as do the Northerners of more effete Dallas. San Antonio just cannot see how there might be too much of such a good thing as music.

Politically, however, the well-fed North-Side inhabitants draw but little water in San Antonio's elections, where the formula for success is: Split the South Side and carry the West Side. The North Side is apathetic, doesn't care, doesn't count.

But San Antonio's domestic problems, long turbulent, have never in peacetime dissuaded the influx of tourists. And if you visit San Antonio, you will want to know what you will see and where you will stay.

San Antonio has scads of tourist courts, many of them handsome and comfortable, others mere vice arenas. In the near-by Bandera country, there are dude ranches with all the trimmings: horses, scenery, swimming pools, wonderful food. But the main stand-by of the tourist is San Antonio's group of hotels. Both the Plaza and the

White Plaza are comfortable and pleasant. The historic old Menger, built Spanish style around a central patio, has recently been modernized. The Army hangs out at the Gunter. So do the cattlemen who, when in convention assembled, often push back the chairs and do square dances in the lobby. The Continental is said to be a nice place from which to engineer a Latin-American revolution. But, hotel-wise, San Antonio's finest blossom is the St. Anthony. People who have stayed there once feel good all over when they start back to it. A guest may register in the garage when he drives in, walk a few steps to an elevator, and go directly to his room without passing through the pleasantly ornate lobby. Here the Guernsey-bosomed dowagers listen every afternoon to the music of a Mexican orchestra, and the incoming tourist would hesitate to parade before them in rumpled driving clothes, followed by a lot of dilapidated, car-bunged luggage. His room will be air-conditioned, and the service, which even during the war was above the average, will be superb. The food and music in the tapestried Peraux Room and in the wrought-iron-grilled Anacacho Room will be rewarding, and the feminine clientele sparkling and pretty. The prices will astonish him with their moderation. I know many more expensive hotels than the St. Anthony. But if a good hotel is supposed to leave you alone, and a fine hotel to make you happy, I don't know any finer hotels in New York or Paris or Madrid or on the Riviera.

Once the visitor starts on his rounds he will see one of the most beautiful cities in the land, one of the most distinctive, one of the gayest, one of the richest in dramatic, heart-stopping history.

The thing, of course, in which San Antonio takes greatest pride is the Alamo, where in 1836 less than two hundred Texans against orders, against reason, with every opportunity to leave but with a powerful disinclination to backtrack, fought Santa Anna's six thousand men until the last of the Texans was butchered and burned. In front of the Alamo is a fancy cenotaph to its heroes which makes them look as tame and spirituel as poetasters. The sight of it still gives real-Texas-loving Frank Dobie a hard spell, and it does fit the subject about as well as a tatted halter would fit an outlaw longhorn steer.

San Antonio is as full of "points of interest" as a Mexican dinner is of *cominos* seed: historic missions; museums; the old Spanish Governors' Palace; forts and airfields; La Villita, an ancient village restored, with old adobe houses that seem to have grown, through the centuries, out of the stony earth—all of the pictorial fare of guidebooks.

Here, too, is where Gebhardt's, the General Motors of the Tex-Mex food world, simmers its good canned chile and cranks up its tamales. Oddly enough, though hard-drinking San Antonio has two busy breweries, it has no distillery whatever.

On a pretty day you can have more fun just sitting in a grassy plaza in San Antonio than you could have at a ball game in some towns. At Milam Park, for example, which is the Columbus Circle of San Antonio, you can see little groups gathered around speakers who may be holding forth on anything from *El Comunismo* to Seventh Day Adventism. In the midst of another group someone may be reading a newspaper to persons not having this ability. Elsewhere, for the same reason, a public stenographer will be writing love letters for a fee. Old folks sit in nodding serenity soaking up the good sunshine. If it's Sunday, the statue of Ben Milam, who once stormed San Antonio's forts with two hundred volunteers and wrested the city from fourteen hundred Mexican troops, will be surrounded by shattered bay rum and "Sweet Lucy" bottles. Somehow it seems to have become a custom to bust bottles on the monument to this brave man.

The central vein running through the town is the lovely little San Antonio River, charming almost beyond description, with its stone walks and bubbling springs, its grassy banks, the little studios built beside it.

The river comes into town on the North Side above 320-acre Brackenridge Park, where there is a whopping big zoo with barless bear pits, all sorts of amusements for kids, and a reptile garden at which, every Sunday, just as sure as four o'clock comes around, a lot of people rally round and devour fried rattlesnake, not because they are starving, but as a delicacy.

A little farther on, the river passes Frank Rosengren's house, where, every Sunday, there is a kind of little salon of the bookish or musically or artistically inclined. A pretty fair crowd, including a sprinkling of lonesome soldiers, can usually be found there along about dinner-time on Sunday night.

From Frank's the river, running just as crooked as a San Antonio street, by-passes the Pearl brewery, which seems to have set out to resemble a medieval *Schloss*, and flows on downtown past the Municipal Auditorium, where it' soon becomes its prettiest. Here are even gondolas and gondoliers for hire to abet the romantic tendencies of an already romance-ridden town. The little stream passes near "Joske's of Texas, the largest store in the largest state," and then runs squarely through an open-air theater which has its stage on one side of the river and its audience on the other, so that the catfish and the turtles get the best view of all performances. After wandering on past the Library, it passes the thirty-story Smith-Young Tower, makes a sharp left turn around the Plaza Hotel, and heads on out of town.

But while the river is one of the most engaging things in town, the market place, as dark falls, becomes perhaps the liveliest part of the city as the fleets of trucks roll in from the Rio Grande Valley. In 1945 they hauled in $26,000,000 worth of garden sass.

The market place, after dark, is headquarters for the *mariachi* singers, or strolling troubadours, who usually travel in threes, and pass from car to car playing their guitars and singing their Mexican songs and ballads. Many citizens of San Antonio have their pet groups in the market place and always select the same singers. But any group of them will sing better for *botínes*-wearing, Texas-struck Holland McCombs than for anybody else, not merely because he pays well but because he knows just when to give the happy little yelps of appreciation that bring out the best in the artists.

For a hundred years there were ladies known as "chile queens" who, with the coming of night, set up their little charcoal braziers here in the market place, spread tables with red-and-white cloths and, mid the plink of guitars and the lifting of song, served out *enchiladas* and the like to their hungry clientele of truckers and tourists and just plain people who knew a good thing when they saw it. But the public-health service kept plaguing them until it finally drove them out of the market. Of course, nobody ever expected the chile queens to be sanitary. You knew you were taking your life in your hands when you ate there. You were willing to take the chance because it was night in San Antonio and nothing would quiet the peculiar hunger inside you except the market place, its tumultuousness and music and the chile queens' tasty, albeit germy, wares.

Since the queens are gone, it's pretty much every man for himself on the subject of where to eat Mexican food in San Antonio. La Fonda, the Original, Jalisco, and the Mexican Manhattan all have their disciples. If you have a Mexican friend who inivtes you to his home, perhaps you may taste *nopales:* tender young cactus, first dehorned, then cut up, dipped in egg batter and fried. Or perhaps there will be *menudo:* tripe and hominy. Or plain *frijoles:* beans, first boiled and then fried, or that exquisitely delicious Mexican dish, *cabrito:* the roast ribs of baby goat. During the war, whenever San Antonio boys met overseas, the one dish that was the broad common denominator to eating back home, the thing they cried out for and had to have, was chile con carne, which, at least so far as San Antonians are concerned, does seem to be habit forming. On any wartime Christmas, chile, in tens of thousands of cans, went out from San Antonio to impair the digestion and elevate the spirits of her fighting men.

But if there were any one scene that haunted a lonely San Antonian on the wrong side of an ocean, it must surely have been that most spectacular, stunning and cyclonic phenomena that is the spontaneous expression of the combined elements that compose San Antonio. And that is Houston Street around twelve or one o'clock on payday Saturday night. No fiesta, nothing staged, could compare with its intensity: the blaring music; the glaring yellow and red and green lights; the curio shops with displays of every kind of gaudy junk; the uniforms containing young men in every degree of confidence and bewilderment, the veteran with his battle stars on his chest and the scars in his eyes; sight-seeing sailors from Corpus Christi, tractable before overwhelming odds; the pin-wheel games where you have a chance of winning a felt pennant, a Kewpie doll, a bright satin pillow stamped "Souvenir of San Antonio"; the dust; the smell of alcohol, of chili peppers, of onions frying, of packed hot bodies;

the fist fights; the very air dynamically charged with sexual impulse; the savage beat of the inner tempo of the town itself.

And then there is the denouement of Sunday morning in which San Antonio is mild and repentant and gentle as a lamb. Old church bells ring softly. A little brass band goes tootling through the streets to call forth the dozing parishioners of Our Lady of Guadalupe. Everywhere virtue, felt and radiant, is in the ascendancy.

Since billeting and, oddly, entertaining, the military is one of San Antonio's biggest businesses, the one in particular which saved her during the depression, many of her military installations are permanent parts of the town, installations such as Randolph and Kelly Fields, as well as three-thousand-acre Fort Sam Houston, which San Antonio bills as the largest Army post in the United States. San Antonio's present overall population, military and civilian, is about half a million. She expected a greater postwar decline in population than has actually occurred. San Antonio believes her war-inflated cost of living will go back to a more comfortable level, and that her natural attractiveness to vacationers and sight-seers will reassert itself. Old soldiers, who have remained active beyond their allotted time, will swarm in. Military hospitalization has to some degree taken up the slack that resulted from a decline in Army training operations. The district's good land goes on raising cotton and corn and steers.

Certain elements in San Antonio are strongly opposed to the coming of big industry to their town. With it will come fuller unionization of labor, which they feel will jack up wages in existing enterprises. And since most other communities are anxious for industry and will make concessions to get it, it is more than probable, if this group prevails, that San Antonio's golden air will remain unsullied by the blight of factory smoke. Industry wishing to set up shop in South Texas will, in that case, probably gravitate to up-and-jumping Corpus Christi, whose population has bean-stalked from 10,000 to 110,000 in the last twenty years and whose emergence as a real competitor for South Texas' business San Antonio neither worries about nor finds very dignified.

San Antonio's Chamber of Commerce, however, under the influence of a younger group, is committed in favor of the acquisition of light industry, says it does not try to sell San Antonio as a cheap-labor town. It has secured the intersection at San Antonio of two of the big trans-regional speedways. Further, chemurgy is to the Chamber of Commerce these days what ukuleles were to Joe College twenty-five years ago. It points out that at near-by New Braunfels a plant is making camphor and extracting oils from cedar, which San Antonio possesses abundantly, and the value of these products is reported to be greater than that of the land on which the trees grew.

Another plant is producing salad oil from pecan shells, of which, of course, San Antonio has an oceanic supply. From what's left of the shells after the oil has been removed, it makes tannic acid. The ultimate residuum is made into activated carbon. And if San Antonio can just find some use for mesquite trees which will pay for their removal from the land, one of her fondest dreams will have come true.

Another fascinating possibility is the building of a highway to Mazatlán. Mazatlán is a Mexican Pacific port to which San Antonio is nearer by six hundred miles than she is to any American West Coast port. And there are San Antonians who point out that half the cost of the freight traffic to China is the rail cost to the Coast, that the governments of Mexico and the United States are so chummy that the transborder shipping factor could be easily ironed out, and that San Antonio, with access to the Atlantic through Gulf-port Corpus Christi on one hand and to the Pacific through Mazatlán on the other, would become a great ambidextrous, two-ocean inland port of entry standing astride the shank of the nation and at the gateway between North and Central America.

But to the San Antonian long away from home who wonders how much his town has changed, the answer is: very little. San Antonio has gone right on in its old way, being an Army post, a merchandising and handicraft town by day, by night making love and music, unswervingly being itself and having a rousing and rowdy good time.

12: *Cincinnati*

CINCINNATI is a city with the straightforward simplicity of the Middle West, along with much of the grace of its cross-the-river neighbor, the South. It has little either of the rawness of the West, or its ebullience. Many of its manners and menus, as well as its maturity of viewpoint, are European. Its government machinery, to those accustomed to the old toe-to-toe methods of two-party government, smacks slightly of Graustark—at least until one gets used to the idea. As a city, it has many feathers in its cap and, in the form of huge and bewildering problems, many a sharp thorn in the seat of its pants.

Cincinnati has a certain rhythm that must be sensed if the city is to be understood. In the *dramatis personae* of American cities, Cincinnati is a curious, somehow Dickensian character. It's calm, and has a kind of simple poise, which its most circumspect elements describe as serenity, and which its progressive forces call complaceny.

Though quietly merry, it is somehow deliberate and legalistic, instead of being either intuitive or impulsive. It's a lot like one of its leading families, the Tafts—resembling in its rubicund jollity, President William Howard; in its abiding, all-prevading conservatism, Senator Robert; and in its reformist desire to inject morality and efficiency into its government, it most closely resembles Midwesternly handsome Charles Taft, head of Cincinnati's Charter party.

One reason for Cincinnati's conservatism is that, as Midwestern cities go, Cincinnati is old. And age tells on a city, just as it does on a woman. There is no blush of newness and expectancy upon Cincinnati's buildings, which are, on the average, from ten to twenty years older than those of other Ohio cities. Too, when most U. S. cities reach a certain age, their rising population curve—with all that means in terms of booming real-estate values and general bullishness of viewpoint—begins to level off. That of Cincinnati, which contains about 450,000 people inside its corporate limits and about 350,000 more in its metropolitan district, began leveling off long ago. Moreover, Cincinnati's people are themselves old. It has been reported to have the same number of persons over sixty-five as Cleveland, which is twice as large.

With increasing frequency these days, Cincinnatians raise troubled voices in public and ask if their city is not sick. They ask whether, as a result of declining vitality or indecision in meeting civic problems, the city has not lost much of whatever it is that makes a city magnetic and compelling—the thing that enables it either to acquire or create the new enterprise essential to a city's continued regeneration.

But if Cincinnati's present is in some respects tinctured with apprehensiveness, she has, nevertheless, in the past known glory. In her younger days, when Longfellow called her the "Queen City of the West," he was not indulging in mere polite flattery, but declaring a fact. There was a time when she was the biggest, the richest, the gayest city in the region, when she could take Chicago or Cleveland or St. Louis across her knee whenever she got good and ready.

As early as 1800, Cincinnati had finished her Indian killing and had things fairly well tidied up. There were schools, churches, a newspaper, more than a hundred log cabins, and a handful of rough frame houses. The town nestled on the north bank of the Ohio River between the Great Miami River on the west and the Little Miami River on the east. From the Kentucky side, the Licking River was pointed as straight in Cincinnati's face as any perverse child ever aimed a water pistol at a bishop's hat. However, the flat basin was surrounded on every hand by convenient hills to which the five hundred townsfolk could repair when the rivers became obstreperous.

Cincinnati first intruded upon the world's consciousness when citizen Daniel Drake, a medico, published a book in 1815 called *Picture of Cincinnati*. It had wide distribution, and was instrumental in bringing thousands of Europeans to Cincinnati. In the excitement of witnessing the first steamboat runs, it was only natural that the town should take little notice of a local taxidermist named John James Audubon, who was stuffing birds and animals at the Western Museum, though somewhat later, bookkeeper Stephen Foster would gain his first prominence in Cincinnati on the strength of his early ditties.

By 1828, Mrs. Frances Trollope had hit town and opened a bazaar, which she naïvely stocked with goods bought from local merchants at retail prices and then, in turn, marked up. Naturally the enterprise soon folded, and Mrs. Trollope returned to England, carrying with her a little opus called *Domestic Manners of the Americans,* which was to give Cincinnati still more publicity, this time as a wallow for barbarians. But this black eye was subsequently to have beefsteak enthusiastically applied to it by Mrs. Trollope's fellow-countryman, Charles Dickens, who found Cincinnati one of the few places in America to his liking. In 1832 the preaching Beechers blew in to take the town, theologically, to the cleaners, and it was in Cincinnati that daughter Harriet first began to be aware of such matters as the Underground Railroad, whose leading spirit in smuggling slaves to Canada was Levi Coffin, a Cincinnati merchant.

By 1850 Cincinnati, with a population of well over 100,000, was a rich, happy, largely Teutonic city, full of *Bauvereins, Turnvereins,* choirs and German bands. Most especially in the German district known as Over-the-Rhine, the very air was pierced by Gothic spires and was adance with *Gemütlichkeit.*

It had but little of the complexion of an inland city. It was linked by canal to Lake Erie, and, a little later, by rail with Columbus, Cleveland and Philadelphia. But the main trade plied the river between Cincinnati and Pittsburgh, St. Louis and New Orleans. German craftsmen were busily at work in foundries and were brewing beer as mellow as the woodwinds accompanying a *Sängerfest.* The excess corpulence of some half-million hogs a year enriched the city's soap-making enterprises. At the same time, hams with a Westphalian accent and the sausages for which Cincinnati was famous brought delight to the whole Central Valley. Moreover, the city had become a great building center for steamboats, which it turned out in increasing numbers and luxuriousness right up to the Civil War. It made stoves and shoes and clothing in enormous quantities. It sold more barrels of whisky than any other American city. Combined imports and exports coquetted about the $200,000,000 mark annually; half the capital invested in Ohio industry had been risked in Cincinnati.

For some time now, the first Mr. Nicholas Longworth had been demonstrating his uncommon ability for coming out on the right side of a real-estate deal. He became Cincinnati's first millionaire and was on the way to becoming one of the richest men in the nation.

As in most communities with large immigrant populations, attacks both physical and political were made upon the newcomers by the America-for-Americans crowd. But both the Germans and the large numbers of Irish exhibited so spirited a disinclination to being pushed around that the attacks were abandoned, and the city went on in its own happy, beery way.

Of course the greatest emotional and political issue here, as elsewhere in the nation, was abolition. And when Harriet Beecher Stowe's *Uncle Tom's Cabin* was published, this best seller was a key factor in the ignition of the Civil War.

During the war, Cincinnati busily fortified her heights, hospitalized the wounded, supplied the Union Army, and was given the fantods by Morgan's mercurial Raiders. But the principal effect of the war on Cincinnati was the destruction of her most important customer, the South. The railroads, originally built as feeders for the steamship lines, destroyed not only Cincinnati's great shipping industry, but her vast shipyards as well. In order for the city to restore commercial contact with what was left of the South, it became necessary for Cincinnati to build its own 350-mile railroad to Chattanooga, a road, incidentally, which the city still owns.

Other economic bad breaks lay in the offing. Later, Henry Ford would blast out of existence the city's huge wagon-and-carriage-building industry, which had represented half the nation's output. And finally, when the old city was groggy and reeling, Andy Volstead would deal it the unkindest cut of all, would vote its great beer and whisky industries into silent death, would leave battered Cincinnati with nothing to moisten its pretzels but its tears.

Yet, during this succession of economic disasters, Cincinnati made strides as the cultural capital of the Ohio Valley. It brought the great Theodore Thomas to conduct the orchestral music for its May Festivals, where the choral singing couldn't be touched by any other city. In 1895, it organized its own symphony orchestra, which, by 1909, under the baton of dramatic Leopold Stokowski, was bringing great prestige to the city, as its distinguished old Conservatory of Music had been doing for nearly fifty years.

Politically, on the national scene, Cincinnati was sending Tafts to Washington. Locally, the city was in the clutch of the Cox Republican machine, and languished in it for more than twenty years. Ultimately, Cincinnati voted itself a charter form of government with a city manager.

But a city which in its earlier days had been able to take the lead in making boats and wagons and stoves was bound to have certain industrial resources that change could not kill, merely re-express. This was true in regard to Cincinnati's machine-tool industry, which blossomed in both World Wars, and most particularly in World War II.

Today Cincinnati's factories turn out products worth in excess of $700,000,000 a year. The city claims to make more machine tools, playing cards and soap than any other city in the world. Incidentally, Cincinnati's Procter & Gamble pioneered not only in making soap float, but labor purr. This company was one of the first corporations to give Saturday afternoon holidays (1885), pension-and-benefit plans (1887), and guaranteed forty-eight-week years with paid vacations in 1923. Along with soap, other important Cincinnati items are paper and paper products, including books, for which early citizen William Holmes McGuffey set the pace by hawking some 122,000,000 of his Readers, although it is said that McGuffey's take from this huge enterprise was almost nil. The city's healthily varied industries produce, among many other things, such articles as shoes, processed meats, laundry equipment, pianos and radios.

If it hadn't been for radios, Cincinnati's ex-bicycle mechanic, Powel Crosley, Jr., who currently manufactures automotive doodle-buggies, could not have afforded such trinkets as Cincinnati's ball park and America's original professional baseball team, launched in 1869 as the Cincinnati Red Stockings. And since Cincinnatians grew melancholy, lost not only bets but their eagerness to buy tickets to Crosley Field when the Reds were losing, Crosley hired as general manager Larry

McPhail, who initiated such factors as night baseball, beer, usherettes, brass bands, fireworks and clowns, so that the fans would have a good time even when the team couldn't win. By these means, McPhail put the Reds in the black. This, in turn, meant more and more money for players and, in 1940, a world championship.

But Cincinnati has many immediate problems that can't be solved by an umpire at Crosley Field. Some of these problems are common to almost every American city in the post-World War II period, others common to the whole Middle West, and still others peculiarly Cincinnati's own. Every morning, just under its masthead, the *Enquirer*, which stands politically in the middle of the road, with the *Post* on its left and the Taft-family-owned *Times-Star* on its right, carries its platform for Cincinnati. It wants something done about river purification, rapid transit, flood protection, airport facilities and the smoke nuisance.

Each of these demands is plausible and of great importance to Cincinnati. For example, the Ohio River, from which the city draws its water, is an open sewer from its source. Cincinnati's own untreated sewage goes into the river only a few hundred yards below the intakes for the city's water plant. A system of dams, which maintain a nine-foot navigation level on the river, sometimes holds the river in pool at low water. At these periods, manifestly, Cincinnati's water comes from its own septic tank. And no matter how thoroughly or adequately purified the water may be, each time Cincinnatians drink it, they have difficulty in keeping out of their minds the fact that it is, after all, secondhand. However, there's hope that a river-purification pact can be reached among all the states polluting the river, and Cincinnati's projected sewage-disposal plants will, when they're built, treat the city's sewage before dumping it into the river.

Like virtually every American city, most of whose streets were originally built to give passage to a small number of horse-drawn vehicles, Cincinnati has a staggering traffic problem. Yet, it is one of the few American cities which possess a $6,000,000, twenty-year-old, abandoned hole in the ground that was primarily designed for interurban cars. City Manager Wilbur R. Kellogg expects this system

CITIES OF AMERICA

A Portfolio of Pictures

Royal Street in New Orleans' French Quarter

New Orleans water front and sky line

Salt Lake City business street

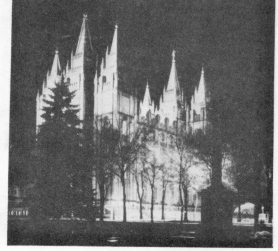

The Mormon Temple at night

Washington Monument in Baltimore

Baltimore row houses with white marble steps

allas

ort Worth

San Francisco's Golden Gate Bridge

Cable car on California street

Chicago's Michigan Avenue

.The Gold Coast

Philadelphia's Independence Hall on a rainy night

Cadillac Square in Detroit

Congress Street, Portland

H. W. FECHNER

Portland Head Light on Cape Elizabeth

The Alamo, San Antonio

Downtown Cincinnati

Ohio River levee

Seattle, looking from Queen Anne Hill toward Mount Rainier

ARTHUR GRIFFIN. FROM "THE BOSTON BOOK" BY ARTHUR GRIFFIN AND ESTHER FORBES, PUBLISHED BY HOUGHTON MIFFLIN COMPANY. REPRINTED BY SPECIAL PERMISSION OF THE SATURDAY EVENING POST, COPYRIGHT, 1946, BY THE CURTIS PUBLISHING COMPANY

"Brimstone Corner" in Boston

Denver Civic Center, from dome of Capitol

State Capitol at Atlanta

Campus of Atlanta University Center for Negroes

Pittsburgh steel mills at night

University of Pittsburgh's
"Cathedral of Learning"

Madison, Lake Monona in foreground and Lake Mendota in background

Upper Campus, University of Wisconsin

Courtyard of Union Station,
Los Angeles

Los Angeles
City Hall

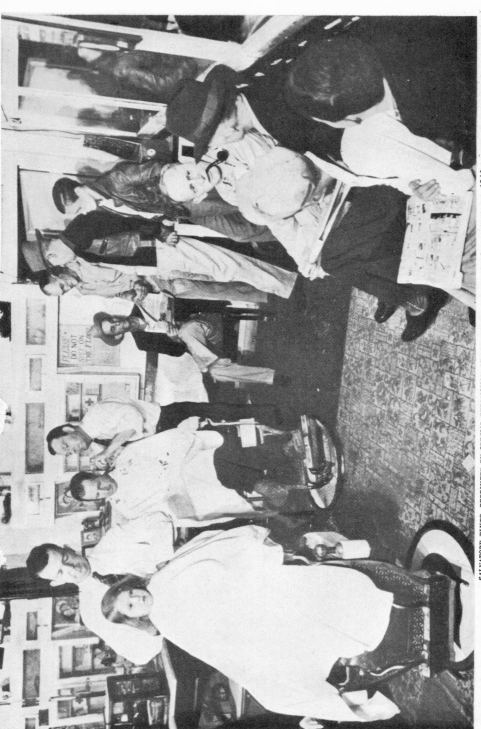

Bounds Brothers Barber Shop, Rockdale, Texas, on Saturday afternoon

Washington from the air

eventually to carry passengers below the surface of the downtown area, and freight on its outer reaches.

But if the subway project is at present quiescent, the Ohio River is only intermittently so. In the great flood of 1937, a sixth of Cincinnati was inundated; property damage ran into the multiple tens of millions; fires raged and the waterworks was drowned out. Some of the more impulsive Cincinnatians feel that this sort of thing just won't do. Others, realizing that most of the water-front property is the oldest, most obsolete and least tax-bearing in town, feel that it is not worth the cost of a huge engineering project to prevent its occasional baptism. However, Cincinnati's richest industrial area, Mill Creek Valley, has been given some measure of protection by a barrier dam, erected to keep the Ohio out of the Valley. This dam is equipped with powerful pumps for the purpose of snatching flash-flood water out of the Creek and dumping it into the Ohio before it can pile up.

As for airport facilities, Cincinnati comes closer than almost any other large American city to having no airport whatever. Its Lunken Airport, too small, and subject at times to flooding, is built in a cup of such high and precipitous surrounding hills that the airlines flatly refuse to jeopardize their personnel and four-motor equipment by landing there. Special landing and take-off techniques have to be employed even to bring in twin-motor planes. But informed Cincinnatians believe that in another three or four years, a new airport, for which the land has yet to be bought, can be opened.

Yet many citizens who wonder how their city could have slept so soundly through this period of fast-expanding aviation realize that the city's smoke problem is really tough. In the first place, Cincinnati regards itself as the bituminous-coal capital of the United States, annually handling 500,000 cars by rail and 4,000,000 tons on the river. She must burn this coal in order to earn a living and keep from freezing. She has a largely toothless smoke-reducing ordinance unlike the sharp-fanged St. Louis one, which makes every coal dealer responsible for selling only that type of fuel which can be burned smokelessly in the type of equipment the customer owns. So far, Cincinnati soft-coal interests, not wholly without the sympathy of the average Cincinnatian, who is somewhat sentimental about coal as a major foundation stone in the city's economy, have succeeded in blocking the passage of such a measure in Cincinnati. The result is that the city is smeared with soot, and the blinding smoke, on many a winter day, browns out the whole basin.

The remaining planks in the *Enquirer's* platform for Cincinnati call for the acceleration of such steps in the right direction as extension of its boulevard-lighting plan (nicest of all seem the three thousand-odd soft gaslights still in use), advancement of Cincinnati's prestige as a national art center, and, finally, the perpetuation of good government.

Cincinnati's much-discussed government consists of a city council of nine, and a city manager, hired at a salary of $25,000 a year by the council for his administrative abilities and his aloofness from politics. The council names one of its members as mayor, to look after ceremonial chores.

When the Cincinnati voter goes to the polls to elect members of council, his ballot sheet contains merely the candidates' names, with no indication of their political affiliations. The voter makes his selection, according to choices, voting first choice for the candidate he is most eager to have in council, second choice for the one he is next most eager to have, and so on.

Anybody in Cincinnati with enough names on a petition can run for a seat in council. But most often candidates are proposed by the powerful Republican machine—in national elections Cincinnati is the most consistently Republican of any major city—or by the Charter party, which is to say that mélange of reformers, disgruntled Republicans, and the Democratic machine, which must make common and reasonably humble cause with these fractional groups in order to get a look-in.

As this is written, the Republican machine has a majority in council. Yet it is and has been the experience of Cincinnati that, in practice, the city manager really manages, without any noteworthy political hindrance.

From the standpoint of city government solvency, Cincinnati's charter government has been an all-out, hands-down success. It has substantially reduced the city's bonded debt, has kept current expenditures smaller than income—all this, be it noted, while Cincinnati goes on paying virtually the lowest city tax of any important American city.

Whether Cincinnati's government has been too economical, and has, in fact, denied the city refertilizing expenditures necessary to its healthy metabolism, is a frequent subject of debate in such fetching old suds-shops as Grammer's Café and Mecklenburg's Beer Garden. Some Cincinnatians wonder if the whole basic concept of their government is not, in the last analysis, more logical than practical, since economy and efficiency are but two of the elements necessary to successful government.

They believe dynamic leadership to be of equal importance—and that they do not have. In fact, their government, by placing the principal power in the hands of a city manager, who for practical purposes is an efficiency expert, is designed to preclude such leadership. For in Cincinnati there is an extremely confused chain of responsibility from government through political party to the electorate.

In most American elections, the voter, when all the campaign shibboleths have faded from his mind, votes, in effect, for his own salvation and happiness. He expects, and will hold his candidate accountable for, the working of such incidental miracles as are essential to that end. But in Cincinnati one votes merely for one of two shades of efficiency. Yet the majority of Cincinnati Republicans, whose local machine, were it not for the charter, could probably take over without difficulty, would not go back to the old form of government even if they had the chance.

Due to its peculiar terrain, Cincinnati has dozens of wonderful vantage points from which to look out upon the city. A pleasant way to reach one of them is to take a trip up the "incline," a cable-drawn platform which hoists cars, streetcars or pedestrians up the sheer face of Mount Adams. At the crest, if you wish, you can visit the famous old Rookwood pottery, creator of the Tiger Eye vases which were the rage during the 'Nineties. But if you are in downtown Cincinnati and wish to have no nonsense about your sight-seeing, you can simply catch an elevator and scoot to the top of the forty-eight-story Carew

Tower, and from that point look out upon the panorama of the whole city. Almost straight down is the top of Cincinnati's extraordinarily fine skyscraper hotel, the Netherland Plaza, which, when I was there, had a really outstanding corps of waiters. Close by is a large excavation where the Emery family, which owns all these properties, has started work on an eight-story department store building, atop which will roost not pigeons, but a four-hundred-room hotel to be known as the Netherland Terrace. Also you will see many beautiful government buildings in the central downtown area.

But there is no more pleasing sight in this or any other section than the late home of Mr. and Mrs. Charles P. Taft, which has been given to the city, along with its exquisite furniture, fine collection of paintings, *objets d'art*, and a large sum of money, as a museum. The house itself, which is alleged to have been designed by the architect of the White House, is that rare admixture of majesty and delicacy which could receive and assimilate these great paintings with grace and without awe, not deigning to become a museum, but completely remaining one of America's most beautiful homes.

Surrounding Cincinnati's central cluster of skyscrapers, which contain, on their lower levels, uncommonly attractive stores, is the moat of blighted area that is a familiar and melancholy pattern in American cities. Some 40 per cent of Cincinnati's homes, mostly, of course, in its slum area, are in need of either private baths or major repairs. On the downhill edge of this area there is the Ohio River, where barges are loading and unloading, where the steamer *Island Queen* is waiting to take holiday crowds to a river pleasure-ground called Coney Island. At the Public Landing are the Greene Line packets, which still make long journeys, carrying passengers and freight, up and down the river. It was this line on which Mary Becker Greene, Cincinnati's own Steamboat Annie, did her worthy stuff. The tugboats, which push long strings of barges, are as often as not sternwheelers, which somehow have more appeal than those with mere propellers.

On the other side of the river, in Kentucky, are Covington and Newport, where gambling is not legalized, but does opulently occur, and where Cincinnati does most of its night-clubbing. Certainly the most exquisite religious edifice in the area is Covington's St. Mary's Cathedral, reminiscent of Notre Dame in Paris. In it, incidentally, are three frescoes by Covington's own Frank Duveneck, who later became a pillar of the Cincinnati Museum. But perhaps the most touching things in Covington are the genuinely grand old houses of the steamboat captains, with their widow's walks on top, which the ravages of time and flood have caused to fall into wrack and ruin.

But on the Ohio side of the river this feeling of retrogression and decay is absent as one passes among the modern buildings of the University of Cincinnati. This school—the world's largest municipal university—is a strapping giant with eleven or so thousand students. It was at U.C. that Dean Herman Schneider inaugurated the co-operative plan of education, by which engineering students alternate between study in the University and work in industrial shops and factories, where they not only get practical experience but earn part of their way through school—a plan which has subsequently gained wide currency. U.C. is more or less above and beyond the smoky part of the city, as is smaller, beautiful St. Francis Xavier University.

Just as handsome and, in its own way, more impressive is Cincinnati's Union Terminal. This station is a monument to years of work on the part of George D. Crabbs, who undertook the job of unifying the station facilities of Cincinnati's seven railroads, a job which cost some $41,000,000. The station's fountain-bathed foreground, its huge central corridor, its splendid murals, its unobtrusive seating arrangement, its manifold services, its beautifully integrated architectural impact, combine to make it an absolute knockout of a railroad station.

Among the city's parks, Ault Park is probably the town's handsomest beauty spot and shows most explicitly what can be done with Cincinnati's steep hillsides. Yet no outdoor spot means more to Cincinnatians than their zoo. This results not only from the presence of Susie, said to be the world's one trained gorilla, and her animal neighbors, but because the zoo is the home of Cincinnati's famous summer opera, which in 1946 celebrated its Silver Jubilee.

In winter, of course, one goes for musical refreshment to Cincinnati's massive old Music Hall, the sight of which couldn't be more

German if it were made of pumpernickel bricks with *Schmierkäse* mortar. Here, each Friday afternoon and Saturday evening during the season, Cincinnati's great musical tradition becomes a living thing as, while the audience applauds, suave Maestro Eugene Goossens mounts the podium, bows, lifts his baton and awakens the voice of his eighty-eight-piece Symphony Orchestra.

The Saturday-night audiences are composed of everybody from bobby-soxers to dowagers, and if you watch their faces, you can see them soaking up this great music like so many rapt sponges. An indication of how much Cincinnati loves its orchestra is found in the fact that each year the Woman's Committee for the Orchestra sells more advance tickets for the season's concerts than are sold for any other orchestra in the nation.

But just as Cincinnati is proud of its Orchestra, so, also, can it be proud of its co-ordinated health program, to which Bleecker Marquette has devoted the last twenty-five years of his life. The inquiring Rockefeller Foundation has declared Cincinnati's and Cleveland's health programs to be the most effective ones in the land.

In fact, Cincinnati likes co-ordinating next only to planning, which it adores. It was the first American city with an official city plan and has recently plunked down $100,000 for a new Master Plan, which is already well along toward completion. One of the most interesting aspects of this plan is its comprehensiveness, since it plans not merely for the city, but for the city's thickly populated environs as well.

Acquiescing to the presence of Cincinnati's seven community-dividing hills as well as to common sense, the planners assume that no place is as pleasant to live in as a small town, if it provides the services of a city. New six-lane express-ways are proposed not only to handle the main currents of traffic, but to serve as effective barriers between industrial and residential areas. The aspirations of Mr. Sherwood Reeder, director of the Plan, for rehabilitating Cincinnati's tawdry water front are breath-takingly ambitious and will, if carried out, tend to make Cincinnati's water front as beautiful as Chicago's. One of the more interesting features is a group of apartment and public buildings built on stilts, with their above-ground basement walls serving as dikes.

Cincinnati has voted bond issues aggregating $41,000,000, a substantial part of which will be used to give expression to the preliminary aspects of the Plan. And it's noted as an encouraging sign, by those most eager for the city to bestir itself, that more than 80 per cent of Cincinnati's thrifty voters favored laying out this money.

Industrially, the Cincinnati that was slipping before the war is today, according to Mayor James G. Stewart, soundly back on its feet. As a counterbalance for those industries that have drifted away, "Cincinnati has," still according to its mayor, "been picked by 130 new permanent industries, which add approximately $12,000,000 to the gross pay roll." Financially, Cincinnati's government is shiningly solvent. Culturally, it is still in the forefront. And physically, realizing that it is in want of refurbishing, it is preparing to mold itself into the beautiful city its planners have designed—not immediately, mind you, not hurriedly, but with due Cincinnati circumspection.

1 3 : *Seattle*

T HE CENTRAL fact about Seattle, the thing that particularly differentiates it from most other cities in the United States, is that it is situated back of, beyond, away from almost anywhere else. From such Eastern centers of population as Baltimore, New York and Boston, it is just about as long a way to Seattle as it is to Tipperary. The Wright brothers have moved Mt. Rainier closer to Manhattan in terms of time, but not a millimeter closer in space. And you'll never have a personal feel of the somehow soul-expanding enormity of this intervening land mass until you have traversed its astonishingly dissimilar surface at ground level.

When you leave the populous east-north-central area, the last large city you see is Minneapolis. Then for hundreds of miles you roll across the rich flat black plains of western Minnesota and North Dakota, smooth land that is adorned in summer with billions of yellow blossoms of wild mustard and oceans of blue-green spring wheat. In western North Dakota the earth begins to go into convulsions, and you are in the Bad Lands. Here, and on across the broad reaches of Montana, the towns are multiple scores of miles apart. Each is a kind of miniature Reno, with lots of boots and bars and clinking silver dollars, lots of rugged, weather-cured people. All the salutations you receive are in loud, friendly voices. You sense in the. people an exhilarating pride-without-smugness.

By the time you reach that alfresco Maginot line, the Rocky Mountains, you can no longer hear the names of Lewis and Clark without doffing your hat and coming to attention. For they explored all this without benefit of A.A.A., Duncan Hines or internal-combustion engines. Even today there are only the highway signs and the sight of American farm machinery working in the valleys to remind you that you haven't, through some ill-starred fluke, wandered off into Tibet to have your misadventures posthumously recorded by James Hilton.

Spokane, Seattle's inland outpost—and you may be sure that is not the way Spokane thinks of herself—is the first city of more than 40,000 you've seen in well over a thousand miles. Then you cross a desert, pass through some magnificent timber and over the Cascade Mountains. Finally, almost unbelievably, there, doubly enchanted by nature and distance, lies Seattle.

You pass into the city over a concrete floating bridge, the world's largest floating structure. It spans Lake Washington, which is twenty-five miles long and more or less forms the eastern border of the city. Like almost all Northwestern lakes, this one is beautiful, deep and bluest blue, surrounded by fortunate dwellings.

Once inside the city, you note that the streets don't quite match up. In the old days when the original proprietors plotted the land into city blocks, one went by the points of the compass, while the other two ran their streets parallel with the harbor.

Your eye is peeled for the Western note, so predominant in Montana and Idaho. But your eye has difficulty in corroborating your mind's preconception. Somehow Seattle isn't quite the West—or any of the other stereotyped categories.

When you pick up the newspapers, the *Times*, the *Star*, Hearst's *Post-Intelligencer*, you realize, once and for all, that Seattle is a screwy place, because the papers keep talking Alaska this and Alaska that. Anybody knows that Alaska belongs not all over the morning papers but in geography books. Yet it turns out that Alaska is virtually an outlying ward of Seattle. To cap the queasy climax, Information Please comes on the radio in the afternoon.

So Seattle seems strange to most Americans from the population belt. To a new arrival it has the quality of a distant railroad station which, in order to fulfill its peculiar destiny, is dependent upon the passage of strangers, upon the unpredictable occurrence of wars, or the "folly" of some deceased Secretary of State and a coincidental discovery of gold. It has the feeling of a place where you lay your plans to do something somewhere else. For eloquent testimony of this point, listen to the leaving whistles of train or ship at night, whistles that endlessly unwind your imagination and set your heart to pounding.

In this city of hills and waterways, surrounded by visible, snowy mountain peaks, it is almost impossible to build a house without a view. For that reason, there are lots of big picture windows in most of the houses, the newer ones of which seem to follow a kind of modified California type of architecture. The names of much of the stunningly luxuriant shrubbery that adorns the lawns have an unfamiliar ring to the average visitor.

Seattle's main drags, Second, Third, Fourth and Fifth avenues, are laid in successively higher tiers on the wedding-cake hillside, which rises so steeply from the bay that some of the cross-street sidewalks have built-in cleats. Its tallest building is the forty-two-story Smith Tower. Yet if you enter Seattle from the sea, its hill-heightened skyline gives the impression of reaching almost to the clouds.

The town is acrawl with hotels. Its most opulent and imposing one, and a very nice place to stay, is the Olympic, named for the mountains across the bay. But there's not a highball for sale in any of them. Seattleites whose thirst can't be quenched by beer and wine are dependent either on the state-owned liquor stores or on their private clubs for a taste of the ardent. And, as you'd suppose, some of the best stories in town can be heard at the constricted but hospitable and pleasant Press Club, and more especially at its club within a club, the Round Table. Here most afternoons Phil O'Neill of the Seattle *Times* acts as moderator and, when more than one of the members are talking at once, he raps on the table and declares the place to be a "Portuguese boardinghouse." Among other things, they like to talk about the election when the *Times* ran the jazz-band leader, Victor A. Myers, as a burlesque candidate for mayor to embarrass the opposition. Myers garnered a surprising amount of votes and got the political bug. In a subsequent election he ran for lieutenant governor, and today presides over the Senate at Olympia.

Seattle's social elect do their clubbing at the Rainier, but if you're an old Alaska hand, perhaps you'd prefer the Arctic Club, where, through the big, leaded-glass dome over the dining room, Northern lights romp and play. However, membership in either one would fail to impress old-line Tacomans, who look on Seattle as an arena for the cavorting *nouveau riche*, its citizenry generally as ragtag and bobtail. Yet Seattle, with its score of foreign consulates, is not without a diplomatic set to decorate the social scene with formal functions.

When the Seattleite is fretful and bored, but is in no mood for the movies, he can attend either the Showboat or Penthouse theaters, both under the aegis of the University of Washington and founded by Glenn Hughes, director of the Division of Drama. It was here that Frances Farmer, Ella Raines and Jean Heather got their early dramatic training. Though there are commercial stages in town, Seattle is too far from taw to attract road shows more than once in a healthy coon's age. Perhaps the Seattleite will be diverted by the Seattle Symphony, for several years conducted by that *enfant terrible* of the podium, Sir Thomas Beecham.

Seattle goes in for totem poles, Chinatown and endlessly intriguing public markets where both the vegetables and the fishes have strikingly handsome complexions. A good many of its furnaces burn sawdust, and many of its busses burn Diesel oil with an attendant ruckus that is awesome. Its water front, mainly along Alaskan Way, is a colorful mélange of moving shipping, tooting ferries, hypnotic smells, curio shops, live-octopus peep shows, frozen-fish museums, foreign seamen, the piled nets of fishermen, ship chandlers' and sail makers' and riggers' stalls, ladies of susceptibility, fish and oyster booths.

There are all sorts of pleasing little cruises to be taken in the Sound: the one-hour ferry trip to Bremerton, home of the Puget Sound Navy Yard, the hour and three-quarter run to Tacoma, the eleven-hour trip to Canada's Vancouver, with a stopover at Victoria. On the way you have to detour to keep from running over the San Juan Islands, themselves a noted Puget Sound playground.

King County, which contains Seattle, is dotted with 205 lakes and streams and most other types of recreational facilities on a large scale. Perhaps that's why its people seem so sun-tinged and healthy. On a summer holiday Seattleites shuck off their clothes and go swimming by the thousands in either fresh or salt water. Others take to field or mountain stream. Only a person with corked ears can fail to

hear the call of the wild at such a time. For the unregenerately sedentary, there are lovely shaded drives around the lakes and hills that
soothe the wrung-out spirit.

The region that Seattle dominates is incredibly beautiful. If it's
possible for you to get too much really breath-taking scenery, then
the Pacific Northwest can make you holler "uncle." Its national parks
are studded with truly mighty forests which yet, when seen in relation to the colossal, snow-covered peaks that dominate them, are reduced to so much mossy green fuzz. In these parks are working,
moving glaciers and vast areas of lowland that are aflame with wild
flowers. There's almost no recognized use to which a canoe paddle, a
sporting gun or a fly rod can be put that would not be profitable in
these surroundings.

And it gives pause to this observer to learn that the city which
dominates this wilderness was earlier charged by one lady visitor with
being a mere road-show New York. Beyond the fact that in both
New York and Seattle the citizens wear clothes and, in the main,
speak English, the similarity of these cities is not too apparent to the
naked eye. When a city is new and busy and bewildered, lives in an
air-conditioned climate, has its chief commercial intercourse with the
Orient rather than the Occident, when redskins from twenty-seven
tribes are no strangers to its streets, and when, in normal times, the
cry is not a nerve-shattered plaint for "*Lebensraum*" but the exuberant whoop of "*tim*-ber!", then that city is a lot less likely to resemble
the suave metropolis on the Hudson than, say, Seattle, Washington.

Many Seattleites are a little miffed at the outside world for its lack
of knowledge and understanding of the town's exact place in North
American geography, as well as its assorted wonders. Seattleites are
also extremely touchy about any outside criticism. To point up this
sensitiveness, Nancy Wilson Ross, in her book, *Farthest Reach*, reports, "Lewis Mumford, requested to say what he thought of the
way the town was laid out, implied that it was too bad it couldn't be
torn down and a fresh start made. . . . When Mumford left for
Hawaii a local paper bitterly commented that the critic had sailed for
Honolulu 'which up to this time has been known as the pearl of the
Pacific.' "

One reason for the Seattleites' sensitiveness is their feeling of active participation, both by themselves and by their parents, in the shaping and development of this still young city.

Less than a hundred years ago, the population of Seattle was exactly one: a nineteen-year-old lad named David Denny, who was sick, without food, and living in a log cabin that had no roof. The exact location for Seattle was made a little later by David and his brother, Arthur, and their friends, Carson Boren and William Bell. Using Arthur's wife's hundred-foot clothesline and a horseshoe for a weight, they went looking for the bottom of Elliott Bay, on the eastern side of Puget Sound, and couldn't find it. They knew they had verified the presence of a great harbor, and very soon they were in business, supplying pilings and building timber for fast-growing San Francisco. It was simple. Fell the great trees into the harbor, float them to the ships and send them away, along with orders for needed supplies to be returned by the lumber ship. Then when Henry Yesler set up his steam sawmill and Dr. David Maynard his salmon-packing plant, where he ineffectively cured the fish that the Indians caught, Seattle's growth rapidly increased.

Seattle had two other profound advantages besides an excellent harbor and superb timber. Despite the fact she had a latitudinal equality with Quebec, she was warmed by the Japan Current and had glorious weather. It might wet you oftener than you thought necessary, but it would never cook you nor freeze you. Lastly, she had a mountain pass, the Snoqualmie, which, at 3,000 feet, was a thousand feet lower than any of the other Northwest passes inviting ingress from the broad interior of the nation.

By 1853 the wagons were rolling toward Seattle. Cholera haunted the inhumanly long trail, which began to be lined with graves. In the Cascade Mountains it was sometimes necessary to slaughter the oxen and plait their hides into cables for lowering the wagons down the sheer declivities. But pioneering had become a lust and a craze that nothing but the western limits of the frontier itself could stop. The wagons rolled on.

Seattle was named for a great and wise and sad Indian chief who, like Pétain, knew when he had met his masters. Nevertheless the town successfully prosecuted an opera bouffe war with some of the Indians and, in 1861, pre-empted the territorial university by presenting the government with a *fait accompli*. Its first president and teacher was Asa Mercer, who subsequently distinguished himself by ministering to other of the town's needs besides its hankering for intellectual refreshment.

Like most frontier towns, Seattle's citizenry was mostly male, and the tortures of springtime were acute. As one of the early settlers of Seattle, Asa Mercer wanted to see it thrive, know harmony and multiplication beyond immigration. In order to circumvent virtual spontaneous combustion of this virile citizenry, he went prospecting into the East to find wives for the lonely pioneers. Mercer was a decent man, a kind of rawhide Cupid, convinced that what he was doing would brighten the lot of all concerned at both ends of the line, since the man-devouring Civil War had blighted many of the Eastern girls' connubial aspirations. .

On his first trip Mercer brought back eleven girls. You can imagine the excitement they caused in the little frontier town. On his second trip he brought back a hundred. The reception these girls got in Seattle, the understanding of their courage, their need for the immediate friendship of the few established families, and the mutual admiration of pioneer for pioneer was touching and wonderful. And the success of the mission is proved by the number of present-day citizens of Seattle who proudly claim to be descended from "Mercer's girls."

Perhaps even more ladies could be persuaded to venture out when the Northern Pacific should get rolling. Seattle bid $700,000 for the right to become its western terminus. At the time Seattle contained less than 2,000 souls, and the $700,000 was to be paid principally in real estate. But Seattle's hopes were dashed. The N.P. decided in favor of Tacoma. Seattle, however, was not to be denied. The townsfolk determined to build a railroad with their own hands and did— as far as the coal mines out on the edge of town. Then they decided to ship through Canada and were making headway when the harassed Northern Pacific finally brought its tracks into town. Seattle's primary problem, communication with the rest of the nation by rail, was for the time solved.

On July 15, 1897, the first omen of Seattle's great impending adventure electrified the nation. On that day the steamship *Excelsior* reached San Francisco carrying prospectors from the Yukon. One man had gold worth $115,000, another $130,000, and had been offered $2,000,000 for his claim. A few days later, the *Portland* blew into Seattle carrying a ton and a half of gold and excited stories about the Klondike, where gold was to be found not in mere dust but in pellets and nuggets. One man had washed eight hundred dollars' worth out of a single pan of gravel.

All over the country every man not already rich, every man who hated his own humdrum job or was bored with a humdrum wife or life, found that here was a valid excuse for escape and adventure. Seattle was, of course, the logical jumping-off place and, according to Archie Binns' excellent *Northwest Gateway*, it promptly became bedlam, too full of people and money and mass hysteria. Every available ship was chartered to haul the prospectors north to Alaska. Twelve stern-wheelers were being built in one Seattle shipyard for the same purpose. Camping equipment, freshly bought, covered blocks of streets. Schools were opened to teach prospectors some of the more rudimentary tricks of the trade: how to wash gold out of a pan of gravel and how to make a team of Huskies mush.

Within ten years gold worth $174,000,000 came out of Alaska. How many men died along the frozen trails, or were liquidated by cohorts who coveted their pokes, will never be known. But since that time a lot of tidewater has flowed in and out of Puget Sound.

Today, Seattle is a city of slightly less than half a million. For purposes of comparison, Tacoma, at the south end of the Sound, and inland Spokane are about a third of that figure. Portland, just across the state line in Oregon, is the second largest city in the Northwest and has only a few score thousand less citizens than Seattle.

As has long been the case, the state of Washington's forests of spruce and Douglas fir, of cedar, hemlock and pine, are her most abundant and readily negotiable source of wealth. More than 50 per cent of Washington's income has customarily derived from the sale or processing of her forest products. Her paper business started before she became a state, and years before the last war began, her plywood and pressed-wood industry was making long strides. At that time, according to W. E. Difford, managing director of the Douglas Fir Plywood Association, it had become a $75,000,000 a year business, capable of supplying a third of a million all-plywood houses. An almost microscopic part of her red cedar went into some of the world's finest racing shells built by George Pocock for every big American boat-racing university except Yale, which is supplied by his half-brother.

Of course the city of Seattle's heaviest commercial nugget is her extraordinarily fine port. Elliott Bay is linked by canal with Lake Union and Lake Washington, giving Seattle a total deep-water frontage of almost two hundred miles. Here a vessel that has been so long at sea that her bottom is foul with marine growth needn't go through an expensive dry-docking process. She has simply to pull up into Lake Washington where, for want of salinity, the barnacles will give up both the ghost and their grip on the ship.

Not only does a heavy freight and passenger business pass through the port; so does the exotic harvest of Northwest fisheries. And however unbelievable it may seem, two of her biggest customers for halibut are already-fish-ridden Boston and New York. Seattle catches and cans considerable Sockeye salmon right in Puget Sound, but it is the influx of the gigantic Alaskan catch which makes salmon and Seattle almost synonymous.

Although Washington state doesn't set the world afire agriculturally, it, nevertheless, has a thriving livestock and dairy industry and produces exportable quantities of wheat and some of the finest fruits, berries and vegetables to be obtained anywhere. From her orchards, mainly in the irrigated Wenatchee and Yakima valleys, comes one fourth of the nation's commercial apple crop.

The Pacific Northwest long had one undeveloped resource of almost frightening immensity: its potential hydroelectric power. This amounted to 40 per cent of that of the nation as a whole, and seemed a kind of divine compensation to its citizens for their having to climb up and down so many mountains. For some time the cities of the Northwest had been supplied principally with hydroelectric power developed by private concerns. Then the United States government lit into the Columbia River and imprisoned it behind the mighty Bonneville and Grand Coulee dams, so that it must henceforth work to earn fulfillment for its yearning for the sea. By the time the Japanese let go on Pearl Harbor, the whole interconnected Northwestern power system, composed both of public and private systems, was aquiver with dynamism, was just waiting, as the Westerners say, for somebody "to make a track." Whatever could be done electrically, the Northwest could do with emphasis and impact.

At this time we were desperately in need of aluminum, needed it in quantities never dreamed of before. The electrolytic reduction of alumina to aluminum on the required scale called for huge funds of electric power, preferably cheap. And the mills began to beat a path to the door of the high-voltaged Northwest. They kept coming until the region had a rated capacity of 550,000,000 pounds of pig aluminum a year and the ability to roll about half of it. That, plus a magnesium plant which produces eight times as much as the entire nation did before the war.

Speculating on Seattle's future is one of those fascinating games of which the first rule is: hold onto your hat. The factors involved are endlessly diverse and magnificently unpredictable.

In isolating the weaknesses of her position, it is manifest that Japan, one of her best prewar customers, is busted. Her lumber industry, though still going strong, has passed its peak, and the high premium she must pay for steel is a chronic deficiency. Then there is the blunt unarguable fact that Seattle has no important population pools close at hand to buy her goods and services. Her Northwestern bailiwick of Alaska, Washington, Oregon, Idaho and Montana contains only about 3 per cent of the nation's inhabitants. Viewed politically, this miniscule electorate cannot pack a very big wallop in the struggles of the Northwest to affect Federal policy. Finally, she has a national reputation for labor strife and high labor costs.

But the men who spark Seattle today, while aware of these difficulties, are just as aware of her remarkable promise.

In the first place, they do not feel that Dave Beck, boss of Seattle's strategic Teamsters' Union, plus important affiliates, will find it necessary to take the place apart. These days Beck sits so squarely in the driver's seat, and has the town so tightly organized, that he is full of affability and kindness to the industrialists he has brought to heel. Though Washington probably has more Communists than any one state deserves, Beck, perfectly aware that there is no place in Communism for a really up-and-coming labor leader, is a private-enterprise man from the word go.

Dave Beck is blue-eyed, pink-faced, abstinent and personable. He talks to two men in much the same way he would to two thousand, his voice growing louder than he realizes, leaning heavily on the phrase "in my judgment." He is built like a forty-five slug. He is tough, but he is also exceptionally able. He demonstrated his ability to bring the old-time labor baiters to their knees during the early 'Thirties when both sides were marshaling and deploying their goons. He has just as emphatically shown his ability to keep his own communicants in line. And this in itself is no mean feat when you think of the rumbling vitality of American truck drivers and cabbies.

Beck has created a peculiar state of affairs in which, as of the present, he has both Seattle capital and labor joyfully eating out of his hand. He has gained extraordinarily high wages for his workers. But by keeping them steadily on the job, he has been able to convince the industrialists, whose money has paid for the contentment of the workers, that production costs are lower than in some other sections of the country.

Throughout the financially foolproof 'Forties this Beck-guided economic arrangement has paid off for all concerned. Whether this all-round *Gemütlichkeit* can withstand the ravages of a depression, when the pickings are slim and there is blood in every competitor's eye, remains to be seen. But however transitory or permanent this honeymoon between Seattle's capital and labor may be, Beck apparently is there to stay, since sweet-talking is but a single arrow in his bulging quiver. For Seattle lives by transportation, and Beck controls that last crucial mile between rail station or dock and customer's warehouse.

Seattle's lifelines now consist of four transcontinental rail lines and some seventy sea lines that span the globe. Then there is the new dimension of the air. The most direct airline route from the United States to Vladivostok, Hong Kong, Manila or Singapore lies squarely across Seattle. Seattle and Tacoma have buried the hatchet to the extent of going into cahoots on a new $10,000,000 airport being built on the No Man's Land between these neighboring cities.

Northwest industry is poised to compete for the markets of Siberia and China not on a basis of gigantic, rigid, low-cost production-line manufacturing of the Detroit type, which must inevitably be designed primarily for America's great home market, but with custom-built goods. These goods will be created on a thesis rare in our export trade: that the customer, having to operate face to face with divergent local conditions, is right in demanding divergent specifications, and that he's willing to pay more to get what he wants.

The Northwest is also working to establish a "foreign trade area." That means an area into which she can import foreign produce tariff-free, grade it, clean it, repackage or, as in the case of oil nuts, refine it, and ship it out again with the value of processing and profit added, without having paid any customs duty whatever. This would tend to make all the world hers, both as a mine of resources and as a market.

Washington's growing paper and plywood business will give increasing support to her budding chemical industry. Already those Gold Dust twins of the future, plywood and light metals, are going into new rail rolling stock, both for passengers and freight. Undoubtedly, both will play a big part in the nation's efforts to house itself properly. Moreover, Seattle will not be content merely to send her aluminum pigs to Eastern markets for final processing. She is bound and determined to make lots of the nation's pots and pans and other profitable gadgets right here on the West Coast, to create a completely integrated light-metals industry. In terms of labor, every single worker on the pig-aluminum level would have to be complemented by an estimated seventeen workers on the fabricating level. And though the realization of this integrated light-metals industry involves the working of at least half a dozen future wonders, and is at this time largely a gleam in Seattle's big dreamy eyes, she is determined to make it a reality. In any case, Boeing, which has already bought a major portion of its Seattle plant from the government, will continue to be a factor on the finished-goods level.

As a further development of the Columbia River project, the Bureau of Reclamation is proceeding with plans to irrigate an area of 1,200,000 acres of fertile land in the Big Bend of the Columbia River which is expected to support a total population of 250,000 people. There is an estimated total, according to Paul W. Hand of the Bonneville Power Administration, of over 3,000,000 acres of land in the Pacific Northwest that can ultimately be irrigated, with potential agricultural products to the value of $350,000,000. And the plangent hum of the Bonneville dynamos, in a nation whose petroleum deposits are being fast expended, promises creative energy in perpetuity, and is as full of magic potentialities as Aladdin's lamp.

For a dreamer, an imaginer, actually for a pioneer, and particularly for one who is adept at shrinking distances, Seattle and the Northwest are mighty hard places to keep away from. Surely the people of no American city have a more profound conviction that the future is their friend.

14: *Boston*

Boston is complex and fascinating and, in many respects, one of the most distinctive cities in this republic which she helped so much to found, protect and nourish. Boston is three centuries, and she has two basic cultures which are, in numerous ways, antipathetic. Half a dozen other cultures are thrown in for good measure and cacophony.

She is full of almost benumbing contrasts. Her people are rich, her government is poor. She has a reputation for both bigotry and intellectual eminence. Former Mayor Maurice J. Tobin, and more latterly governor of Massachusetts, says he has never known of a labor racket in New England during his political life. Yet for the last decade Americans have become accustomed to reading in newspapers of recurrent squabbles between Boston management and Boston labor. Her Yankee minority has a serene conviction that it is the elect of the Unitarian God, while Irish wits speak of their own people as the "poor, downtrodden majority."

Boston considers herself the third most important money market in the nation. Moreover, much of the money and skills that developed many of the nation's newer cities flowed originally from Boston.

The automobile which made Detroit great, the textiles which now go so far toward supporting the South, the steel that became Pittsburgh, the shoes that helped to boom St. Louis, the finance that gave Kansas City and many another Western town its start—all had their American origin in Boston. Our world-wide sea trade began in Boston bottoms. Boston passed the first educational legislation, set up the first college and provided America with the foundations of a national literature.

Boston got its start in business when her mariners began peddling fish and ice, and Yankee-trading all over the globe. She was first ramrodded by the Puritans who, in their high-handed disciplinary actions against the less pure, made a piker out of Oliver Cromwell. The American Revolution got its prime impetus as well as many of its leaders and rank-and-file fighters from Boston. The clipper ship, developed after that war, for a time gave the Yankees a speed advantage over the rest of the world's ships.

Small, diverse industries were springing up. Boston's sons were becoming renowned as statesmen, preachers, soldiers, writers, painters, governors and thinkers. The city was beginning to feel her oats. She was becoming more and more justified in regarding herself as the Athens of America. Then, as the intellectual and moral leader of the nation, she led the fight to free the slaves whom her merchants had previously sold to the planters of the South. In the process of supplying the Union Army, she created still more Boston fortunes.

Meanwhile, across the Atlantic, potato crops were failing in Ireland, and pogroms were raging in Russia and Poland. Life for the poor in Sicily and southern Italy had long been a hungry dog's life. Word of American opportunity, often exaggerated, found its way around Europe. The mighty procession of immigration got under way.

Of the 2,500,000 people who live in metropolitan Boston today, those of recent foreign origin engulf the native stock, which is almost pure English lineage. Foreign-language-press figures show that in Greater Boston there are 200,000 Italians, about the same number of Jews, about 50,000 Poles, 30,000 Swedes, 25,000 Germans, 20,000 Lithuanians and 17,000 Greeks. Not shown in these figures are 30,000 Negroes, a large group of Canadians—and the Irish.

Boston proper is an Irish city, from which the simon-pure Yankees have largely fled to build residences in the outlying suburbs. They commute to their city offices. Yet it should be noted that the figures quoted above include not only the foreign-born but their American-born children, and many of them feel as former Ambassador Joe Kennedy felt when the newspapers referred to him as an Irishman. He looked up in bewilderment and said, "I was born here. My children were born here. What the hell do I have to do to get to be an American?"

The Boston which was first Puritan, then Unitarian, is now predominantly Roman Catholic. It is widely presumed that the frequent accession of Irish Catholic mayors and the more or less permanent incumbency of the Irish in subordinate public offices is the dynastic outcome of effective machine politics. Yet both former Governor Joseph B. Ely and Boston's politically omniscient W. E. Mullins say that if there is any man in Boston who can deliver 1,500 votes, they don't know who he is.

For the same reason, no politician is powerful enough to protect organized vice, once it comes to light. The principal reason Boston has had so many Irish Catholics in her government is simply that there are so many Irish Catholic voters and that the holding of public office is a passion among the Boston Irish, many of whom arrived in a strange land with little or no money and saw hope of security in the city's civil service.

But an Irish Catholic candidate has slim reason to take victory for granted merely because of his ties with Eire and the Church. Dyed-in-the-wool-Yankee Leverett Saltonstall defeats Irish Catholic opponents in Boston almost as readily as he does Unitarian Protestants. Boston just likes him.

The late Cardinal O'Connell was, in some respects, the most politically powerful man in town. He was a conservative, aristocratic churchman who seldom used his power, and then only when he considered moral issues to be at stake. Archbishop Richard J. Cushing, who now heads the Boston archdiocese, is younger and less conservative and remote than his distinguished predecessor. He hobnobs with the poor, visits the prisons, and he went out of his way to assure the General Court (the state legislature) that he favored passage of anti-discrimination legislation which was pending before it. Though he has not been head of the archdiocese long, Cushing has Boston's hot, emotional Irish heart securely in his pocket.

Boston has the highest per-capita cost of government of any large American city—more than twice that of St. Louis, for instance. But the herds of visitors that come to Boston from all over the nation are not interested in the city's housekeeping problems. They come to see a national shrine.

If the visitor comes by automobile, his indoctrination will begin as he enters southern New England and passes through quiet, dignified little villages celebrating their tercentennials with ox-pulling contests. He will see the steepled churches and village greens with their enormous old elms, the clapboarded saltbox and Cape Cod houses sporting little signs that tell how many hundred years the structures have stood. If the visitor comes from a part of the country where any building fifty years old is considered ancient, he will find his standards and viewpoint subtly changed. Then when he reaches Boston and starts looking for the physical relics of America's past, he will realize promptly that he's hit the historical jack pot.

First off he can tell, by the scores of graveyards everywhere to be found, that Boston's antiquity is no put-up job. In these graves lie a number of the signers of the Declaration of Independence, as well as the parents of Ben Franklin, who, as a boy, decamped to Philadelphia to become that city's Public Asset Number One.

The tallest building in today's Boston is the Customs House Tower, its tallest monument the one which honors the battle of Bunker Hill. From the Bunker Hill monument you can see "Old Ironsides," the frigate *Constitution*, lying in Boston's mammoth navy yard. She looks somehow proud and ready, after having been restored by contributions from the school kids of America when the only alternatives were to junk her or, *nail to the mast her holy flag, set every threadbare sail, and give her to the god of storms, the lightning and the gale.*

Over in downtown Boston is Faneuil Hall, called "The Cradle of Liberty" because in her second story Sam Adams and other leading revolutionists met to plot and plan such enterprises as the Boston Tea Party. The spot where the tea chests were actually jettisoned is now dry land, dredged up to enlarge Boston's business district.

If the visitor's interests embrace old Boston's literary adventures, he can make pilgrimages to the homes of its great authors. The Emerson house and the Longfellow house, as well as the Hawthorne houses, stand in good repair. So does the Alcott house, where Louisa May wrote *Little Women.*

Once the visitor really gets prying around in Boston, he'll find that Paul Revere was to Boston pretty much what Franklin was to Philadelphia—the busiest man in town, with a finger in most of its pies. Revere, also, did his bit of publishing and politicking, and he turned out a great variety of products from his workshop, among them the copper plates which shield the dome of Massachusetts' Bulfinch-designed State House on blue-blooded Beacon Hill. This one was finished in 1798, but is known as the "new" State House to distinguish it from its still-extant predecessor, in front of which the Boston Massacre occurred.

Bulfinch was not merely the first American architect; he was a very able one. You can stand before the State House nowadays and see that the Bulfinch walls, made of hand-struck brick, pierced here and there by fan-shaped windows, have a kind of living, quietly emotional quality. The granite and marble wings, which were added much later, could just as well have been built to enclose a house of correction.

Regilding jobs for the dome cost $12,000 and were usually postponed by such Yankee string-savers as Governors Coolidge and Saltonstall. Much of the interior of the State House is paneled in white oak and is extremely handsome, but the most Boston-like object there is the four-foot-long "Sacred Codfish," which symbolizes Massachusetts' first basic industry. It hangs in the House of Representatives. It was filched by collegians a few years ago, but once it was located by the cops, the young scholars were allowed to return it with no questions asked and no charges filed.

Many of the houses on Beacon Hill, which is social Boston's final redoubt, were also designed by Bulfinch, with upstairs living rooms and downstairs dining rooms. Since Bulfinch received his training in an England which once had a tax on windows, the bay window, which gave you most for your money, abounds here, as it does all over Boston. The Women's City Club is one of the half-dozen buildings on Beacon Street with genuine, age-purpled panes, the result of a chemical eccentricity in a certain batch of glass shipped from England back in Boston's girlhood. Some of the lavender panes you see are, alack, phonies.

Next door to the City Club is the snooty old Somerset Club, where only members and guests from more than a hundred miles away may enter by the front door. Local guests, of whatever eminence, may enter only by a side door and may not, under any circumstance, go into the club's main dining or reading rooms.

Spread out in front of the State House are the nearly fifty acres of the Boston Common, which was first set aside as a place of common pasturage for the townsfolk's cattle. It's still all there, green and lovely, in the city's heart, just as it was back in Emerson's cowherding boyhood. Remarkably domineering pigeons make power dives at your face. Little gray squirrels gingerly panhandle peanuts beside the Frog Pond in which nagging wives once were ducked. Here, as in many other places in Boston, are statues and bronze tablets to commemorate Boston's great of other years. This spate of statuary is one of the pleasantest, most Athenian attributes of the town. It keeps history living before your eyes, exemplifies Boston's gratitude for the individual endowments that contributed to her greatness.

Just across Charles Street from the Common is the Public Garden where, among graceful old wineglass elms, a bronze George Washington sits astride a bronze horse. Near by is a little lake traversed by prim swan boats. The swan boats have benches that span two pontoons and are propelled by young men who sit back inside a much-larger-than-life, artificial swan's folded wings and pedal the paddle wheel that pushes the boat.

People feel free to wander at will over the grass in the Common, but take no such liberties in the Public Garden, which is more buttoned up and formally landscaped.

Every tree in the Common and the Public Garden has its family designated on a plate in Latin and English. But where Boston really gets down to the business of growing trees is in the 265-acre Arnold Arboretum, with its 6,500 varieties of trees, shrubs, and vines, and one of the largest horticultural-botanical libraries in the world.

Yet if social Boston makes a point of visiting the flower beds in the Public Garden in the summer, it makes an even more emphatic one of attending, in the wintertime, the Friday-afternoon concerts of the superb Boston Symphony under the direction of Serge Koussevitzky. The Symphony occupies a large place in Boston life. It gives summer-night, open-air concerts from a bandstand beside the Charles River and also holds a six-weeks spring festival called "Pops" in Symphony Hall, where tables are trundled in and where everything is claret punch and merriment. The Symphony, in its less sober manifestations, is directed not by the great Serge, but by Arthur Fiedler. It is also at Symphony Hall that the *Boston Herald's* annual Book Fair is held, and to which its literary editor, Alice Dixon Bond, dragoons most of such folk of letters as the country currently affords.

Boston's Public Library, which faces triangular Copley Square, is huge and impressive, but if you really want to read in the company of Brahmins, you take out a "proprietorship" in Boston's famed Athenaeum, a society that bought George Washington's library. Since well-bred Boston likes neither display, the abandonment of tradition nor the final farewell to a dollar bill, tea and buns still have a going price of three cents at the Athenaeum.

Across the Charles River in Cambridge is Harvard University, which has been improving young men's minds and social standings for hundreds of years. A few miles to the northwest are first Lexington and then Concord, where the embattled farmers stood and fired that famous shot.

Almost everywhere through Boston's outlying districts are ancient inns. The one with the most captivating atmosphere is the Wayside Inn in Sudbury, near Concord. Henry Ford has bought it and restored it as nearly as possible to the condition in which Longfellow found and loved it. Yet the one most famous for its food is the Toll House in Whitman, where the meringue on the lemon pie is three inches thick. And for those Boston visitors who look upon the cod and the bean as the Jukeses and Kallikaks of human fare, it's worth noting that the Hotels Vendome and the Copley Plaza have genuinely gifted French chefs, and of course the home of honeycomb tripe and delicious, hinged rolls is the famed Parker House. Some travelers regard the sleek Boston Ritz as America's finest hotel. Both Locke-Ober's and the Oyster House on Dock Square are informal but respected eateries, and just in case you're hungry for a plate of good old New England shishkebab, you might look in at the Athens. S. S. Pierce, which sounds like a steamboat, is the town's most famous grocer, and traffics in all the world's delicacies.

Boston's downtown streets are as crooked and narrow as her Commonwealth Avenue is spacious and pretty. Downtown crowds abandon the narrow sidewalks and wander in dreamy hordes in the streets. Outside some of the newspaper offices, bulletins are chalked on the walls, just as they were when Sherman was giving it to Georgia. Boston newspapers, like English ones, carry a good deal of advertising matter on their front pages. Boston's Louisburg Square would do credit to any of London's better neighborhoods with no change whatever. It was used by Hollywood as one of the sets in filming Thackeray's *Vanity Fair*.

The badge of social confidence among many old-school Boston ladies is an ensemble consisting of a lavender hat, a black velvet ribbon around the neck, a green bag for carrying parcels and any dress old and out of style. If it happens to have leg-o'-mutton sleeves, not only the wearer but all beholders feel good about it. The streets are full of trim and pretty colleens, too, but that's another matter. Many of Boston's stylish upper middle class buy their clothes from the Boston branches of New York shops, but most old-line Boston ladies shop at Boston's own R. H. Stearns'—except, apparently, for their hats. A Bostonian, when asked by a visitor where Boston ladies bought their hats, said in astonishment, "My deah, we don't *buy* our hats. We *have* our hats."

Boston has always been less interested in personal adornment than in running her mills and plants. Last census reports show the Boston industrial area, comprising four counties with the pretty English names of Essex, Middlesex, Norfolk and Suffolk, spun and wove woolens worth $125,000,000 and processed food products worth $100,000,000. With such exceptions as Little, Brown and Company, Houghton Mifflin, and the Atlantic Monthly, trade publishing and magazine publishing have largely abandoned a too closely Watch-and-Ward-watched Boston for New York. But Boston's standing in the academic world helps her to remain a great textbook center.

She does, in all, $90,000,000 worth of publishing a year. Diversification of her industries is still a major strength—industries which make lots of shoes, machinery, chemical products, transportation equipment and oil, coal and rubber products. Metropolitan Boston's 1942 manufactures reached $3,000,000,000.

But her leaders realize that the future has, industrially speaking, a bear trap baited for Boston. Until recently, she has competed with an America that was, in large areas, industrially illiterate and without the physical means to process native raw materials. Today it's a different story. As a result of war training, the South, the Southwest and the Middle West have plenty of skilled workers. They also have plants and finance, and they are aggressively on the make for new industries, to add the manufactured value to their own raw materials and to supply their own markets with finished goods. Boston is worried and is rallying her industrial Minute Men to do something about it.

Commercial aviation's limitless promise has also changed Boston's outlook. In the past, Boston and New England rather enjoyed living on a fairly quiet siding of America's main, thundering traffic lines between New York and the West Coast. A far less complacent contemporary Boston gets just as worked up over the establishment of a direct airline to Cleveland and the West Coast as, in earlier times, it got over a shipment of scenic wallpaper from General Lafayette to the numerous Boston ladies who had entertained him—which is not meant to imply that old-line Bostonians want to *go* to Cleveland or the West Coast, even on a visit.

Boston's air ambitions are impressive. She is the nearest large American city to London and Paris, and is fighting, under the leadership of the Massachusetts Development and Industrial Commission, to become the "Hub of the Air Universe." She has already changed the name of her Logan Airport, which is but ten minutes from the heart of town, to the Logan International Airport. Current improvements, principally three seven-thousand-foot runways to receive giant airliners, will run up the cost of the airport, much of it made-land, to around $40,000,-000. At least one airline, TWA, has already applied for a world-encircling route that would make Boston the first American port of call from Europe.

But if the outcome of Boston's struggle for a dominant place in the commercial air world remains to be seen, she nevertheless faces the future with many economic trumps. In the first place, there's her port, second in imports and eighth in general business among those of the nation. The port has scores of miles of water front, lies but six miles from the open sea, has been improved by Army and Navy expenditures and is to get further improvements from the state.

Her fish business, older than the town itself, was long exploited by the Indians, who ate what they could and used the rest for fertilizer. Today, Boston and Gloucester, which is in her orbit, haul in some $20,000,000 worth of fish a year. Gloucester gets mainly perch, which it fillets. To Boston's famous Fish Pier, which her Chamber of Commerce admits is the most up to date on earth, come principally cod, haddock and lobster.

Boston's insurance business is a bedrock, here-today, here-tomorrow business.

Another equally permanent undertaking seldom thought of as big business, is Boston's prep schools, colleges and universities. Besides Harvard, which normally has 8,500 paying guests and an endowment of $160,000,000, and Boston University with 10,000 students, there are such schools as the famous Massachusetts Institute of Technology, Boston College, Wellesley, Radcliffe and Tufts, as well as scores of smaller schools scattered around in Greater Boston.

Of genuine importance in Boston's economy, both as a source of wealth and as a stabilizing factor, are the invested savings of fifteen generations of thrifty, industrious Yankees which run into tens of billions and keep many superannuated New Englanders amply supplied with fish balls and beans.

Yet more productive are the skills of New England's people, which Bostonians insist are matched nowhere outside her region. It is the possession of these skills that Boston considers her greatest asset in the fight for industry. She points out that industrial processes will become more and more complicated, entailing more and more precision operations that require abilities which just aren't to be found in the boll-weevil states or out where the tall corn grows. Realizing that her ultimate strength is her people, New England has wisely refertilized that resource with education. According to the last census, it has the highest educational level of any section.

Boston and New England clean up on their summer tourist trade. The region offers a choice of mountains or seashore, historical lore and exhilarating summer weather. It is somehow more restful, less garish and bustling than most of the rest of the nation. It provides a peculiar kind of going-home, an odd escape from a present that has not been too easygoing lately into a past that belongs to all America.

Every old house is a story, a simple, compelling story built around a great fireplace with Dutch ovens, a crane for suspending kettles, a spit that was turned by the pull of weights. The chimney, in addition to being the source of warmth and daily bread, the spiritual center of gravity of the family, literally held the house up, supporting heavy, hand-hewn oak beams. These old New England houses, surrounded by stone walls that represent thousands of backaches, offer, when seen in conjunction with New England's churches and flowering literature, an approach to the spirit that animated old Boston, a spirit that maintained it and made it great.

Ultimately, there isn't just one Boston. There are many. But fundamentally there are two—today's commercial heterogeneous Boston, and the seventeenth-eighteenth-century Yankee Boston racked with violent artesian urges of creation, of expression and growth which could flow at all only through the tightly constricted nozzle of stern moral and religious restraint. And it is impossible to walk down a Boston street today without seeing them both in continual, ever-startling proximity.

15: *Denver*

DENVER, perched on a high plateau at the foot of the Rockies, out where the word "Divide" is as much a geographical as a mathematical term, and where peaches most often come in cans, is one of those Western towns that is sufficiently civilized to make living there a pleasure, while, at the same time, it retains its easy Western ways, its flamboyant terrain, and its clean, dry, up-perking air. Yet, oddly, it has a conservatism of viewpoint somewhat singular for a city that is only eighty-odd years old and is situated in the heart of the high-betting West.

To the whole Rocky Mountain Empire, which composes more than a quarter of the nation, Denver is what London is to the British Empire. In this sparsely settled area, Denver's population of 375,000 is a staggeringly huge clot of humanity which towers beyond comparison with Salt Lake City's 150,000, Phoenix's 65,000, Butte's 37,000 or Cheyenne's 22,000.

While Denver itself is a mile above sea level, its buildings, though not squatty, give anything but an impression of skyscraping. The general feeling of the city is one of substantialness and of being widely spread.

The first things that will probably strike you about Denver, after you have duly oh-ed and ah-ed over its mountain backdrop, are its cleanliness, its extraordinarily large but still deficient number of hotels, and its system of street identification, which is one of the least informative and most frustrating in America. You'll unavoidably note that many of Denver's shops are full of silver gewgaws, many of which only a savage Comanche far gone in drink would find in good taste. At the same time, if you've come by way of Reno, you may be surprised to learn that in Denver people work for a living, rather than preying on man's weakness for red-eye, roulette, and the other fellow's wife.

For a city its size, an extremely large percentage of its people own their own homes, which are built almost exclusively of brick, and keep their lawns green, trim, and lighted by blossoms. And since trees, in a state of nature, are a rarity on the plain which Denver occupies, the city's thousands of carefully planted and tended trees seem especially beautiful to you where they occur in double lines on each side of the long, wide streets.

However, it is these same trees which help hide from you the more attractive parts of the city when you've paid your twelve cents for a glimpse of it from the top of the twenty-story Daniels and Fisher Tower. Yet if you don't focus your attention on the shabby areas between the downtown district and the stockyards, or on the pathological fungi of shacks and honkytonks that seem to attach themselves to the perimeters of all resort towns, you'll find that Denver is an astonishingly handsome city.

Denver's system of parks is outstanding in the nation. In City Park, whose elm-covered acres resemble Boston Common, you can take your animals dead or alive by prowling either in the zoo or in the really top-flight Colorado Museum of Natural History, where the exhibits are staged with great skill and excellence. And if you've nothing planned on a summer's evening, you can stay right there in City Park and hear a band concert. There are numerous other lovely, well-kept parks, all of them under the direction of Mr. George Cranmer, the man who won't put up decent street signs.

You'll also find that Denver, to which tuberculosis has made its tragic contribution, is a considerable medical center and the home of, to name only a few, the Army's big Fitzsimons General Hospital, the Colorado General, the Denver General, the National Jewish, and the Children's Hospital, the last named of which is as modern and shiny with glass and tile as any of Denver's new apartment buildings.

To an equal extent, Denver is a Western capital of learning. Within its limits are the University of Denver, with almost six thousand students, Colorado Woman's College, Regis College, and the Boettcher School for crippled children, which stands adjacent to the Children's

Hospital. The largest and most unusual of these schools is the Emily Griffith Opportunity School, a "people's school," which has no entrance requirements, but will teach its twelve thousand students of all ages almost anything they want to learn. Out at the near-by town of Golden, is the unexcelled Colorado School of Mines. But from the standpoint of sheer physical plant, Denver's public school system, which was rebuilt during the 'Twenties, will knock your eye out and make that of most comparable cities look like two cents.

Yet where downtown Denver shows off to finest advantage is at her Civic Center. Here she went all-out Athenian, and, around a broad central area of green lawn, built her majestic municipal building on the west, facing, on the east, the State Capitol, the dome of which has been lavishly dolloped with gold. Then, spotting in each where it would do the most good in forming an harmonic whole, Denver built a Greek theater, the Memorial Colonnade, the Denver Public Library, handsome but too small to carry the load, the State Historial Museum, and the U. S. Mint, which squats, gooselike, on a golden egg second only to that at Fort Knox.

Not too far away is beautified Cherry Creek, now trickling, now racing, toward its rendezvous with the South Platte River, down behind the Union Station, where the streamliners wind up their fifteen-hour journey from Chicago. From the Union Station, it's only a couple of jumps to the Municipal Auditorium, which the Denver *Post*, under the new leadership of Palmer Hoyt, late of Portland's *Oregonian*, thinks isn't nearly large enough, just as it deplores the fact that Denver is one of the only American cities its size which has no organized baseball. What makes the *Post* howl for a new coliseum is that there is at present no place in town big enough to hold the crowds which flock each year to the A.A.U. championship basketball tournament and to the National Western Rodeo, Horse and Livestock Shows.

But both to Denver's visitors and her home folks such town doings are but a part of their reason for being there, since the countryside is full of wonders. On any clear day you have only to look toward the west to see the Rockies beckoning for skiing or hunting in the winter, for fishing or camping or perhaps mountain-climbing in the summer.

There are fifty-one mountains more than fourteen thousand feet high in the state, and Denver's Mr. and Mrs. Paul Gorham have shinnied up the last frazzling one of them. Of course Pikes Peak isn't the tallest, but being something of an individualist, and doing its towering away from its chief competitors, it has managed to gain for itself the better press agents.

Yet perhaps Denver's unique and most pleasing attribute is its chain of mountain parks, comprising more than twenty thousand acres, where its people can, when they get sick of the sight of one another, go and find solitude. It is in Denver's Red Rocks Park, only a few minutes from town, that you'll find the city's huge new outdoor theater, which will seat ten thousand and which is so arranged between red sandstone precipices that its acoustics are said to be perfect. At the moment, since Denver's Symphony chooses to *spiel* only when winter's winds doth blow, the city is hard put to figure a way to utilize this splendid amphitheater. But since it is spectacularly beautiful, Denver is sure something will come along and put it to good use.

One of the things Denver's people and visitors make a great point of seeing is the three-week summer Play Festival at near-by Central City, where the presence of such artists as Ruth Gordon, Lillian Gish, Gladys Swarthout, and Richard Bonelli has long given assurance that the stuff would be mellow. Right in town, the Elitch Gardens Theater is still going strong, bearing the footprints on its boards of almost everybody from Mrs. Fiske to Fredric March. And speaking of big names, Denver has, at one time or another, been the stomping ground of such of the journalistic great as Eugene Field, Courtney Ryley Cooper, Gene Fowler, Forrest Davis, George Creel, Clyde Brion Davis, and Damon Runyon who, under the spell of Denver's rarefied air, knocked out a couple of volumes of poetry during his stay.

For ghost-town *aficionados,* the possibilities of adventure and discovery are unlimited. By hopping over the mountains to the Western Slope, they can find the vacated apartments of the Cliff Dwellers, if by that time none of our homeless contemporaries have moved in.

For the air-minded, Denver is laying out a soaring field from which, after your glider has been got into the air, you will be able, it is believed, to ride to your heart's content by employing the elevator-like thermal eccentricities of the air above the mountains. This field will overlook the beginnings of Prospectors Trail, a 153-mile round-trip route which will take you to the top of Lookout Mountain, there to gaze upon the grave of that engaging old showman, Buffalo Bill, past dude ranches, with which the state is infested, and over the highest automobile road in America to the very summit of 14,260-foot Mount Evans, with all that implies in awesome scenery and hair-raising hairpin turns. This trail also goes through many of the old mining towns, whose citizens played such a lively and vital part in the early history both of Colorado and of Denver.

For contemporary, white-collar Denver, comfortable and handsome and civilized, might today have been just so much cow pasture except for the guts, greed, caliber and luck of the scaly old prospectors and freebooters who built it.

Not until 1858, a very short time ago for the birth of an American city, could the settlement which was later to become Denver be said even remotely to have resembled a town. By that time, word had got abroad that gold had been discovered near the confluence of the South Platte and Cherry Creek. This rumor completely neglected to mention that, in quantity, about enough had been discovered to fill a tooth. On the strength of this rumor, a party of Kansans moved in, built cabins, and in time realized they had been sold a glittering bill of goods. Later, a second party founded a town in the vicinity. Finally, the Denver City Town Company was formed, taking its name from the territorial governor of Kansas, General James W. Denver, whom, by this action, it very sensibly sought to butter up.

By 1859 this collection of skimpy villages not only possessed two saloons, a mud-and-log hotel, and a bank that charged from 10 to 25 per cent interest a month on loans, but was witnessing the arrival of stage coaches of the Leavenworth and Pikes Peak Express. One of the most colorful personages to arrive at this time was Professor O. J. Goldrick, decked in plug hat, frock coat and yellow gloves. Soon the Professor, one of the greatest enemies of clear, simple, English prose the world has ever seen, started the state's first school with thirteen pupils.

In this same year, more deluded gold hunters swelled the population.

Denver City and the town of Auraria across Cherry Creek were fighting so hard for dominance that the first newspaper, the *Rocky Mountain News*, discreetly built its offices on pilings in the bed of the creek that separated these embattled rivals. Even so, it was necessary for the printers to rack their rifles near the type fonts and for ye ed. to keep his shootin' irons handy.

Meanwhile, the newcomers were showing a disquieting resentment over the absence of the gold they had come to dig. Many of those who, on their way out to Colorado had shouted, "Pikes Peak or bust," now, busted, pronounced a pox on the "Pikes Peak Hoax" and started dragging back to the States. Then, providentially, on May 6, 1859, John H. Gregory of Georgia really struck gold on the North Fork of Clear Creek, some thirty-five miles away. But if this new rush tended to ease the social pressure, it also tended to depopulate the town.

The *Rocky Mountain News* quoted Horace Greeley in the following tribute to the Denver of this period. There were, he said, "more brawls, more pistol shots with criminal intent in this log city of 150 dwellings, not three-fourths of them completed, nor two-thirds of them inhabited, nor one-third fit to be, than in any community of equal numbers on earth."

Denver pretty much had its own fish to fry during the Civil War. It was divided in its sympathies, but nevertheless contributed three regiments of troops to the Union cause. However, these were chiefly utilized in keeping open the trails, in hounding and, with a fine disregard for age or sex, massacring the Indians.

In 1864, Denver, where ordinarily the only excess moisture was the water in its mining stocks, was very nearly washed away by a flood which came roaring down Cherry Creek. It drowned twenty citizens of the now consolidated town, to say nothing of unseating and thoroughly dousing the creek-straddling *Rocky Mountain News*.

By 1867 the town had a private mint and a new hook-and-ladder company, as well as intermittent telegraph service—intermittent, since roaming buffaloes, gnawed no doubt by Rocky mountain fever ticks, found the telegraph poles so good to rub against that they snapped off the poles in great numbers.

But Denver's principal trouble was isolation. She had dreamed that the Union Pacific might come through town, but had had that dream reduced to powder when the U. P. chose instead the less precipitous grades that would take it by Cheyenne. And at once an exodus of the more expedient Denver merchants got under way.

This was a time of black despair. But the Denverites of that day, who'd paid fifty cents a barrel for water, had washed the kids in a single tubful on Saturday night, then tossed lye in the greasy bath water and boiled it into soap for Monday's washing, were a reasonably unconquerable breed. They raised $300,000 and themselves agreed to build a road bed to Cheyenne, on which the railroad in turn agreed to lay tracks. This spur to the U. P.'s main line was finished in 1870.

In the ten years following, the easily mined gold deposits, which had kept Denver going as an outfitting station, began to play out. As yet, Colorado agriculture amounted to very little. Once more it appeared the town was going to pot, when the great silver strikes began to be made at Leadville, Aspen, Creede, and others.

Between 1880 and 1890, Denver's population jumped from 35,000 to 106,000. The city's manufactures, mainly smelting and mine machinery, tripled in value. Denver became a millionaires' town, and even the acid pen of Eugene Field could not whittle them down to size nor dampen their exuberant lavishness and sometimes simian display. It was in 1881, with Denver's elite turned out in all its spangles, that the Tabor Grand Opera House opened its doors. It had been erected by H. A. W. Tabor, a former Vermont stonecutter, who, over in Leadville, had run a seventeen-dollar grubstake up to many millions of dollars. And when a portrait of Shakespeare was placed in the opera house lobby, Tabor demanded it be replaced with his own, asking disdainfully, "What did Shakespeare ever do for Colorado?"

Denver became so rich in the 'Eighties that it managed, with the help of the Cripple Creek gold strike, to squeak through the financial panic in the 'Nineties.

It was, for example, in 1892 that the still famous and still excellent Brown Palace Hotel opened its doors. It had been built by a Denver ex-carpenter, Henry C. Brown, who'd got dabbling in real estate and had grown so rich that he could easily afford to give the state the site for its capitol. And his nine-story, block-filling hotel was spectacularly elegant. Owing to the somewhat extraordinary hollow-log design of the building, every room was an outside room; also it had had $4,000 spent on its furnishings. The silver was sterling, the china the finest Haviland, and the linens especially woven in Ireland. You could buy a ten-course banquet for a dozen people for $110, and the food, running from consommé Renaissance with Amontillado to and right on through *terrapin en caisse à la Maryland* with Dry Monopole, was so bountiful you couldn't begin to eat it all, and so good you couldn't bear to leave it.

It was also in the 'Nineties that a bold, brash lottery operator from Kansas named F. G. Bonfils and a Dutch Barkeep named H. H. Tammen, who officiated at Denver's high-kicking Windsor Hotel, went into partnership to buy a small newspaper, which they called the Denver *Post*. The paper's platform was almost as aggressive as Mr. Bonfils' haberdashery: "Dedicated in perpetuity to the service of the people, that no good cause shall lack a champion, and that evil shall not thrive unopposed."

Nothing in American journalism has ever quite equalled the gaudy, ruthless performance put on by the aforementioned gents. The sight of the paper itself was enough to lift your feet off the ground. The front page was splashed with huge political cartoons, and it was a rule that every kind of headline type must be used on the front page every day. These headlines were printed not with black ink but with restrained and subtle crimson. The *Post* fought everything spectacularly that it construed to be deleterious either to Denver or to the *Post's* circulation. It fought the *Rocky Mountain News* both with its journalistic Big Berthas and with F. G. Bonfils' very tangible fists shoved into the nose of the opposing publisher.

If a company in which either Tammen or Bonfils owned stock was getting by with anything at the expense of the public, they scalded it too. And though they never showed the faintest hesitancy in putting the blowtorch to their adversaries, they were never stuck for a single libel suit. In fact, the only time they were ever tapped for judicial come-uppance was on one mildly embarrassing occasion when Mr. Tammen was convicted for trying to fix a jury. Frances Belford

Wayne, who's been on the *Post* for thirty-five years and is the daughter of the territorial judge known as "the Red-headed Rooster of the Rockies," says of the *Post's* early publishers, "They were impatient men. The country was a desert. There were irrigation projects and railroads to build. Our methods may have been rough at times—and I, as Bonfils' hatchet woman, have a pretty good idea of just how rough they were—but we always fought for the people."

Another of the giants of this period who also did great things for Denver was Mayor Robert W. Speer. He'd been to Europe and had seen that it was not necessary for a city to look like a spavined mine camp. He wanted to bring civic beauty and dignity to Denver, and was the inspiration for most of her present glory in that department. The *Post* fought him tooth and nail, "not," according to Mrs. Wayne, "because there was anything especially wrong with Speer's program. F. G. just didn't like him. Everything in those days was very, very personal."

Since the turn of the century, Denver has become still larger and more civilized. It has reorganized its government in such a way that it, and not the state, runs the city. However, for twenty years or so, the city has been run by the political machine which, for most of that time, has kept aging, honest, somnolent and unswervable Ben F. Stapleton in the mayor's office. Roughly speaking, Denver's form of city government is a dictatorship, in which the mayor may hire and fire all department heads on his personal say-so. Only the auditor is elected. And Denver, apparently too busy with other matters to take the time to democratize its government, dreads the day when it shall fall into the hands of an unscrupulous mayor.

To see Denver whole, one must realize that its primary function is to serve the Rocky Mountain region and, most particularly, the state of Colorado as doctor, lawyer, merchant and (political) chief, as well as banker, butcher, teacher and supplier of transportation, markets, entertainment, culture and shelter for the transient. Actually, Denver is much more than the capital of Colorado. It is, in a very full sense, Colorado's "front office."

Yet, though Denver is primarily a distributing and financial center and, is, relatively speaking, an un-industrialized city, it, nevertheless, mills Colorado wheat, is so handy with the butcher knife that its stock-yards run neck-and-neck with Fort Worth as the world's leading sheep market, and has even, in the last few years, become something of a wool market, a prerogative which, oddly enough, has hitherto been more or less monopolized by Boston. Its machinery companies, which started out fabricating mining equipment and, later, began building equipment for the refining of beet sugar, have now, while still continuing their old lines, graduated into the oilfield-equipment business. In spite of the fact that these companies must first import steel and then export the finished product over considerable distances to the user, they manage profitably to stay in business.

Charles O. Voigt, president of Denver's General Iron Works, be-lieves the answer lies in the fact that Denver workers live close to the plants that employ them, and that Denver's climate and recrea-tional facilities make a man really feel like working when he's on the job. Mr. Voigt points out that Denver's war plants received far more than their fair share of Army and Navy "E" Awards and that the Department of Labor found Denver's man-hours in industry 20 per cent more productive than those of the nation as a whole. Incidentally, the General Iron Works is a co-operative mill, owned by three com-peting sales companies, who find that this joint manufacturing scheme flattens the seasonal production curve and results in considerable economy.

Denver is, furthermore, the home of the Gates Rubber Company, which in all likelihood made the fan belt on your car. But despite the fact that it claims to be the nation's sixth largest maker of rubber goods, it is, nevertheless, a peanut in comparison to any one of rubber's Big Four.

Today the goose hangs high in Denver. The elegant pascal celery that grows in its environs, along with its famous carnations, which have adorned the buttonholes of many of London's best-dressed Bertie Woosters, is in high demand. It has in excess of two hundred Federal bureaus—more, Denver claims, than any other city outside of Wash-ington—and these bureaus bring the town a $20,000,000 a year pay roll. It is nothing for the Sunday Denver *Post* to carry fourteen pages of classified ads. And since the Rocky Mountain regions have so many more U. S. Senators per capita than the rest of the nation, Colorado's sugar and silver prices are well protected by the government. In as much as silver usually occurs in the same ores as gold, lead, copper, zinc, and so on, a high price for silver inevitably raises the margin of profit on the production of all these other metals.

Denver's future, except for one mildly sour note, is pleasant to contemplate. The one dissonance is the fact that most of the old giants and miracle-makers which Colorado siphoned off in the latter 1800s are no longer there. Denver and its fortunes lie in the hands of the second and third generations, who are, according to expert testimony, nice, successful people, who manage to stay wealthy and, at the same time, do their bit for good works and civic causes. But, according to the daughter of the Red-headed Rooster of the Rockies, "Our people have come of age at the expense of being interesting. They're worthy, but undramatic. You never get a surprise any more. The trouble is," she added a little wistfully, "they have no rampage left in them."

Recently the *Rocky Mountain News* editorialized:

Denver's chief danger right now lies in a state of mind—a tendency to resist any sort of change.

It's the same sort of thinking that opposed the Civic Center in Mayor Speer's day, that objected to purchase of land for a municipal airport, that even worked against the expansion of the water supply that was necessary to Denver's very life.

This negation, this defeatism, isn't confined to any one group or any single sort of proposal, but is manifest too often when change is proposed —and, of course, any civic improvement necessitates some sort of change.

Yet aside from the temperament of the people who made and now inhabit it, there has seldom been anything wrong with Denver that enough water, salable goods and markets wouldn't cure.

At present, there are a number of projects in various stages that, when completed, will vastly increase the amount of water available for irrigating Colorado farms, which are, by all odds, the source of her greatest wealth. One such project, supplying water from the Colorado River, will boldly cross the Divide, just as Denver's .Moffat Water Tunnel already does, bringing in much of the city's drinking water from the Western Slope. Another project will divert water from the upper tributaries of the Blue River into the South Platte. And the effect of these and other irrigation ventures will, in stimulating and expanding the general economy both of Colorado and of Denver, be mighty.

In the second place, Denver, which the war pushed into fairly advanced, and hitherto untried, industrial techniques, has gained a new industrial confidence which is prompting it to make its first major drive for industry.

Though Denver was born out of reach of the big population pools and has acquired most of her present transportation facilities the hard way, her transport position has steadily improved. In recent years her rail passenger time to Chicago has been halved and, by the expenditure of public funds for tunnels and cutoffs, she has maneuvered herself onto a transcontinental line. Within the last year she has rounded out her airlines network by gaining a direct line to Los Angeles. And these vital improvements make it just as much easier for John Tourist to get in as for Denver's goods to get out.

Denver's future, just like its present, was more or less predetermined long ago when, on one hand, her climate and natural resources came into being and, on the other, back in the 'Eighties and 'Nineties when the Browns, Tammens, Bonfils, Moffatts, Speers and Tabors made Denver the giant of the Rocky Mountain region. For when a city so far outdistances its competitors in sheer mass that no close comparison can be made, an endless variety of fat plums, such as Denver's ever-increasing regional headquarters and assembly plants for national companies, will inevitably, almost automatically, accrue to it.

In a word, Denver, top hand of the Rocky Mountain region, and foreman of a state that is outstandingly rich in unexpended resources, is sitting pretty in the saddle, single-footing right along toward the fulfillment of its apparently comfortable, if not particularly exciting, future.

16: *Atlanta*

A TLANTA is hardly that way at all. The Thespian gallantries, the fierce chauvinism, the do-nothing poor-but-proud, the powerful preoccupation with genealogy, simply are not there, except in her museums and books and occasional heated meetings of the Daughters of the Confederacy. Generally speaking, she is far less "Southern" than Richmond or Charleston or Savannah, all of which look with a mildly shocked hauteur at Atlanta's brash vitality. According to Hal Steed's *Georgia: Unfinished State*, Savannahians says, "Atlanta has the nerve of a Government mule. If it could suck as hard as it can blow, it could bring the ocean to it and become a seaport."

Atlanta, capital of the biggest state east of the Mississippi, is a pushing, growing, young man's town, which, unlike Augusta and Macon, does not go home to lunch, but grabs a sandwich or maybe lunches with the Lions, Kiwanis or Rotary, where hardly 25 per cent of the members are native-born Atlantans, then goes back to the office and hits the ball. Much of its vitality is Yankee vitality. When the Federals took the town in 'Sixty-four, the Carpetbaggers were not far behind, and have been coming ever since. There are no Yankee Negroes or Yankee poor whites, but where the power lies, Atlanta is a good half Yankee, and that is why you will not find in Atlanta the integrated character you might expect there. The only differences between heterogeneous Atlanta and heterogeneous Houston are unimportant ones. Pre-Civil War Atlanta and contemporary Atlanta, not merely materially but in character and feeling, are as different as day and night, as Chicago and an earlier Versailles.

There are, of course, old-line Atlantans left who are still mighty proud of the spunky fight their granddaddies put up against Sherman, who burned the town during the wah. All the townfolk are proud of the city's twenty golf courses, and of ex-Governor Ellis Arnall, the South's most dynamic leader in its endless, hitherto fruitless fight for a "fair" freight-rate structure, for honesty and progress in government, and the realization of the real, and long-latent, fruitfulness of the South. They are not very proud of the fact that Woodrow Wilson practiced law there, because he thought the Atlantans ignorant, and they that he was a prig. They are proud of Atlanta's thousands of pretty homes, her hundreds of thousands of beautiful trees, her current prosperity.

Her greatest claims to fame are, in the order of their occurrence: (1) the Ku Klux Klan, which had its beginning in the bed sheets of post-Civil War Atlanta; (2) that carbonated gold mine of Atlanta's Candler family, Coca-Cola; (3) grand-slamming Bobby Jones, who at forty-three declared himself an ex-golfer, went out and shot a sizzling sixty-five; and (4) Margaret Mitchell's *Gone with the Wind*. But if these are Atlanta's four most famous phenomena, tennis star Bitsy Grant and the Federal penitentiary, which arches its eyebrows at forgetful Atlantans at income-tax time, are not far behind.

Virtually all her people are Protestant, native-born Americans. The Baptists and the Methodists run the town and the state as well. Her half-million people are, by races, one-third black, two-thirds white, and almost all her soil is red. The viscosity of her accent is not so heavily Southern as Vicksburg's or Montgomery's, but it's nice and drawly. "Sugar" is still the nickname of lots of nice children, and the *r* in cawn pone is as silent as the tomb. She is a hot-bread, boiled-greens, fried-chicken-and-cream-gravy town, where you are apt to get a dish of hot grits for breakfast, extra for free, whether you order it or not. But she's no longer a town of formal calls, as some in the Old South still are. This custom began to peter out about 1910, along with the habit of going home at two o'clock for a big hot midday Southern dinner. Busy Atlanta has other fish to fry. Today's newcomer to Georgia's capital is apt to find time heavy on his hands until he goes out and makes himself some friends.

Atlanta ladies are still talking about the first real servant problem that has hit the town since the Civil War. World War I did not seriously disrupt Atlanta's servant supply. But during World War II Atlanta women who had never done anything more strenuous than give orders to Negroes were running their own houses, raising their mammyless children and dreaming for the first time of secondhand washing machines.

Atlanta's downtown business district is less attractive than Birmingham's, and one of the easiest places in metropolitan America to get lost. It was laid out by the cows that made the trails that served as the first streets, cows that had apparently received their previous training in laying out Boston. These cow trails converged at Five Points because there was a spring there.

Atlanta's famed Peachtree Street was an Indian trail that followed the highest ridge in town on its way through the Cherokee Nation toward Chattanooga. There's some difference of opinion as to the derivation of its name. Old Indian maps show that it crossed the Chattahoochee River near a landmark called "Standing Peachtree," which could have given the street its name. Others say the trail crossed a creek at a place where there was a big tree at which friends gathered to pass the time of day and toss knives at a mark on its side, that it was called "the pitch tree," which later became rearticulated as "Peachtree," and was retained in that form as the name of both the creek and the street. At any rate, Peachtree Street is one of the main arteries of traffic through both the labyrinthine business district and the older residential district which sprawls over the wooded hills with a feeling of pleasant spaciousness.

Although Atlanta's most spectacular private fortunes have derived from Coca-Cola and well-timed maneuvering in local real-estate deals, she makes her living, in the main, by being a branch-house town. Like most such cities, she is a white-collar town, full of office workers. She has about 25,000 government employees. And since mules have largely been tractored out of the Midwest, Kansas City's scepter has been passed on to Atlanta, which today reigns, market-wise, as the mule queen of America. She has some nine hundred factories of varied size and importance, which manufacture everything from gingham for Georgia peaches to cheese for Georgia Crackers. For that matter, the value of her manufactured products is greater than that of her huffing, puffing, industrialized sister, Birmingham, but since her manufacturing plants are numerous and small, she is more open shop than is her smoky sister. Nevertheless, Atlanta's principal business is wholesaling.

She has one of the finest regional-distribution systems in the nation. It came into being, like the very town itself, because of the railroads. When, just after the Civil War, Sherman was asked why he selected Atlanta as his prime target, he said, "Atlanta was like my hand. The palm was the city, or hub. The fingers were its spokes—in this case, the railroads. I knew that if I could destroy those railroads, the last link of the Confederacy would be broken." As a matter of fact, Atlanta, which was first, for obvious reasons, called Terminus, took her present name from the Western and Atlantic Railroad. In addition to her eight rail systems, which operate fifteen trunk lines, she is served by nine airlines. And while Atlanta has private interior problems and struggles and victories, all her really vital interests and problems involve the whole Southeast, which is her customer.

Georgia, which is roughly synonymous with the rest of the Southeast, was born poor, first settled by Oglethorpe's company, largely from the debtor prisons of England, made good, and grew rich. Then the Civil War left it busted. It was devoid not only of wealth but of tools. There was nothing much for it to do except scratch the earth and tighten its belt. The only way it lived at all was "on the principal," by spending not the increment of its natural resources but any and everything it could sell—mostly cotton, the culture of which devoured the fertility of its land.

The Southeast's first post-Civil War taste of marked prosperity or even boom times came in World War I, when the price of cotton skyrocketed. But this prosperity was short-lived, and by the time the great depression of the early 'Thirties came, the South was being spoken of as the nation's number one economic problem. One of the reasons for its plight has been graphically described by Henry W. Grady, the late editor of the Atlanta *Constitution*, when he wrote:

I attended a funeral once in Pickens County in my state. It was a poor "one-gallus" fellow. They buried him in the midst of a marble quarry; they cut through marble to dig his grave; and yet a little tombstone they put above him was from Vermont. They buried him in a pine forest, yet the pine coffin was imported from Cincinnati. . . . They buried him in a New York coat and in Boston shoes, in a pair of breeches from Chicago and a shirt from Cincinnati. The South didn't furnish a thing for that funeral but the corpse and the hole in the ground.

Excluding the special case of Birmingham, the South's first industrialization on a scale greater than loft and sweatshop operations occurred when the Northern textile manufacturers began moving toward the cheap labor to be found there.

As for the town of Atlanta, she was benefiting by a trend toward the decentralization of large national businesses into regional subdivisions. Her central location, plentiful labor and splendid transportation made her a natural to profit by this trend. By the late 1920s she already had a good start. Today she possesses some three thousand of these regional branch houses, with the promise of more to come.

But her one customer, the Southeast, has a moderately uncertain outlook. The region finds itself with much of its supply of natural resources expended and without sufficient industry to counterbalance its present weak agricultural position.

Georgia, like Italy, has for a long time been a labor market. One of its biggest crops has always been babies. And this resource has likewise been expended. Between 1920 and 1940 more than half of its young people left the state. They left because of lack of economic opportunity and bad living conditions. In 1940 the average per-capita income of the United States was $575. Georgia's per-capita income was $315. In a typical Georgia county, in 1941, 61 per cent of the houses were unpainted, and a quarter of them had no windowpanes. Ninety-eight per cent of all Georgia's farm buildings needed either to be replaced or extensively repaired in 1943. A recent United States survey showed that more than half of Georgia's incorporated towns have no public water system; even more have no public sewer system.

As the last war ended, Georgians felt that the best and quickest way of getting the state back on its feet was to attract and hold its roughly one-third of a million young service people as they were demobilized. That group possessed not only vigor and new skills but that even scarcer commodity, money. By applying for funds available to it under the G.I. Bill of Rights, this group would have $700,000,000, or twice the valuation of Georgia's present industrial plant, to spend—where?

If the returning veterans invested that sum in small businesses and small farms in Georgia, it would give the state powerful commercial impetus, give her a breathing spell in which to undertake longer-range schemes for her salvation. And knowing the reasons why she failed to hold her young people before the war, Georgia, principally under the leadership of a "heartless, absentee-owned corporation," the Georgia Power Company—which is a subsidiary of Commonwealth and Southern—was launching a determined campaign to make the state attractive enough to hang on to its returning service folk and their hundreds of millions of dollars.

This campaign was called the "Georgia Better Home Towns Program." It was an intricate, carefully thought out plan which began with picking up trash and getting the grease off filling-station floors, and ended with what amounted to a state-wide face lifting. It wasn't aimed directly at the acquisition of huge industries. Its fundamental objective was to make Georgia fit to live in, which its migration figures —one out of every four Georgians lives outside the state—implied that it had not been in the past. As one leading Georgia executive told me— and he was a man whose life, money, memories and loyalties were all invested in Georgia—"Unless the principles this plan represents are translated into reality, Georgia, in my opinion, will be through."

If Atlanta's prosperity and outlook seem brighter than those of Georgia itself, the difference lies chiefly in the fact that there is more money in manufacturing and wholesaling than there is in farming Southeastern lands. But the Southeast can never go wholly broke without taking Atlanta, albeit on its shoulders. along with it to the poorhouse.

The difficulties of Atlanta's Negroes since the Civil War have, of course, been even more severe than those of white Atlantans. In 1935 to 1936, the average family income of the white population was around $1,500. At the same time, a Negro family averaged $476. In 1940, the average adult white Atlantan had had ten years' schooling, the average Negro five and a half. The white kids were having a dollar per school day spent on their education, the Negroes thirty-four cents. And, as in the case of every city which has large slum areas packed with great numbers of underprivileged, these conditions were reflected in Atlanta's health and crime.

Figures in 1943 showed that incidence of venereal diseases in the Atlanta area was four times that of the United States as a whole. In the early stages of the war, 16.2 per cent of Atlanta selectees were rejected because they were infected with syphilis. According to 1942 FBI figures, Atlanta outmurdered every other American city except Chicago and New York.

Atlanta's Negro population has been prospering, along with the rest of the town. A good maid in Atlanta has been getting about fifteen dollars a week. And though thousands of Atlanta's Negroes work as house servants and yard men, who do not come under the provisions of the Wage and Hour Act, that act yet remains the biggest and most helpful piece of legislation to the Southern Negroes since Mr. Lincoln set them free. The luckier ones, like the luckier poor whites, live in decent and pleasant low-cost housing units with playgrounds and community centers. Atlanta Negroes also have their small, high-society group, and their scholarly group that lives in the orbit of Atlanta's system of seven schools giving higher education to Negroes, which is said to be the best in the land. Decatur Street, where the fish fries aromatically, is Atlanta's Beale Street.

The one-party system disfranchises the Negro in local Southern elections, since they are decided by a "white man's primary."

Many practical, hardheaded Atlanta leaders are heartily sick of the one-party system, which, with minor exceptions, kept the Solid South safe in Democratic ranks since the Civil War, has kept it standing aside, starved and hungry, while the doubtful states feasted at the trough of Federal patronage. Atlantans complain that, in presidential-election years, "We're lucky even to get a speech." For while the one-party system was designed to disfranchise the Negroes, it has tended, in actual effect, to disfranchise the whole South.

Recently, Birmingham's columnist, John Temple Graves, voiced the opinion of many of the more progressive Southerners when he said that the whole Southeastern realm must take some chances, and the crucial ones were, "A chance on the Negro, encouraging advancement on his side of the line," and a chance on the two-party system.

It is only fair to mention that the votes which re-elected Talmadge, the Negro baiter, came not from Atlanta, but from the outlying counties which, by means of one of the nation's many rotten borough systems, have more power, vote for vote, than do Atlantans. It is for this reason that, though the people of Georgia in 1946 voted gallus-snapping Gene Talmadge down at the polls, he was, nevertheless, able, through Georgia's weird electoral laws, to win the governorship again, even if he did not live to be inaugurated.

Nobody expects Atlanta's Negro problem to be solved by any single magic stroke. In 1944, the Atlanta Chamber of Commerce formed a committee composed of six whites and six Negroes to act as a guide in interracial relations. To date, its steps have been small ones, but all in what would seem to be a constructive direction. As time passes, the education level of Atlanta's Negroes is slowly rising. Their death rate, while still twice as high as that of the whites, has dropped 40 per cent in the last twenty-five years. There is some snail's-pace removal of the economic barriers placed before them; a legislative floor has been put under their wages. Most Southern students of the problem, many of them Negroes and as realistic as Booker T. Washington, believe that the ultimate salvation of the Negro rests with the Negro himself—his own bootstraps, plus what sympathy and help he can get from his white neighbor. He has, in spite of his unequal opportunity, already come a long way, and as the one-party system becomes more and more of a hardship on the South, it will eventually, some Southern leaders believe, disappear. The biggest enemy the Negro has in the South is the poor white, with whom he competes in the labor market. And the poor white frequently has almost as little influence as, and often less respect from the ruling whites than, the Negroes themselves. Yet the election of men like the late Governor Talmadge in Georgia,

Bilbo and Rankin in Mississippi, men who treat the Negro with vituperative contempt, tends to drive, particularly the young, Negroes into intransigent groups that are disillusioned and bitter. Thereby one more barrier, this one psychological, is laid across their already heavily obstructed path.

Though "new money" and "Yankee money" are well represented in Atlanta society, there are still descendants of the old families to be seen taking their toddy at eventide at the exclusive old Piedmont Driving Club, from which, in earlier times, the gentry sallied forth in their tallyhos. They can also be found at the Capital City Club, and in smaller numbers at the Athletic Club.

These people have some of the more interesting attributes of the characters in Miss Mitchell's book, people who still live, at least part of the time, in the spiritual halls of Tara, people to whom Five Points, the crossroads of downtown Atlanta, is a symbol of the deathless resurgence and indomitable will of the Old South. They still live in a world where gallantry and audacity and personal honor are pillars of life, an uncomplicated world of obvious rights and wrongs. And there are those who say flatly that Julius, the Negro headwaiter at the Driving Club, is the smartest man in town and has the largest mental dossier on the foibles of her leading citizens. But even in the clubs, the spirit of today's Atlanta is dominant.

The industries Atlanta is most eager for herself and Georgia to get are ones that will process the things for which Georgia produces the raw materials and extensively consumes. For example, anybody looking for clay would naturally go to Georgia, yet the dishes on Atlanta's tables were made outside the state and probably from Georgia clays, which are shipped out in their raw form to be used for many ceramic purposes. She'd like to process almost all her own food, with the exception of Georgia peaches, which don't lend themselves to canning as well as the California variety. She'd like more paper mills and furniture factories to process the nation's finest timber stand. Florida has a little more acreage in timber, but a lot of it is in the swamps and too hard to get out.

Another incipient processing industry is the dehydration of sweet potatoes for animal food. Georgia has, to a large extent, turned her back on cotton in favor of tending swine and kine and poultry. In this enterprise she is embarrassed by the fact that her land and climate are not good for corn, that her average acre yields but ten bushels. Yet that same average acre will yield eighty-four bushels of sweet potatoes, which, when dehydrated, is the rough equivalent in carbohydrates of thirty bushels of corn. In the light of these facts, Georgia's acquisition of a yam-dehydration industry would seem to be assured.

And when a cow-feed-conscious Atlantan says "Kudzu," it is not necessary to reply *"Gesundheit!"* He has not sneezed, but mentioned the wonder vine, "earth's best friend," on which Georgia is pinning her highest hopes of arresting the erosion of her red hills, and which, at the same time, grows two and a half tons of good hay to the acre—hay that is almost as nutritious as alfalfa.

One of Atlanta's burning ambitions is to become a great tourist center. In the first place, most surface traffic between New York and New Orleans, Florida and the Midwest passes through town anyway. The Georgia Agriculture and Industrial Development Board plans for its tourist panel to spend $100,000 a year in national advertising. To non-tourist-minded Georgians the panel points out: "Tourists are easier to pick than cotton."

One of Atlanta's attractions that is not widely known is her climate. She has the highest altitude of any American city her size or larger, excepting only mile-high Denver.

No matter how blistering her summer days, the nights are said to be delightful. She has a huge outdoor recreation plant incorporating many handsome parks, and Georgia Tech has a way of putting out mighty interesting football teams.

There are lots of rivers and lakes in the near-by hills, and Atlanta's annual rainfall, which is in excess of four feet, is plenty to keep them supplied with water. There are, of course, countless points of historic interest and others which have become important because they played a part in *Gone with the Wind,* whose author, in case you've been wondering, has been too busy with Atlanta Red Cross work to write another book. At Grant Park there is the cyclorama of the Battle of Atlanta. The panorama painting, into which the three-dimensional figures in the foreground are skillfully merged, is fifty feet high, four hundred feet in circumference, and manages to be really effective and felt.

Atlanta has a good many pretty nice hotels, but some Atlantans feel that if she's going into the tourist business in a big way she will need to build a new super hotel where a brisk and winning battle will be carried on against the soiling effects of Atlanta's somewhat sooty air. For that matter, Atlanta could do with two or three really distinguished restaurants. There are several nice teahouses and fried-chicken places, and the food in the better hotels will do. Also, there is a place out near the bomber plant that makes toasted-corn-bread patties which would make Sherman lay that blowtorch down.

Atlanta has a number of fine women's shops, and when Atlanta's women go shopping, they don't parade around in frowsy aprons, but wear at least their second-best bib and tucker and are a handsome sight.

The one big disappointment to the tourist coming to Atlanta—the tourist who has so often seen on picture post cards that gallant procession of Confederate soldiers in the wake of Marse Robert and Traveller sculptured across Stone Mountain—will be that it just isn't there. Instead, there is only a hideous gash in the mountain's granite face, the tentative outlines of a man and a horse. Gutzon Borglum chiseled and blasted away at Stone Mountain until Lee's head was finished and on the general's birthday in 1924 served breakfast on his shoulder to distinguished guests. But the task was hard and dragged slowly. More and more money was needed. Endless difficulties and perplexities arose. Finally, Borglum fell out with his employers, took an ax and busted his models to pieces, then left the state.

Also, be it noted, there is no such place as Tara, and the tourist who pays twenty-five cents to see Scarlett's bedroom in a Georgia farmhouse is being hoodwinked.

If the tourist's literary interests do not end with *Gone with the Wind,* he may visit the Wren's Nest, home of Joel Chandler Harris, the Uncle Remus man. And if he reads the Atlanta *Journal,* which "covers Dixie like the dew," he'll be reading a paper where Margaret Mitchell, Don Marquis and Erskine Caldwell all did their stints. Atlanta, generally speaking, doesn't care for *Tobacco Road*—which, by the way, is a real place—though the show, over protest and in diluted versions, has played there twice. The Chattahoochee River, which, according to Sidney Lanier, flows "out of the hills of Habersham, down the valleys of Hall," supplies the visitor's drinking water, which is the softest water to be found in any American city.

Atlanta has lots of colleges. In addition to the Negro college system already mentioned, there are Georgia Tech, Emory University, Oglethorpe University, Agnes Scott College, seminaries, night and professional schools.

Despite the fact Atlanta has multitudinous liquor stores and a good many bars, she is not much of a night-club town and there's a law that bar drinks must not exceed the wallop of wine.

But her people are friendly and hospitable, and their houses, in great number, are inviting and handsome, mostly red brick in Georgian style, set well back from the street among hickories and pines and maples and flowering dogwood. Atlanta gardens are pretty and the result of a lot of work. The town has more than a hundred garden clubs. But lawn grass is a problem, since Bermuda grass, which grows best there, can't stand the dense shade of Atlanta's trees. One of her less appealing houses is the cold gray granite Governor's Mansion, in the backyard of which vote-wise Gene Talmadge raised chickens and cows. But the charm of many of Atlanta's houses even seduced Bible-belt-belting Henry Mencken into declaring Atlanta to be one of the loveliest cities in America. Julian Street said it was one of the nation's twelve most distinctive.

She hasn't struck oil, as have New Orleans and Jackson, Mississippi, but she has come out of the war temporarily well heeled, and with an almost unbeatable chance to remain the Southeast's dominant central city.

She is still saddled with the one-party system. Her Negro problem is still unsolved.

But win, lose or draw, Atlanta is confident. Nothing that happens in the foreseeable future can, she feels, be as soul-trying as the rocky, so often hellishly hard and disheartening road she has already traveled.

17: *Pittsburgh*

SPRING comes to Pittsburgh not when the first strawberries grace her table, nor with the blush of the earliest rose, but when the first strings of gondola cars, wound like beads around her neck, bloom red with the season's first Mesabi ore.

For Pittsburgh—that fruitful, filthy monster—has long had one principal forte: building much of the steel spine upon which the United States has worn the clothes of democracy, prosperity and power. The story of Pittsburgh is the kernel of America's industrial might. From her has come a giant's share of the steel not only to build America's railroads, automobiles and the ribs of its skyscrapers, but to gainsay the seldom gainsayable will of the British in 1812; to conquer the gallant and rebellious South in the 'Sixties; in World War I, to beat the brains out of Germany's great Krupp cartel; and in World War II both to retake Krupp, along with Skoda *et al.*, and to close the vise on Nippon's Mitsubishis. Whether, in the last war, Pittsburgh made a greater contribution to victory than some of the more distinguished combat groups, whether in peace she creates more wealth than certain of our great regions, would be interesting and possibly tactless questions. In any case, this mighty town is the world's champ, the Paul Bunyan, of heavy industry.

To feed Greater Pittsburgh's nearly two million people, and to feed the flames that make her nights lurid and her days besmirched by smoke, this capital of the Pennsylvania Ruhr possesses some thirty-five steel mills and 350 coal mines, some sixty-odd glass factories and more than a hundred chemical plants, while some 30,000,000 tons of cargo pass through her river harbor each year. She produces mountainous quantities of electrical equipment and clay products, aluminum, coke by-products, and bituminous coal. In most of these, she leads either the nation or the world. And, finally, since she is the home town of Mr. H. J. Heinz, who was as puissant as the horse-radish he bottled as a boy, Pittsburgh is naturally the Abou Ben Adhem of international gherkin circles.

Yet despite, and often because of, this cornucopian industrial fecundity, Pittsburgh has troubles swarming round her head like squadrons of disgruntled hornets. Since her industrial eggs are so highly concentrated in one brittle steel basket, a break in the steel market or a prolonged strike in the steel mills can result in a city-wide calamity. There is a definite shift of the steel-consuming industries from the Pittsburgh region to the south and westward. She has, moreover, contrived to get herself the name of a strike-happy labor town. The city suffers from acute hardening of its traffic arteries, and its government doesn't take in enough money to give the city the kind of services it needs. The quickest and most thorough way to get polluted in Pittsburgh is not by boozing in her dives but by diving in her rivers. These same rivers have a disquieting way of rising up and washing out the town.

Yet these are secondary troubles. The greatest handicap, within the area of remedial ills, of this municipal plunderbund, from whose anguished guts so many huge fortunes have been wrenched, is that, in the minds of millions upon millions of Americans, it is not a tolerable place in which to live.

To most Americans, Pittsburgh, aside from her great and actual earning and producing power, is a city in which individual man has long since become a particle absorbed in the industrialized, unionized mass to be unwittingly marched and counter-marched by the war lords of management and labor. It is generally accepted that there is something in the Pittsburgh air which ripens a slum just as that of Virginia does a ham. Her housing shortage is no war baby. She has had housing crises since the 1830s, and a fairly constant housing shortage since the end of the last century. According to the 1940 census, 43.5 per cent of her dwellings were either in bad order or in need of major repairs.

Her culture is popularly supposed to be strictly of the mill-end variety, and her grime is legendary. In a recent movie Groucho Marx alluded to Pittsburgh's most famous malady. Eying the rings of cigar smoke he was busily blowing, he remarked, "This is like living in Pittsburgh—if you can call that living."

Yet the multiple scuttles of soot one must devour per annum as a part of the price of living in Pittsburgh are no laughing matter. Instead, they are a hellish, tormenting, disease-abetting and spirit-wilting thing. If you know Pittsburgh well, the very name will granulate in your mouth and your nostrils sting from the memory of the somehow acid quality of its air.

There was a time in the history of the nation and of Pittsburgh when the hordes of immigrants, driven by the destitution in their old homes and lured by the blandishments of those who had use for them, would eagerly settle in any spot in America that offered them jobs. That is emphatically not the case now. There is no longer an influx of job-desperate, undiscriminating immigrants, and the nation is, at least for the time, so rich that its people relocate themselves as much on a basis of the attractiveness of living conditions as on that of economic opportunity. This is a fact that looms very large in Pittsburgh's mind at a time when experts estimate that 20 per cent of America's productive plant is "floating," seeking to locate or relocate, and when no expert is needed to point out that these plants can't go where people, among them plant executives' wives, won't live. Again, the war sent thousands of young Pittsburghers to live for awhile in the bright and sprightly cities of the West and Southwest. As one young Pittsburgh veteran told me, referring to his own new outlook, "We are like the old mule that was finally brought out of the mine. We have just found out that there is such a thing as daylight."

This situation, and the dire threats implicit in it, has got old Pittsburgh's coat tails popping, and the city's various factions are showing a tendency to co-operate that has not been a Pittsburgh phenomenon for a good many years.

Pittsburgh's extraordinarily powerful Chamber of Commerce, whose membership rolls have contained such names as Andrew Carnegie, Charles M. Schwab, Henry Clay Frick, Andrew Mellon and H. J. Heinz, has been, since the beginning of the Roosevelt Labor Revolution in 1933, the embattled citadel of "the interests," while City Hall has been more or less regarded as GHQ of the liberal-labor junta.

But that fissure has begun to heal. Recently the Chamber of Commerce not only gave Pittsburgh's new Democratic mayor, David L. Lawrence, some lunch, but a chance to make a speech, in which he declared, "I think we have certain stereotyped images to dispel. To a great many people the term politician is a term of reproach . . . and since government is operated by politicians, the less that good citizens have to do with it, the longer their good citizenship will remain unsullied.

"And there are still others who think of a Chamber of Commerce as stuffed shirts, . . . phoney statistics, . . . and economic royalists bent on grinding down the face of the poor.

"I want you to join me on the Pittsburgh team.

". . . In this critical era we must work for Pittsburgh as we have never worked before. Pittsburgh is not alone in its problems. But it will be alone—at the bottom of the heap—unless we unite to solve them."

Due to the circumstances of Pittsburgh *real-politik,* of which more later, there were good reasons why this invitation might be accepted. There is also good reason to believe that Pittsburgh is in the beginning stages of one of the most dramatic periods of municipal renaissance that any great American city is likely to undergo in the next decade.

But in order to see where she's going, it's best to know where she's been.

Pittsburgh came into being as a warlike town when the British Colonial Government undertook in 1754 to build a fort where the Monongahela and Allegheny rivers meet to form the headwaters of the Ohio. But before the British could finish, the French and their Indian allies swept down on the fort, captured it, and named it after Canada's governor-general, the Marquis Du Quesne.

They kept it until 1758 when, under pressure from the British-American forces, among them Colonel George Washington, the French set it afire and fled down the river. The victorious General Forbes gave the settlement its present name in honor of the British statesman, William Pitt, the elder.

Before long, a new fort was built, but, during the Revolutionary War, backwoods Pittsburgh was so gingerly engaged in keeping the top of its head off some Indian's belt that it cut no very great figure in the national picture, though the march of the half-naked, half-starved Pittsburgh regiment through the deep snows across the Allegheny Mountains was filled with great suffering and heroism in its triumph over sheer agony. Meanwhile, saucy Virginia tried to snitch the settlement, and would have kept it but for the restraining hand of the Continental Congress, which gave it back to Pennsylvania in 1780. By 1794 mad Anthony Wayne had licked the Indians decisively. About the same time, President Washington had thoroughly quelled Western Pennsylvanians' rebellious refusal to pay the excise tax on the rye whisky they distilled. The community of Pittsburgh could finally lay down its arms and take up its tools in a genuinely businesslike way.

In the War of 1812, the doughty jacktars of Commodore Perry were skinning up and down rigging that had come from Pittsburgh's ropewalks, just as the shot for Jackson's cannon in New Orleans was coming down the river from Pittsburgh's furnaces.

Very soon Pittsburgh's industrial prowess was to become so great and her ears so grimy that visitors would remark on the Pittsburgh women's dress, usually black, frosted perhaps by an occasional white frill that was doomed to spend most of its life in the wash pot.

The pattern of growth the town took began at the coves where mills were set up. The mill owners, varying in personal background and in industrial needs, imported foreign workers and settled them around the mill. Around one mill would be an Irish community, around another, German, and so forth, so that on the future day when they should merge, they would amount more to a federation of small nations than an integrated political body. Pittsburgh, as it would long continue to be, was being built primarily as a place to work, not to live. In fact, leisure and recreation were regarded as somehow immoral by the people who led and formed opinion.

By 1850, when Pittsburgh's metropolitan population approximated 50,000 and the value of her manufactures was $50,000,000, she had sustained a great fire, finally been reached by the telegraph line, bridged the rivers, entertained such distinguished guests as Daniel Webster and Henry Clay, and had discovered that every time President Jackson and his like got fooling with hard money or high tariffs, Pittsburgh was pretty sure to have a panic.

More or less until the 1850s Pittsburgh had been blessed with such vile transportation facilities between herself and Philadelphia that she became a "make-it-yourself" town, and whatever was left over could always be floated down the river and sold.

During the Civil War, of course, the munitions orders the Yankee government fed to Pittsburgh's metal industries fattened them mightily. Meanwhile, after having forced the old town to buy great quantities of bonds, both the B. & O. and the Pennsylvania Railroad had reached her with their tracks.

But the Pennsy line failed to endear itself to Pittsburgh, and when, in 1877, the railroad started cutting wages and doubling the length of trains, a strike was called, trouble started, and before the townfolk had got done with the railroad, they had burned down the roundhouse, the Union Station, destroyed 104 locomotives, 66 passenger coaches, and 1,383 freight cars. Damage claims were finally settled for a little less than $3,000,000, and it's interesting to note that only in recent years has Pittsburgh finally got the Pennsy and other property owners paid off.

Four years after the great railway strike of 1877, the union that was subsequently to become the AFL was formed in Pittsburgh. Unions in the steel industry had their work cut out for them, since it was a standard tactic in the industry for the companies to invade new trade territories by underselling those who had the business. Cuts in steel prices might have been made gradually on a basis of increasing industrial efficiency. But, according to Tom C. Campbell, an editor of the steel industry's magazine, *The Iron Age*, a sudden cut in steel prices, demanded by the companies' selling policy, was often followed by a wage cut.

The bitterness between management and labor reached a fever pitch in the 'Nineties. In 1892, the workers at Carnegie Steel in the little town of Homestead, seven miles from Pittsburgh, walked out. Carnegie was in Europe. His associate, Henry Clay Frick, who'd made a million dollars out of coke and railroads by the time he was thirty, handled the strike, which culminated in a pitched battle when the company undertook to execute an amphibious landing of three hundred armed guards. The workers repulsed the landing at a total cost to both sides of ten killed and some sixty wounded. But, in the end, state troops were brought in to maintain order, and the strike was broken.

An event of seismic proportions occurred in 1937, when the United States Supreme Court validated the Wagner Act, and when, without spilling a drop of blood, John L. Lewis, with a toss of the blackberry bushes that adorn his brow, signed a union contract with Big Steel. And Little Steel, including Jones and Laughlin Steel Corporation, which employs nearly 30,000 Pittsburghers, was, like the little lamb, not far behind.

Lewis' right-hand man at that time, a Pittsburgher of Irish descent who'd come up from the mines and through the labor battles, was Philip Murray, who is now president of the CIO, and who, as it happens, adores Pittsburgh.

Mr. Murray is much admired by, and friendly with, the head of Pittsburgh's new liberal-labor government, David Lawrence, the powerful and skillful politician upon whom so much of Pittsburgh's hopeful future depends.

As it happens, Dave Lawrence not only sits in the mayor's chair, but is the leader, which is to say boss, of the Democratic city machine, and his influence is heavily felt through the county and state organizations, and in Washington. Among his personal political assets, he has an excellent radio voice and a photogenic face which, in press photos, looks ten years younger than his actual age of fifty-seven.

Since it is the custom of political bosses to select, elect and rule candidates, rather than take office themselves, observers in many quarters feel that the only reason Lawrence sought his present job was because he believed that the next four years offered him a chance to be the greatest mayor Pittsburgh ever had. For machine bosses who are independently wealthy, men such as Lawrence and Ed Kelly, men who like to win at whatever they undertake, sometimes fall in love with a town and like to make it great, as well as rule it. Moreover,

Lawrence has a couple of graft indictments on his record, though he was both times acquitted. Some who know him best believe these indictments are two of the sharpest spurs that drive him on in his zeal to be an effective public servant.

Lawrence had hardly been in office long enough to raise the temperature of the mayoral chair up to a proper 98.3 degrees of Fahrenheit before Pittsburgh had got the promise of a new flood-control dam to be built on the Conemaugh River which, along with other dams now abuilding or already built, will bring down the crests of future Pittsburgh floods by something like nine feet. This means a saving of many millions of dollars a foot, since Pittsburgh's great industries, like much of its 330-acre Golden Triangle, are built almost entirely in the flats and since, as has been demonstrated in previous floods, they won't float.

Getting this vital Conemaugh dam was a result of teamwork. Lawrence marshaled his legislators on the Democratic side. The Chamber of Commerce whistled up its friends on the Republican side, and this phalanx got the dam. Moreover, Pittsburgh is going to build sewage-treatment plants that will not only render the decreased floods of the future less defiling for Pittsburgh, but will almost certainly raise a hail from downstream Cincinnati's puckered lips.

The main hope of substantial Pittsburgh slum clearance lies in gaining Federal grants for that purpose. Already Pittsburgh's faithful Democratic government has secured 5,600 units of government low-cost permanent housing. These apartment houses are built in groups, themselves the size of a small city, that must appear to anyone, whatever his political coloration, as substantial diamonds in Pittsburgh's slummy roughs.

Yet Pittsburgh's present administration, so strategically situated in the fight for Pennsylvania's big block of presidential electoral votes, is out to get 7,000 more such slum-effacing units.

The means proposed by City Hall to remedy the emptiness of the city government's pockets is to get more refunds from the state government, whose treasury at the moment contains a $200,000,000 surplus.

In regard to building Pittsburgh's proposed colossal four-block-square public auditorium, which will also house rent-paying industrial exhibits, it is hard to tell whether City Hall or the Chamber of Commerce exceeds the other in enthusiasm. While the Mellons go ahead building the Mellon family seat into a city park—Richard K. Mellon and his sister, Sarah Mellon Scaife, have only recently added more land and another $100,000 to this civic project—both the Chamber of Commerce and City Hall are full of excitement over the prospect of building a new and beautiful park at the now somewhat shabby point of the Golden Triangle at the forks of the rivers, where, among other things, a replica of Fort Duquesne will be built on its original location. Though the two wet sides of the Triangle are already framed in imposing highway structures resembling those which encircle Manhattan, and though the city has untold millions invested in fine bridges and tunnels, it plans, in conjunction with Allegheny County and the Pennsylvania Department of Highways, to build a new beautified highway that will connect the proposed Point Park with the famed Pennsylvania Turnpike. Over this new highway, through traffic will be guided around the Triangle by this impressive scenic route. This will not only result in easing the traffic burden of the Triangle's often narrow and confusing streets, but will give the passing stranger an impression of Pittsburgh that will be highly pleasing and at considerable variance with what he may have been led to expect. Just in case the tourist is in a hurry, another freeway will cut directly across the base of the gilded tricorn.

But if he has time to tarry, he will be well advised to visit the Civic Center and look upon the beauties, of which the flowers in Phipps Conservatory are not the least, of Pittsburgh's midtown Schenley Park. Though Duquesne University is situated elsewhere in the city, the stranger will find, here at the Civic Center, such handsome structures as the colonnaded Mellon Institute for industrial research, the marble memorial to Pittsburgh's George Westinghouse, who invented the airbrake and went on from there, the huge Syria Mosque, where Pittsburgh's Shriners shine, a whole group of important medical buildings, Soldiers' and Sailors' Memorial Hall, Carnegie Institute of Technology, and the Carnegie Library, the old nest egg from which were hatched so many others that dot the nation. Yet towering over all these structures, and with the Stephen Foster Memorial and the Heinz Memorial Chapel nestling near by, is the University of Pittsburgh's forty-two-story skyscraper, which is somewhat clammily entitled "The Cathedral of Learning."

If an examination of this academic bean pole has caused no crick in the tourist's neck, he can survey other impressive skyscrapers as well as churches in the Golden Triangle. The forty-two-story Gulf Building stands on the spot where the oil-refining industry in America got its start. Across the street is the impressive thirty-four-story, copper-trimmed Koppers Building. There's a public observation deck on the thirty-seventh floor of the Grant Building, from which the tourist can get an elegant view of the mighty, hill-bulged, river-striped city. The interior of the near-by Mellon Bank will please his esthetic sensibilities if he's the kind of person who can keep from being uncomfortable in the presence of $600,000,000.

A little way up the hill, he'll find the Allegheny County Court House and Jail, which is in appearance one of the sternest, most forbidding and somehow terrifying dungeons this side of Madrid. From this pause-giving pokey, it is a five-minute ride to the Bühl Planetarium, where stars can be seen in the daytime and atoms are split to individual order.

The tourist will find that the people of Pittsburgh, who in earlier days were somewhat ungenerously thought of as Polacks, Hunkies, Wops and Micks, sweaty, dirty, harried, toilers who spoke pidgin English, are today mostly second and third generation Americans, whose minds have been milled by the same standard American schools and press as those of the tourist himself, and that they are people with as much leisure as he has to pursue the sweeter pastimes which have nothing to do with puddling pig iron. For example, if the day offers sufficient visibility, they can go out to Forbes Field and watch the Pirates play. Pittsburgh's biggest minority, her Negroes, are represented by two Negro National League teams, the Pittsburgh Crawfords and the Homestead Grays.

Those in search of manifestations of Pittsburgh's culture will find that it has a strapping Symphony Orchestra, now under the distinguished direction of Fritz Reiner, which for years took its cues from the baton of Victor Herbert who, in his spare time, managed to knock out an occasional new operetta. The Carnegie International Art Show causes as much comment and attention in painting circles as did a new book by Pittsburgh-born Gertrude Stein in the more specialized reading circles. For that matter, Willa Cather, Robinson Jeffers and Hervey Allen have all spent parts of their lives in Pittsburgh, and Gladys Schmitt, author of the best-seller, *David the King*, still lives there. Not only has Pittsburgh just held her fourth annual Grand Opera Festival, but something new has been added to Pittsburgh culture. Kaufmann's Department Store has plunked down $50,000 to guarantee an eight-week season of light opera at Pitt Stadium.

But the biggest, most exciting news concerns something that is to be subtracted from the Pittsburgh scene: SMOKE. When the tourist arrives in 1948 or 1949, it is almost a cinch he will find that the air is pure and sweet and exhilarating. Pittsburgh's historic and diabolical defiler is on the way out, is going to get from Pittsburgh just what it got from St. Louis when, led by the smokeless-flame-spitting St. Louis *Post-Dispatch*, it dragged itself out of the soot and smog.

This decision will cost Pittsburgh many millions of dollars in initial expense, but that figure will happily amount, in the long run, to a microscopic fraction of her saving in cleaning, smoke damage and health bills, along with the profits of business retained and gained. St. Louis figured that its annual bill for smoke damage alone was $19,000,000.

In Pittsburgh the ordinance is already on the books. Enforcement against industrial smoke-makers was scheduled to begin in October of 1946, and against one and two-family houses in October, 1947. There were other reasons for this delay than the busy lobby of those with a vested interest in smoke. The only ways to avoid smoke are (1) to use smokeless fuel—oil, gas, electricity, low-volatile coal or high-volatile coal that has been treated—or (2) to employ apparatus that will burn ordinarily smoky fuel in a smokeless way. And there was neither enough smokeless fuel nor smoke-eliminating apparatus available to supply the whole city at the time the ordinance was passed.

There will naturally be a battle royal for further delays in enforcing this law, but its champions form a combination which, there is every reason to believe, is unbeatable. And perhaps none are more powerful in this fight than the Pittsburgh housewives, "with eyelids heavy and red," and scrub-brush worn to a nub. It will be more than all right with them that their soap bill will take a Brodie, and they can hardly wait to straighten their aching backs, put on a pastel dress, and don a pair of white gloves that the wind won't dye while they're on their way to the party.

The Chamber of Commerce, having duly figured the percentages, has taken an anti-smoke position. So have all three of Pittsburgh's newspapers: Paul Block's *Post-Gazette*, Hearst's *Sun-Telegraph*, and with the Scripps-Howard *Press*, in the tail-back, ball-toting position.

Now just imagine Pittsburgh on that great day when its smoke, which for so long has perversely preferred going down instead of up, rolls away for the last time. Observers acquainted both with Pittsburgh and with human nature feel that one of the first things that will almost inevitably happen is that Pittsburgh, with the zeal of all newly-converted sinners, will give itself one of the outdoingest scrubbings and scourings any city ever got. Not only that, but prosperous suburbanites, tired of wasting commuting time, will have begun, as the St. Louis folk already have, to move back into town, converting slum property into decent homes and paying taxes to the city. Many civic improvements will have come about from the efforts of its citizens. Some have taken courses at the Institute of Community Planning, recently inaugurated at the University of Pittsburgh; others have manned such community-improvement councils as the Allegheny Conference on Community Development, the over-all co-ordinating umbrella under which work such groups as the Pittsburgh Regional Planning Association, which is sparked at the top by President Richard Mellon. If this last-named body has its way, you'll also find still more new greenery in the downtown section than that already mentioned. Rows of stately trees will shade Duquesne Way and the Boulevard of the Allies, while the already partially empty block in front of the sixteen-hundred-room William Penn Hotel will be San Francisco-ized, which is to say, converted into a grassy, flowered green, beneath which will lie a many-tiered ramp where hundreds of automobiles can be parked.

Pittsburgh will be modern, in many ways beautiful, with an historic past and a spectacular natural setting, sending its manufactures down an Ohio that is not only pure but which flows at all times just as gently as Sweet Afton. In fact, with all those clear streams and new reservoir lakes and a summer climate that tends amicably to remain in the seventies, and one of the world's most dramatic industrial shows running fifty-two weeks in the year, old Pittsburgh may look up and find herself something of a resort.

More unlikely and unbelievable things have happened in this land of miracles. If that happens—if Pittsburgh ever overcomes its self-destroying schizophrenia and becomes a first-rate place to live—this achievement will rank not too far behind the conquering of the frontier by the pioneers as one of the major miracles in the story of the nation.

18: *Madison, Wisconsin*

MADISON, WISCONSIN, is both a fact and a symbol that stands for many of the finest traits in the American character. It is a place where independent people get up on their hind legs and have their say. Again, it is a seat of serious learning. Moreover, it is surrounded by that basic harmony that derives from good land that has been treated intelligently and with respect. Finally, Madison's people are almost spectacularly unapathetic. They are concerned, interested, and willing to do something about almost any public question. In many ways Madison and its environs are a miniature model of the ideal America of which most of us dream.

Though Madison is a town that would give the ordinary thrill-seeker the screaming meemies in one quiet week end, it is a genuinely exciting mecca to other kinds of people. It is most exciting, perhaps, to the young university-bound Wisconsinite with his tennis racket strapped to his suitcase, his train ticket in his pocket, his heart in his mouth, wondering if his suit's in style, if he'll make a fraternity, if he'll be able to keep his head through the benumbing, bewildering process of matriculation, and whether or not he'll wow the girls. Madison is almost as exciting to the young lawmaker when he first comes to his state capital to sit in the legislature, to enter into mortal combat with "the interests," and to catch the eye of those who know good gubernatorial and United States Senate timber when they see it. It is also exciting to the young university professor, whether he comes to teach or to devote his life to research, to attack that most formidable of all enemies, the unknown, and wrest from it a newly known thing.

To all these, to visitors and residents alike, Madison is almost other-worldly in its quiet beauty. It is built on an isthmus, three to six thousand feet wide, between two of a group of four lakes. Its business section is long and narrow, with Lake Mendota—Indian talk for "evening"—on the north, and Lake Monona—"morning"—on the south. They are connected by the little Yahara River, which winds through the parks at the eastern end of the isthmus.

Almost everywhere there are graceful, stately old elms and maples, beautiful lake vistas. The view of Lake Mendota from Observatory Hill looking over toward Picnic Point, a long, wooded peninsula to which trysting is not news, will convince you that sometimes Nature is the best possible landscaper. The residential and industrial sections bulge out at each end of the isthmus, so that the town has roughly the shape of a dumbbell, with the University of Wisconsin in the western end.

Though the odd shape of the city tends to widen the distance between those essentially separate worlds, "town and gown," town is, nevertheless, mightily affected by gown, in much the same way as are the hundreds of other college towns where this country's three and a half million grads wore their rented caps and gowns, faced the future with a diploma in their hands, confusion in their hearts, and the shine of Polaris in their eyes. For a college education is not a thing that acts only on students. The faculty, with its own insular civilization throbbing with internecine politics, personalities, and teas, shares hugely in the experience. Actually nobody in a college town gets off scot-free. Somebody has to attend the ball games, look upon the evergreen spirit of sartorial experimentation, and get silly signs painted on his fence, as, in Madison, does Economics Professor William H. ("Wild Bill" to his back) Kiekhofer. He still doesn't take it lying down and has the constabulary fall upon the miscreants. Yet he is such a stimulating lecturer that many of his classes are preceded by a "skyrocket": a Wisconsin yell reserved for its heroes.

Then there are the traditional roughhouse days in any college town. One of Madison's is on St. Patrick's Day, when the engineers parade and the law students try to break it up. Again, on the night before the Homecoming Game, the entire student body parades and subsequently crashes the movies. Sometimes it riots—and then the cops let go with tear gas, and the firemen level down with their hoses.

At the other pole of these recurrent manifestations of young-animal spirits, there is the quiet touch of the academic, of the theoretical side of life as opposed to the sweaty, hurrying, elbowing quality of such genuinely commercial or industrial towns as, say, Madison's sudsy sister, Milwaukee. For while reason and truth can better be isolated in the cool, objective analysis of the schoolroom, it's still the bull pen as opposed to the pitcher's box, is, to a degree, a preparation for life rather than life full-blown.

Wisconsin University's campus is one of the most beautiful in the realm, even though many of its buildings are old and a little groggy from time's attrition. Nevertheless, the University has about it the exhilarating air of academic freedom. Beside the door of Bascom Hall, looking down from the heights on the rest of the University, is a bronze tablet bearing the words President Charles Kendall Adams wrote in 1894 when one of his own economists was under fire for unorthodox views on labor's rights: "Whatever may be the limitations which trammel inquiry elsewhere, we believe that the great state University of Wisconsin should ever encourage that continual and fearless sifting and winnowing by which alone the truth can be found."

On a straight basis of scholarship the University of Wisconsin can look any other institution squarely in the eye. It thinks nothing of turning out ninety-nine Grade-*A* Ph.D.'s in a single year. It has a staff of 675 full professors, a junior staff slightly in excess of a thousand, and five hundred "fellows and scholars." Its average student body is around 11,500.

President E. B. Fred feels the University's function is not only to disseminate knowledge, but through research to acquire new knowledge and to see that it finds a place in the lives of the people. The University medical school is striving to develop country doctors to attend the often-doctorless hamlets. It not only interns its students to hospitals, but externs them to selected country doctors to learn the small-town ropes and to acquaint themselves with some of the factors in preventive medicine that would be less readily seen in a hospital. The medical school is also working with the agricultural school as a team on many of the diseases that infect both man and the larger farm animals, diseases such as undulant fever, tuberculosis and lockjaw. It is the agricultural school which most aggressively carries out the University's determination to incorporate its findings into the lives of the people. It has a direct pipeline to them, in as much as it controls the appointments of Wisconsin's county agents and home demonstrators who, in turn, harangue Wisconsin's Honest Yohn and Johann Farmer on the miracles of scientific farming.

Wisconsin's Ag School is perhaps world supreme as a place to learn to psychoanalyze old Bossie, grow her feed, guide her sex life, and coax her into flooding the pail with snowy nectar. Besides the University's regular work in agriculture and dairying, it has long held a fifteen-week winter short course for farmers young and old. While imbuing some ten thousand of them with the whys and wherefores of grassland farming or giving them the latest word on Vicland oats, which the University has developed, it has probably circumvented many an emotional blowup. For the Wisconsin winter is no joke; the cold, which promptly freezes the accessories off brass billy goats, drives the farmer indoors to brood. Then, just as the breaking point approaches, he packs up and goes to the bright lights of Madison. But in case his trip falls through, he can sweat it out at home painting pictures under the guidance of the University's rural art program, which, until his recent death, was directed by no less a personage than Maestro John Steuart Curry.

The University's year-round students find artistic expression in the regular art school and in the dramatic productions of the Wisconsin Players. Too, the University holds writers' conferences on creative writing with distinguished lecturers who are leaders in their field. Just as it has its own newspaper, the *Daily Cardinal*, it also runs its own non-commercial radio station, WHA.

In the more homey realm of keeping house and turning out three good meals a day, the University has a handsome residence, about the sort you'd expect the mayor of a small American city to live in, which is exclusively devoted to being a kind of tackling dummy for the Home Ec girls. They move in in squads of eight and show they can do their stuff without the destruction of stomachs and furniture. Just in case things are not looking up for the sweet girl graduate, either professionally or matrimonially, there is a secretarial school a few blocks away where she can make her peace with the touch system.

The University does very well in basketball, and in football might be a frequent champ in another league. But it seems to have bit off more than it can chew in the Big Ten, where greedy Minnesota and Michigan and Ohio seem determined not to let anybody else win.

In the "rushing" system of the Greek-letter fraternities the football great are high-priority objectives. But Madison is less heavily populated with fraternities and sororities these days since during the depression many of them, having overbuilt on credit, went broke. Those that remain are currently angry at having been poked up by Mrs. Glenn Frank. In an article called "Heartbreak on the Campus" which appeared in a national magazine, she chided these Hellenic clans by pleading the case of the crushed kid on the outside looking in.

The students' Union Building is the center of University social life on its most democratic plane, and is fun for everybody. Here's a huge Rathskeller where our old friend, three-point-two beer, is on tap. Food is cheap and life is new and almost more than you can stand. Casual half-hours are spent chattering, dreaming, making dates, dreading exams, being, in your own eyes, that fabulous thing: a University man or woman.

One wing of this two-thirds Italian Renaissance building is the "modernistic" theater and movie house. Sinclair Lewis has called it the most beautiful theater in the world. Looking at the entire building, modern and Renaissance combined, is pretty much like reading a poem in which Dante wrote the first two stanzas and T. S. Eliot took it up from there. Out back there's a terrace overlooking lake and beach which, when seen in the summer months, does something to you. Monte Carlo is just as beautiful, but it's cynical, old, decadent. Here everything—the time of year, the time of life, the natural beauty— generates a kind of incandescent well-being which thousands of Wisconsin graduates must be unable to remember without a sharp acceleration of their pulse.

Along State Street are the sandwich joints, the movies, the sporting-goods stores, the secondhand-book stores, the music stores, the clothes shops that usually nestle around universities. The Rennebohm drugstore is "the Pharm." A favorite hang-out is The Cabin, with a yard in the back for summer singing. The Flame is a bar-grill where the lads gather after dates, have a stein or two of beer, and bare their hearts. The students and faculty also infiltrate into Madison's downtown stores, theaters and restaurants.

Economically, Madison is in a peculiarly sweet and perennial sort of clover. It would make Beulah Land, as a place to live, work, and do business, have to get up and hump. It is the county seat of Dane County, which is one of the richest agricultural counties in the United States. It does some manufacturing, but mostly the kind that depends on brains and skill rather than hordes of unskilled labor: such precision manufacturing as the making of machine tools, dairy and hospital equipment. Labor-management strife, as exemplified by strikes of any seriousness, is almost unknown. No matter what fluctuations may occur in Madison's industry and agriculture, the paychecks of its nine thousand state and county employees are a profoundly stabilizing influence, and help make Madison business as near panic-proof as possible. Again, student expenditures provide a dead certain income of $9,000,000 or more each year.

Madison's fat income is spread with extraordinary evenness over its entire population of 75,000. Most of its people own their own homes. It can hardly be said to have any slums. True, it has here and there a few dingy, age-ridden houses. They are going down, but they go quietly. In a Federal survey of the median value of homes in thirty-eight cities, Madison rated first. Madisonians send in more income-tax returns per thousand persons, pay tax on a higher median income, than any American city in the fifty- to one-hundred-thousand population brackets. Perhaps its most telling statistic is that it has more oil-burning furnaces per capita than any American city.

Madison's economic condition is not merely the result of local circumstances, but must inevitably reflect that of the state which supports it.

Wisconsin, as Madison's meal ticket, makes a great deal of paper, more maple syrup than you'd think, grows lots of grain, flaxseed, sugar beets, and is the Number One hemp state. It also grows half of the peas that are canned in the nation. Lake Superior fisheries are important. But that smaller number of fish inhabiting its seven thousand lakes, fish which snap at an artificial fly and cause some out-of-state visitor to regard himself as a mixture of Izaak Walton and Einstein, bring much more money into the state. Madison's own lakes offer worth-while catches of bass, perch, and northern pike. And an occasional muskellunge runs off with everything but the rod handle, or maybe your hand.

Wisconsin's once mighty forests have long since almost wholly been sawed up into boards. But the United States Forest Products Laboratory, located in Madison, guides Wisconsin's and the nation's plywood and pressed-wood industries in the wise use of what's left.

However, the leading lady in Wisconsin's economic drama is, of course, the milk cow, which, in moments of piety, Wisconsinites speak of as "the foster mother of the human race." Wisconsin supplies 125,000,000 pounds of the nation's butter and nearly 500,000,000 pounds of cheese. The present tendencies in its cheese industry are toward centralization of small cheese sources into large combines, pasteurization of milk used in cheese-making, and processing, which makes cheese more uniform, less perishable, and, according to connoisseurs, taste like tennis shoes. Eighty per cent of Wisconsin's cheese production is in Cheddar, which is the trade name for rattrap cheese. But sprinkled over the state are many little colonies of Swiss, Italian and French cheese-makers producing the types native to their homelands, and doing a good job of it.

A dairying economy has several basic advantages. In the first place, it's kind to the land. Moreover, in ordinary times, it is based on monthly milk checks and permits farmers, unlike those in a one-crop country, to budget their expenditures with almost as much certainty as a man on a pension.

In Wisconsin, where oleomargarine is a fighting word, its great cheese and dairying business is a frequent subject of legislative conflict in Wisconsin's handsome, cruciform Capitol in the center of Madison. Wisconsin's farmers are perhaps the best informed politically in the nation. They have to be or they'd miss part of the serious fun Wisconsin has always had with politics. Wisconsin's politics have traditionally been uproar politics—full of the yammer, the squawk, the accusing finger, the injured howl. Every voter is an amateur detective, full of zeal to get out and nip a little political iniquity in the bud.

La Follette has, of course, long been the big name in Wisconsin politics, whether that name was borne by the late Old Bob or his sons, Young Bob, until recently of the United States Senate, and Philip, three-times governor of Wisconsin.

Back in the old days, many Wisconsinites were fresh from Germany and Norway, and would still have been there if they had not had the inclination to protest. They also brought with them well-formulated ideas on social and agrarian reforms. The political ball really got twirling when the railroads came into Wisconsin. They had a singularly shadowy idea of what they could get by with, and in their most exuberantly acquisitive moments were charging people fifty cents to haul a seventy-five cent bushel of wheat. At the same time they refused to haul it to any elevators but their own.

It was into this most inviting of scenes for a reformer that Old Bob rode. He had fire in his eye and justice on his side. He lit into the railroads, wove a regulatory straitjacket around them and stopped just short of ripping up the tracks. Then he dusted himself off and looked around to see what other evils needed his attention.

Thereafter, the spirit of protest, which bore the party name of "Progressive," usually rallied around Old Bob. Wisconsin farmers seemed to be haunted by the fear of getting a raw deal. They organized themselves into countless unions and protective societies, out of which began to grow their passion for co-operative enterprises. They looked upon the middleman and felt unenthusiastic about allowing him his cut. They organized co-operative everythings: stores, burial societies, fertilizer supply houses, marketing organizations. These ventures fizzled with appalling regularity. But the Wisconsin farmers kept trying. Today the state has 1,005 co-operatives with nearly a quarter million members. These co-ops do $166,000,000 worth of marketing, $36,000,000 worth of purchasing.

Yet Wisconsin politics, which so often have the appearance of radicalism, are subtly deceiving. Its voters, farmers or not, are mostly small, solvent, energetic businessmen. They hate massed power as such. They believe in home rule, in small, almost one-family business units. They believe in themselves, and, above all, view social and business legislation, in fact all political acts, on a basis of: what's in it, not necessarily for the proletariat, but for me, the working, saving family man, at what precise cost? They pay their debts and are some-times hesitant as a state to accept Federal aid, feeling that some meas-ure of lost sovereignty is the price of accepting charity.

Wisconsin's general political structure roughly resembles a system of soviets in which, through a process of rotten-borough representa-tion, plus a mania for home rule, the rural communities have the upper hand. Individual county boards hold the right to disburse most of the state-highway, welfare and public-school funds through their own local agencies. These county boards have an insatiable hunger for highway money, and when they band together under a single lobbyist who also represents the interest of cement and road-machinery com-panies and contractors, they can apply a heat on the legislature that is withering and well-nigh irresistible. In a recent display of this power, the highway interests, over the Governor's veto, pushed through an act which will impound much of Wisconsin's $30,000,000 war-boom surplus, as well as greater sums of her future income, for highway expenditures. This grab has left the state too poor to provide an ade-quate building program for public institutions, since the state is con-stitutionally prohibited from going in debt more than $100,000, except to suppress insurrection.

Madison's fiery *Capital Times*, with the extraordinary political-mindedness and vitality that characterize the whole Wisconsin press, has declared the highway lobby to be a racket, and has challenged it to an all-out knuckle dusting. It sent reporters and a photographer to crash a victory jamboree at the Club Chanticleer allegedly given by the cement trust for faithful legislators the night after the highway-funds act had become a law. Both guests and host at this soiree fell upon the little band of news gatherers, broke the camera, and en-thusiastically wiped up the earth with their persons. Aldric Revell, the *Capital Times* political reporter, got his jaw plurally socked and his blow-by-blow story spread across the top quarter of page one.

This skirmish came, for a time, to be known as "The Battle of the Chanticleer."

Such high jinks are traditional in Wisconsin politics and news-papering. William T. Evjue, editor of the *Capital Times*, sometimes publishes letters in the paper from outraged readers such as a recent one which declared that he, Evjue, was "the number one oracular windbag and the primary charlatan of the nation." Both Madison papers, the *Times* and the Wisconsin *State Journal,* mirror in detail the state's political strife. When elections impend or the legislature is in session, they are bee-busy clarifying issues, reporting arguments and conflicts already started, putting the finger on shady transactions and flinging in their editorial two cents with a forthrightness that oils neither the waters nor the voters.

Wisconsin is insular, off the nation's main communication routes both physically and politically, and is as isolationist as it is possible to be at this stage of history. It was anti-Roosevelt for the devious reason that Mr. Roosevelt restricted cotton growing in the South, that he not only failed to prevent grass from growing where that cotton no longer was, but gave Southern farmers enough money, for not growing cotton, to buy the cows that gave the milk that stopped the glass tank cars leaving Wisconsin every night for Miami. It was anti-Roosevelt because it wanted no reciprocal trade treaties with Canada that would let in, tariff free, Canadian bacon and paper. It was also anti-Roosevelt because it felt Mr. Roosevelt spoke too grandly, that he had a fondness for deficit spending, and because it felt it had troubles enough without a war which manifestly wasn't Wisconsin's fault and at least might be Mr. Roosevelt's. And the Wisconsin politicians say the simple, effective formula they used in beating Wendell Willkie so thoroughly in a primary that he withdrew his second presidential candidacy was by passing the word, "He's just like Roosevelt."

It is easy to over-simplify Wisconsin politics, to underline their amusing aspects, to assume the role of a precocious Monday-morning quarterback. But to a visitor from one of those parts of the country where elections are determined by the quality of a candidate's fiddle music or the *esprit* of his jug band, the attitude of Wisconsin's sharp-eyed press and electorate seems antiseptic and wholesome. If its voters are to be serenaded, they want oratory rather than musical hoe-downs, and they demand that that oratory have a moderate content of logic. While Atlanta has its Talmadges, Baton Rouge its Huey Longs, Oklahoma City its Alfalfa Bill Murrays, Madison, in its quiet way, is an especially compatible home for government as the expression of an interested, responsible, vigorous people.

In the same way Madison is somehow sympathetic to the processes of learning, a fortuitous greenhouse for the transplantation and ripening of youth. It is a town where the battle lines are drawn against such ageless enemies of man as ignorance and disease, a town where Lincoln could have grown up in harmony with his surroundings, where Galileo could have spoken his mind, and where Demosthenes could have been mayor any day in the week. It is a town where the lakes, at least to Longfellow, were "four lovely handmaids that uphold shining mirrors, rimmed with gold," and in whose cheese-making environs pianist Gunnar Johansen has noted with quiet rapture: "Even the air is nutritious."

★ ☆ ★ ☆ ★ ☆ ★ ☆ ★ ☆ ★ ☆ ★ ☆ ★ ☆ ★ ☆ ★ ☆ ★ ☆ ☆

19: *Los Angeles*

I F YOU gave a child a toy building-set with which to erect a miniature Los Angeles, it would have to contain many broad planes of
stucco the color of oat straw in the sun, many slabs of the clearest
plate glass, barely-slanted areas of red tile roofs, sear brown papier-
mâché hills, and shiny wagon-green globes on stems of varying
lengths to represent citrus, palm and eucalyptus trees. But the principal ingredient, the one with which he'd need to douse the entire
project, would be a Number Two washtub full of the stuff that
dreams are made of. For Los Angeles is a place where the young and
lucky must wear lead soles in their shoes in order to keep their feet
on the ground. To only a slightly lesser degree, this is true of everybody in town.

Los Angeles is one of the most exciting and improbable cities on
earth. It is less a city than a mammoth, perennial convention, and its
citizens, who are largely newcomers from all over the nation, act the
way most people act away from home. It is San Antonio with not so
much tabasco sauce. It's San Francisco with a less integrated character,
an inferior cookbook, and an even brighter future. According to its
most severe critics, it is New York in purple shorts with its brains
knocked out.

Its weather, except when an occasional cloudburst undertakes to
wash the town away, is the velvet blue and gold of summer in
Naples, and many of its buildings are closely akin to the new structures with which Mussolini dotted Italy's anguished, wrinkled face.
Yet, at the same time, it contains numerous architectural freaks, built
in the image of almost everything except an electric fan. These mon-
strosities help wilted portions of the town to become mud-ugly.

Its religions are a mixture of the Orient, the Occident, and Barnum and Bailey. Its politics are a moving, constantly reshaping cloud, now seen to resemble a plate of ham and eggs, a moment later to depict one of Dr. Townsend's foxy septuagenarians with a bulging snap purse the size of a soup bone. Unlike Miami, it's a place where old folks go not to die in peace, but to get young again.

Since Los Angeles is built on a semidesert, it can't get enough of the sight of water. It adores fountains and swimming pools. Its people own more cars, per capita, than those of any other city and drive them right into their favorite eating places, saloons, the bank, and, of course, each other. Its civilization has been declared to caricature, in one way or another, that of the entire nation.

Its Chamber of Commerce, which is the barker for this smash box-office attraction, makes the average Chamber of Commerce look like a gathering of small, tongue-tied children. It knows that, gram for gram, glamour is more valuable than radium. It also knows you can butter bread with Los Angeles' golden climate, and has kept the town doing just that for years.

Los Angeles now contains over three and a third million souls in its metropolitan district, which has become the third largest in the nation. Between 1900 and 1940 California grew five times as fast as the nation as a whole, and most of that growth was in Los Angeles' bailiwick. In area Los Angeles proper is the world's largest city, containing 451 square miles. In certain directions, it's more than a fifty-mile hike across this sprawling municipality, which is often referred to as "nineteen suburbs in search of a city." Los Angeles County is twice as big as Delaware.

Geographically, Los Angeles has been built on the southwestern-most flank of the nation; financially, on oil, movies, citrus fruits, tourists, and, most lately, the production of aircraft. Each of these, with the exception of oil, is tightly linked with California weather.

The movies came there in the first place because the clear atmosphere permitted about 350 shooting days a year, and because almost any scenic requirement could be fished out of the Southern California grab-bag. Douglas Aircraft, now among the largest in the world, was started there, it is said, because Donald Douglas liked the California weather. For that matter, it so bedizens the tourists that, it's claimed,

10 per cent of them either just stay, or before too long after returning home, break under the strain and come tearing back.

It is that same weather which simmers the citrus trees and vineyards into a warm trance of fecundity, and coaxes the truck farms into their year-round yield, with all that implies in rich, out-of-season prices. The value of Los Angeles County's agricultural produce is the highest of any county in the nation. That is also true of the value of its dairy products. And even if you own no more than an acre of almond trees, you are, nevertheless, a bonafide rancher. In California there are no farms, and almost no piece of ground is too small to be called a ranch.

But the movies are, of course, Los Angeles' heart and, a cad might charge, its soul. Financial control of this industry has long since shifted to New York. But the men who discovered it in its infancy, such salesmen and clothiers as Carl Laemmle, Adolph Zukor, Louis B. Mayer and Sam Goldwyn, have grimly hung onto the managerial reins.

Today the movies' ability to affect the world's opinions and manners is a thing of majesty and power. There are probably no four political, military or religious leaders that the world feels it knows, or for that matter just plain likes, as well as it does Bing Crosby, Bob Hope, Clark Gable and Gary Cooper. Due to the current, record-breaking movie viewings, it is almost a certainty that no respiratory area in history has been responsible for more carnal desires than that of Miss Mae West, though in other anatomical regions the championship belongs just as unquestionably to Misses Dorothy Lamour and Betty Grable. It will be remembered that during the war it was necessary for the United States government to request Miss Veronica Lake to assume, in place of her alluring one-eyed hair-do, a more utilitarian one, in order that the thousands of girl war workers who assiduously imitated her might have a little better chance to see what they were doing, and also to avoid being caught and ground up in the machinery.

The movies have created a peculiar sense of intimacy between Los Angeles and the outside world. They titillate the public with a desire to see its heroes in the flesh, to view and, if nobody is looking, even to touch the studios, the lots where such brave and fascinating deeds really took place before the camera's eye. A vast percentage of the earth's peoples has been turned into would-be Johnnies at Los Angeles' stage door.

This powerful appeal of the movies is repackaged in an endless and dazzling variety of forms by both the radio and the press. Aside from the busy doings of the various publicity men, a Los Angeles dateline on a story will, in the nature of things, get more attention from an out-of-town editor than a story of equal news value from Pocatello, Idaho or Vicksburg, Mississippi. For there is an odd vividness in most of the happenings in drama-struck Los Angeles.

In her earlier days, Los Angeles was long one of San Francisco's inconsequential country cousins. When gold was discovered in northern California in 1848, the immediate effect was to drain off much of what little population Los Angeles possessed. Yet as San Francisco grew, it created a market for Los Angeles' cattle, which had previously been salable only as hides and tallow. Then in 1850 the Stars and Stripes, the last flag in a series, rose over California, and, in the same year, Los Angeles was incorporated as a town, with a population of 295 Anglo-Americans and enough Mexicans and Indians to raise the total above 8,000.

In the 'Fifties and 'Sixties, Los Angeles was rough as a cob. When a man was too tough for notoriously rugged San Francisco, Los Angeles inherited him by default. There was usually at least one homicide a day. When the Civil War began, California put in with the Yankees. But Los Angeles' contribution to the cause was far less impressive than was San Francisco's gold, which substantially helped pull the Union through financially.

But by the time the 'Eighties rolled around, the lure of Los Angeles was being felt over the nation—probably because of the ceaseless flow of penny post cards, which may have arrived back East during a sleet storm, saying, "Sure wish you folks were here. We just walk out in the yard and pull oranges right off the trees." A boom began which was further accelerated by a rate war between the Southern Pacific and the Santa Fe during which, at one point, a single silver dollar would buy a ticket from Kansas City to Los Angeles.

When the real-estate boom collapsed in 1888, Los Angeles realized that, in view of its isolated position, it could never become a truly great city without a port, and the town turned to to get one. There was a great fêting of congressmen in the quest for Federal aid, and much heated controversy as to where this hoped-for blessing should be put. In this clamor for a port, fuel right out from under Los Angeles' frontyard was added to the fire. In 1892, Edward L. Doheny and Charles A. Canfield brought in the first oil well, the forerunner of thousands that would be drilled within the city limits in the next few years. Finally, in 1896, Congress voted to build the breakwater which was the beginning of a $60,000,000 series of expenditures at Wilmington and San Pedro that would give Los Angeles one of the finest man-made ports on earth, and one which would one day handle more tonnage than either of the great natural ports at San Francisco and Seattle.

By the turn of the century Los Angeles was a strapping town of 100,000 people. For over a decade the Chamber of Commerce had been thumping the tub in a campaign to increase immigration. This it had done under the inspired, almost divine, leadership of Frank Wiggins, who was probably the most high-voltage booster that ever beckoned the world to Los Angeles. It was he who had built the larger-than-life-sized walnut elephant for Los Angeles' exhibit at the Chicago World's Fair in 1893. Wiggins inundated the nation with stunts, slogans and pamphlets. But there were other boosters too.

In 1907 the Southern Pacific and the California Fruit Growers Exchange, which was subsequently to implant the word "Sunkist" in the nation's consciousness, each kittied in $10,000 to plug the slogan, "Oranges for health—California for wealth." Iowa was picked as a test state. Its consumption of oranges doubled, and immigration from Iowa to California spurted. On that evidence the Exchange raised its ante to $25,000, which since then has been increased many times.

Meanwhile this growing town needed more and more water. A project was begun to bring 258,000 gallons a day from the Owens River, 238 miles away. This supply, in addition to that drawn from her subterranean water basin and other sources, should, Los Angeles felt, put it on Easy Street.

As the town continued its rapid growth, management, sparked by the Los Angeles *Times*, the Chamber of Commerce, and the Merchants and Manufacturers Association, which was organized for the purpose, was fighting powerfully to keep the city open shop. Its methods were strictly non-Geneva-convention, and labor fought back with an equal disregard for the niceties. Then in 1910 bombs blew the *Times* building to smithereens, causing the death of twenty people. When this happened, the structural unions were on a strike the *Times* had been fighting. Burns Agency detectives tracked down and laid the blame for the bombing on John J. McNamara, international secretary of the Iron Workers Union, and his brother, James B. McNamara, in Indianapolis. Over a year later, during the McNamaras' trial, they electrified the country by abruptly changing their plea to guilty, and James wrote a detailed confession. Until this confession, the public had believed the McNamara brothers were being railroaded. Now that its belief had been betrayed, Los Angeles became even more bitterly anti-closed shop.

Throughout the 'Twenties, the migrants kept pouring into the town that everybody said was the new Garden of Eden. The surrounding valleys were green with almost every square inch of irrigable soil producing under forced draft. The movies, like all properly developing youngsters, had learned to talk. Sister Aimee Semple McPherson had gone into action and was knocking Los Angeles for an emotional loop. The local corps of swamis, yogis, crystal-ball gazers, astrologers and assorted cultists was growing apace. Then the depression hit, and as the pinch got tighter in Oklahoma and Arkansas, the jalopy-borne migration of desperation got under way for California.

Under the relentless pressure of poverty, two fundamentally different kinds of people met head-on in almost Biblical conflict: nomads, and the men who plant trees. John Steinbeck, with thundering eloquence, told the story of the nomads in *The Grapes of Wrath* and aroused the nation in their behalf.

Political panaceas sprang up on every hand: join the secret Utopian society; put your faith in technocracy; give the old folks so much money that their spending will break the depression. Upton Sinclair, running on his EPIC plan to End Poverty In California, came within an inch or two of being elected governor. At last, with all hands groggy and on the ropes, the depression ended.

Yet Los Angeles is still morbidly aware of its attractions for the indigent. While it cannot offer too warm a welcome to the well-heeled tourists, who in prewar years usually left Southern California a couple of hundred million dollars to remember them by, Los Angeles wants the boomer, the drifter, the Okie to be warned away. In this struggle, however, it has fought, and will almost certainly continue to fight, a losing battle. Los Angeles is too glamorous and comfortable, and the old concept of just reaching out and picking an orange right off the tree is still shot with magic appeal.

A part of the constant flow of migrants was Los Angeles' quarter of a million Mexicans, and about half that many Negroes, with more arriving every day. Yet at least for the time being, neither group is being subjected to the California Vigilante-ism that its Japanese-American citizens received during the war. One of the more bewildering manifestations of Los Angeles' race tension, if it were race tension, was its series of zoot-suit riots. Nobody has yet given an exact explanation of why the soldiery and the zoot suiters, often Mexican youths, so relentlessly locked horns. Perhaps the most logical reason is that there is just something about a zoot suit that makes you want to swat its wearer.

Although thousands of California's Mexicans work on the truck farms and other less choice jobs, Los Angeles' Negro population is largely working in industry. Even before the war Los Angeles had become a city with a splendidly diversified industry, in nine separate branches of which it was producing goods worth more than $25,-000,000 a year. But today the word "smog" (smoke and fog) is more important than ever in its vocabulary.

Los Angeles makes more oilfield machinery than any other city on earth. Next to Detroit, it assembles more automotive equipment than any other American city. It is hot on the heels of Akron in the production of tires, and has already overtaken Grand Rapids in the manufacture of furniture, and Boston in the canning of fish. It is third in petroleum refining and food processing. Capitalizing on its talent for style, it has become fourth in clothing production, and a world leader in the design and manufacture of sports clothes. Under war pressure its aircraft business became, at least temporarily, bigger than Detroit's automobile industry.

California has almost always had a labor surplus. That is one of the reasons why it's only half organized by the unions. That the surplus of war workers will eventually find jobs is regarded as a certainty by almost everyone in this constantly growing city, whose very growth creates most of her problems—and, almost inevitably, a little further down the line, solves them.

One of California's problems results from the fact that the war fastened itself, like a vampire, onto the state's reserves of the petroleum that has long fed her industry. No new fields have been discovered since 1937. At the current rate of consumption, her reserves could, according to best estimates, last little more than a decade.

Rather than crying over this war-spilt milk, Los Angeles consoles itself by realizing there are important compensations to her fuel picture. California has already-developed hydroelectric power in great abundance, and there's plenty more where that came from. Too, Pacific Lighting Corporation and affiliates, in conjunction with Pacific Gas and Electric Company, are laying a 27¼-inch pipeline, the largest made, to run the thousand miles from Los Angeles to the Texas Panhandle and Hugenon fields. This line will send 300,000,000 cubic feet of natural gas, which is roughly twice as cheap as artificial gas, into California per day. The line will cost $80,000,000 and is tied into gas reserves which, it is claimed, will adequately supply California for thirty years.

And finally, Los Angeles has got water till the world looks level. She finished her four hundred-mile system of aqueducts, siphons and tunnels to the Colorado River in 1941, at a cost of $220,000,000. Today she claims she could supply the water requirements of a population of ten million people.

The fact that the West Coast has to pay at least six dollars a ton more for steel than do Eastern users has long been a weakness in its economy. Henry Kaiser, who is bullish to the last, wants to give the whole West Coast an injection of homemade steel. He says, "We can have an all-Western steel industry if we fight for it—and make no mistake, we will have to fight for it."

Leaving that assertion for the future to affirm, Mr. Kaiser goes on to say, "Light metals also will be produced and fabricated throughout the entire area. I am ready to declare my belief that automobiles will be built in the West." Just in passing, he points out that there is not a highway in California that can meet future traffic requirements, and he is plugging for a six-lane highway between Los Angeles and San Francisco without a single grade crossing. Finally, he has delivered himself of the belief that, once the West gets rolling, it can supply 30,000,000 jobs.

Los Angeles devoutly hopes these wonders come to pass.

But nobody doubts that Los Angeles' tourist business is, and will continue to be, absolutely gigantic. In a recent poll, the Milwaukee *Journal* found that of 58,000 Milwaukee families who planned vacations, a fourth of them were going to spend them in the Los Angeles area. For comparison, the Eastern states, lumped together, ran second with 14.5 per cent.

If you were a tourist driving into Los Angeles today from the north, you'd probably select Highway 101 because it passes as straight through Hollywood as D'Artagnan's sword ever passed through a villain's heart. As you drive out from among the orange and lemon trees of the San Fernando Valley, which became a part of the city to get water for its 48,000 thirsty acres, you begin to notice signs pointing to sideroads: "Warner Brothers Ranch" or, again, "R.K.O. Ranch," designating the spots where most outdoorsy shooting, both of film and blank cartridges, is done.

Then you roll on into Hollywood and pass the Republic lot on your left. Perched on hills everywhere around, there are California-type houses glistening in the sun, their lawns alight with vivid flowers, bathed by twirling sprays. What you won't see is the shaded patios inside them where Angelenos do some of their most comfortable living. In the distance is the Bank of America, which is one of California's principal proprietors.

Soon you reach Hollywood Boulevard, and if you are a confirmed movie addict, you will have touched home plate, arrived at Samarkand, the land of heart's desire. Here you will see people wearing getups in which almost every note, with the exception of conservatism, will be struck. In the line of personal and/or sartorial eccentricity, you can name it and take it on Hollywood Boulevard. Perhaps your gaze fastens upon a bearded, barefooted messiah who is serenely infecting the sidewalk with pestilential fungi. It is a street where, in order to conform, it is necessary to be different. It is also a street that is drenched with talent and ability.

Then if you turn, you enter Sunset Boulevard, and soon pass the pleasure dome *moderne* of NBC, and, a little farther on, that of CBS, monuments to the town's world importance in radio.

Suppose you're staying at the Los Angeles Biltmore, the city's largest hotel, where you may live in high comfort and where even the spittoons wear demure gold bands. If so, you may keep going until you turn right onto Main Street, which is as colorfully tawdry and garish a thoroughfare as you could possibly wish to see. But as you turn onto Fifth, respectability begins to dominate the scene again. Yet you can't help noticing the absence of skyscrapers in this earthquake-conscious city. One of the few buildings in town that exceeds the thirteen-story limit set by city ordinance is the thirty-two-story City Hall.

Once you're settled, you grab the Chandler-owned *Times*, the *Hollywood Reporter*, the tabloid *News*, the Hearst-owned *Examiner* and the *Herald-Express* to see what's going on around town. If it's Saturday, you'll find whole pages devoted to advertisements inviting you to line up with this or that religious personality at such and such a tabernacle. In the field of ecclesiastical showmanship in Los Angeles, the promotion of child preachers is now its brightest feature. One ad urges you to "Hear Little David [aged ten] in the Big Tent," while another touts "Reverend La Deane Murdock," aged eight.

But since Sunday isn't until tomorrow, you'll probably turn to the restaurant and night-club ads. Most visitors hit town with a deathless predetermination to invade the Brown Derby, Ciro's, the Trocadero, Slapsy Maxie Rosenbloom's, Mike Romanoff's, the Cocoanut Grove at the Ambassador, and Earl Carroll's, where both girlies and groceries are given lavish presentation.

Should you become possessed by a hankering for Oriental fare, there are a couple of Chinatowns at hand to dish it out. *Enchilada* fiends, or those who merely want to buy a few Mexican curios in colorful surroundings, will find satisfaction in Olvera Street. Many Angelenos enjoy lunching in the Farmers Market. Here, where the atmosphere of a county fair still prevails, the technique is to eat each item at a different stall until either your capacity or legs become exhausted.

If you're in Los Angeles during the racing season, you can go out to Hollywood Park, Santa Anita, or more distant Del Mar and watch Der Bingle's bang-tails run. On the cultural side, there's the great Huntington Museum, home of Gainsborough's Blue Boy, and, in the Public Library, the Dean Cornwell murals. You can hear such con-ductors as Leopold Stokowski direct the Los Angeles Philharmonic in the fifty-nine-acre Hollywood Bowl. Scholars and football fans may want to visit the University of Southern California, the University of California at Los Angeles, and the California Institute of Technology at Pasadena. If you'll stick around until New Year's Day, there'll be big doings at the Rose Bowl.

If you're feeling athletic, you can go skiing or tobogganing in Big Pines Park, or swim in the blue Pacific at countless beaches. If your heart is set on catching a tuna, this is a good place to do it. But in case you wish to dive for abalone, it is death to let one sit on your thumb. He can hold you longer than you can hold your breath. It's safer just to make faces at him through the glass bottom of a boat at Mr. William Wrigley, Jr.'s Catalina Island. But if you want a truly eerie experience, you can go to Glendale and take a look at huge, ornate Forest Lawn Memorial Park ("The Happy Cemetery"), which seems bent on con-vincing Angelenos that it's fun to be dead.

You can always spend a quiet evening at the movies, say at Grau-man's Chinese Theater, where the feet of the mighty have so visibly trod. But if you want to track those stellar footprints to their lairs, you'll need to go to Beverly Hills, whose femoral artery is spectacular Wilshire Boulevard. And since Hollywood by no means has a monopoly on the studios, you'll also find Twentieth Century Fox in Beverly Hills, MGM in Culver City, and Warner Brothers and Universal in Burbank.

But perhaps the most entertaining thing of all is just being in Los Angeles. It is a marvelous place to go native and confuse yourself with a character in fiction. It's the South Sea Isles of the United States, where the big outside world may soon shrink to a comfortably small unimportance and unreality, a place where once you find that your feet fit a pair of sandals, you may be a goner. Conversely, it's also a place where you may develop an odd dependency on earning two thousand dollars a week and have to spend the rest of your days in an aching strain to keep it up.

Clearly Los Angeles is so varied and manifold that you can find or see in it almost anything you're looking for, including bitter, crushing disappointment. No dreamland could be complete without nightmares. Yet its people may well ask what possible excuse anybody has for living elsewhere, when all the elements of the good life are here, where there is an almost endlessly cheerful and productive climate, where every beauty of nature, from flowers to women, is in lavish abundance, where the way of life is unbelievably casual and easy, and where diversion is on every hand. And finally, even if you're interested in such baubles as riches and fame, where else, asks the confident Angeleno, are you more likely to find them?

☆ ☆ ☆ ☆ ☆ ☆ ☆ ☆ ☆ ☆ ☆ ☆ ☆ ☆ ☆ ☆ ☆ ☆ ☆ ☆

20: *Kansas City*

IN A nation studded with such variegated clots of men and motion as Detroit with its production-line veins, as Denver mid the magic mountains, as Hollywood wearing its chromium heart on its sleeve, as San Antonio daubed with khaki and flushed with sun, as New York with its fever of ideas, Kansas City is probably the most typical of America's big towns.

Kansas City is a kind of interior American crossroads and melting pot where the Southerner, the Northerner, the Easterner and the Westerner meet and become plain John American, with America unfolding, to use one old-timer's rapt expression, "in oceans of glory" in every direction. It got its start on the riches of Boston banks and Western lands and Northern furs. It is not only America's approximate geographical heart, but the center of gravity for her taste and emotion. The soap opera, movie or national magazine that doesn't "take" in Kansas City won't live long in the nation.

Kansas City is a bread-and-meat town. It is interested less in ideas than in things. It has a river and a region, a past, a present and a future, all of them alive and burgeoning and, at least the river and the past, turbulent in spectacular degree. For sheer vitality and bumptiousness, it's almost worse than Texas. In many ways they're much alike. Take size. Kansas City feels itself less a town than the center of the region it dominates: all of Kansas, western Missouri, northern Oklahoma, parts of Iowa, Colorado and Nebraska. Like Texas, it's bursting with "mosts" and "firsts." Its Union Station handles more through trains a day than any other in the United States. People wait for those trains in the biggest waiting room in the land. Kansas City stockyards handle more stockers and feeders—that is, range cattle which are to be further fed and fattened—than any other American market. It is the biggest

244

primary United States market for hard winter wheat, as well as for sorghum grains, and has the largest single grain elevator. And like Texas, its leaders are sluggers, though a few, just now, may point a little self-consciously at the hair on their chests. These days Kansas City's people are like kids out of school. Because Tom Pendergast, who ran the political machine that made Kansas City eat out of its hand during the 'Thirties, is dead.

The machine still controls Jackson County, which contains the city, but the city itself is free. Its Uncle Sam came to its rescue after Tom Pendergast got too big for any local force to tackle. Until that time, Kansas City's slugging leaders called Tom Pendergast "Mister," and meant it. Pendergast was smart, decisive and full of the qualities of command and leadership. He could stuff a ballot box as deftly as a Midwest farm wife can stuff a hen. But his word was good enough for anybody. He went to Mass every morning and then went to his office, from where he ran Kansas City just as wide open as she would run, and the idea of conflict between his professed moral beliefs and his actions never seemed to enter his head.

There were crap games in every pool hall and bookie joint. Whisky was always fifty cents more a bottle in Kansas City than in St. Louis. One of Pendergast's companies sold ready-mixed concrete. You got along fine if you used enough concrete. And the time of his reign is often spoken of as "the concrete age" of Kansas City. One real-estate development has a concrete-floored creek.

During these times, Kansas City's effort to show the visiting salesmen and buyers a good time reached its most florid heights. Under the leadership of Mayor John Gage, Kansas City has subsequently been thoroughly, even dramatically, cleaned up—at the expense, some feel, of the trade of certain gladtime farmers and cattlemen who now prefer Chicago's more frolicsome fleshpots. But back in the roaring 'Thirties there were businessmen's luncheon places in Kansas City where there were strip-tease acts between the shrimp cocktail and the roast beef, acts that went right on to their logical conclusion. In the west bottoms there were cafés with nude waitresses. The biggest crap games between the Missouri and the Rio Grande were roaring continuously—games in which herds of cattle, ranches, even oilfields changed hands.

Clyde Barrow and Bonnie Parker at times graced Kansas City's streets, and citizen John Kaplan attained the distinction in his profession of being nationally recognized as Public Enemy Number One. Pretty Boy Floyd moved to town from the Cookson Hills of Oklahoma. Thus Kansas City, located in the center of three penitentiaries, became a kind of capital and haven for those with extra-legal vocations. Many of these hearties toted their tommy guns in golf bags, and, in those days, a machine-gun-conscious populace could be cleared from the streets instantly by turning on a riveting machine. This was especially true after the Union Station massacre, when five people were mowed down by gunmen seeking to rescue a pal from the clutches of the law.

Finally, the K.C. pickings looked so good that one of the Chicago mobs decided to move in. Soon it was upsetting Kansas City gambling tables and in other ways treating the native racketeers with disrespect, until, late one night, the Chicagoans found themselves let down on ropes and hanging by their feet from the A.S.B. Bridge high above the Missouri River. A conference was held by the K.C. crowd, as the visitors pleaded and as some of the more impetuous Missouri boys whittled on the ropes to pass the time away. Ultimately, however, they yielded to the entreaties of the Illinois delegation, hauled them up and let them retire from the scene with coattails flying. And that was the last invasion from the North.

But Mr. Pendergast, like so many others, entertained the belief that he could guess the outcome of horse races in advance. In fact, he was willing to bet that he could. And it is generally felt that it was a broomtail-busted Pendergast who made the mistake of accepting a $430,000 bribe from a group of insurance companies and neglecting to give the Bureau of Internal Revenue its fair share of the take.

That was the oversight that sent him to the penitentiary for income-tax evasion. Later, sick and broken, he died. One of the machine's most distinguished alumni, then Vice-President of the United States, flew home to help bury his old boss—a gesture of loyalty beyond Pendergast's politically bankrupt grave which set mighty well with many

Kansas Citians, who knew how easily Mr. Truman could have been too busy with affairs of state.

But while Pendergast's shadow is still longer over Kansas City than that of either of those earlier inhabitants of Missouri, Daniel Boone and Jesse James, perhaps the longest shadow was cast by another of the potent individualists who have made Kansas City—William Rockhill Nelson, who, in 1880, founded the great Kansas City *Star*. Nelson had a neck the size of an ordinary man's thigh, and just as stiff. He died not long before Pendergast came into power, and it is a pity that a contest never took place between Pendergast and this rough-and-tumble editor for the heavyweight championship of the forks of the Missouri and the Kaw.

No issue affecting Kansas City ever came to light during Nelson's reign without feeling the impact of his editorial blasts. He carried on an unyielding campaign for improvement in Kansas City—better streets, better homes, better buildings, more parks, playgrounds, museums and civic adornment.

When Nelson died, he left his fortune of $11,000,000 for a Kansas City art gallery. The income from this fund was to be used for the purchase of art objects. The rest of the family furnished the site and $3,500,000 for a building. The gallery is one of the handsomest in America. As usual, Mr. Nelson thought of everything, and provided that the trustees could spend endowment funds only for pictures by artists who had been dead thirty years or more. Consequently, while the gallery abounds with Chinese tomb and temple art and has a skeleton collection of paintings by the European great, there is not a Grant Wood in the place. To express the Midwest, there is a single Tom Benton and a single John Steuart Curry, which some private citizens gave to the gallery.

In his will, Mr. Nelson also directed that the *Star* be sold to the highest bidder on the death of his heirs. At that time, the staff raked and scraped enough money to make a sort of down payment on it. Now the paper is paid for and is virtually wallowing in the black, and the homes of the *Star* men who own it look more like bankers' houses than the usual drear diggings of the Fourth Estate. Among the alumni of the *Star* are editors of many of the nation's leading magazines and some of the best writers. For example, Ernest Hemingway was once a police reporter on the *Star*, and Roy Roberts, the present managing editor, recalls with a chuckle, "not a very good one either."

In the 'Thirties, the *Star* fought Pendergast on almost every issue that arose, just as, back at the turn of the century, it beat the drum for the young Kansas produce peddler who wanted to try to develop the vast and then farm-covered area south of Kansas City that was later to be known as the Country Club District. The young Kansan, J. C. Nichols, was full of ideas, and a go-getter in capital letters printed in red. Between that time and this, Nichols has built good housing around 50,000 Kansas Citians. He lays out and builds whole neighborhoods at a time, so that each house may complement the others, and each neighborhood the others. Shopping centers, schools, churches, and so on, are strategically located. Parking spaces are adequate, and sunken and landscaped around the edges to resemble parks. The streets are laid out to create esplanades and parks of every shape, on which Mr. Nichols has mounted art objects from all over Europe—wellheads, sets of columns and statuary, surrounded by pools and fountains and gardens. This long-range-planned 4,000-acre development, devoted almost entirely to one-family homes, is said to be the largest undertaking of its kind in the world. And Kansas City is immensely proud of the whole thing.

A municipally-planned but Nichols-boosted project is the creation of a vast cultural center that will tie together Kansas City University, the Nelson Gallery, Barstow School for Girls and Rockhurst College, the Midwest Research Institute, and the as yet unbuilt $6,000,000 Linda Hall Library, into a kind of Versailles of the Middle West, with reflecting pools and, in all probability if J. C. Nichols has anything to do with it, a lot of statuary.

Probably the most useful civic building in Kansas City is its block-square Municipal Auditorium, that is as tall as a ten-story building. During one evening, all in the same Gargantuan structure, I saw thousands of yelling people watching a basketball game in the main arena while a delightful performance of *H.M.S. Pinafore* was going on in the beautiful maroon-and-gold Music Hall, which is also where

Kansas City's Philharmonic gives its concerts. Some local organization was meeting in the Exhibition Hall, but this was an off night for the Little Theater, which is tucked in one corner. In all, the auditorium can seat 24,000 people. Incidentally, the machine built it, and spent $6,500,000 in the process, but it provided a meeting place that does credit to one of the nation's most popular convention towns.

But Kansas City is more than any of its political factions, leaders or even its people in general. The keystone in the Kansas City story is geography. In the first place, it boxed St. Louis off from the West. And in the history of the American West the formula has been: population flows west; trade flows east. Once the site of Kansas City had been selected, the only way it could have failed to prosper would have been for the West to remain unpeopled.

In the early days, immigrants traveled as far as Kansas City on the Missouri. By 1836 as many as twenty steamboats were regularly making the trip from St. Louis. At Kansas City the pioneers transferred their baggage and persons to prairie schooners, then hit the Santa Fe Trail. From this time on, men were moving west through Kansas City and sending back their buffalo robes and wool and gold dust to be exchanged for Kansas City's whisky, groceries, prints and notions.

In the latter half of the nineteenth century, the railroads pushed out to Kansas City and kept on going until they extended their prongs to Abilene and Dodge City. And the market had met the range. Soon the great cattle drives up the Chisholm Trail to the railheads were at their height. Already, with transportation and so vast a market, Kansas City was becoming a big branch-house town and wholesaling center. Little by little, a garment industry would grow up to take advantage of the distribution channels of the wholesale system.

Until this time, the lands of Kansas and northern Oklahoma had served in Kansas City's scheme of things principally as pasture land. The homesteaders had tried raising wheat, but the experiment fizzled and farmers were abandoning their lands, when a party of Mennonites brought in thirty bushels of "Turkey red"—rust- and cold- and drought-resistant wheat from the Russian Crimea. It was the answer to Kansas land and climate. Its yield was not only dependable but oceanic. And when Kansas became prosperous, her riches naturally gravitated east toward Kansas City's banks and merchants.

Now the century had turned and more and more light industries were finding their way to Kansas City. That Kansas wheat had to be milled. Milling was becoming almost as important as butchering and packing. Kansas City was also becoming an assembly and distributing point for all the big implement and, later still, automobile companies. Then, as those first plows and cultivators began to fall into disrepair and had to be junked, Kansas City got a steel mill which depended not upon ore, but which straightforwardly stewed up those old riding plows and cultivators and expiring Model T's and fashioned them into new steel shapes.

At every turn, Kansas City's blessed geography served her well. Then her bankers were called upon to bet on something besides cows and grain, to take a new and not so easily calculable kind of risk, and they dropped the ball. The great midcontinent oilfields were beginning to be discovered, and men with a light in their eyes were pouring into the Kansas City banks seeking financial backing to invade this new industry which offered such spectacular rewards. But the "show-me" bankers just couldn't bring themselves to take the plunge. While they hesitated and hemmed and hawed, less-cautious Eastern money poured into the fields and, incidentally, boomed Tulsa, which simply by being there has bit a nice slice out of Kansas City's wholesale-trade territory. Even so, the cross-country pipe lines had to pass through Kansas City, which was able to drain off enough oil to keep a refinery or two humming.

When the war came and Kansas City asked for war industry, Washington laughed out loud. Kansas City, Washington said, had neither skilled industrial labor nor management know-how. But such Kansas City dollar-a-year men as J. C. Nichols and Bob Mehornay spent their days fighting the enemy and their nights fighting the battle for Midwest war plants. They said that if Washington didn't want its war plants bombed, it had better bring them out on the Missouri's secluded banks, that the native ingenuity of Midwestern labor and management would see the projects through. Soon the plants began coming.

There had never been a single Kansas City plant that had handled or needed more than about 3,000 workers at a time. The Kansas City Chamber of Commerce beat the bushes seeking out labor. When Remington's small-arms plant opened and asked for 24,000 workers, it got 75,000 applications. Then North American and Pratt & Whitney came in and sopped up the rest of this manpower and more besides. Still other workers had to be found to build amphibious assault vessels out of Kansas City steel—vessels which were then launched in the Missouri to swim to the sea. Subsequent plants such as the huge Sunflower rocket-powder plant had to hustle mightily for labor.

But Kansas City seemed to remain about as far from the war as you could get in the United States, and showed the minimum signs of war hysteria. It's true that it was pretty nearly impossible to buy a K.C. steak in town, and the Royal American Fat Stock Show, the annual cow Mardi Gras, which is one of Kansas City's greatest social functions, was suspended for the duration. But business thrived on Petticoat Lane, the town's smartest shopping center, and the hospitality at its hostelries, particularly its famous and venerable Muehlebach, was, as far as was humanly possible with the shortage of labor and flood of guests, still genuine and old-fashioned.

One thing about Kansas City life that would strike a visiting New Yorker immediately is the virtual absence of delicatessens. Kansas Citians cook and eat at home, except when, on occasion, they dine out in their country clubs and restaurants.

Twelfth Street, where, in the minds of many a gladtime Oklahoman, Kansas City was always most "up to date," where many went broke and a few would like to be buried, is still one of the main stems, as it was in the days when it inspired *Twelfth Street Rag*. But, in actuality, Kansas City has no "Great White Way," no Fifth Avenue. It has a gridiron business district, built pretty much in the shape of a square, as if a hostile return of the Indians might be expected. Most of Kansas City's downtown streets, with the exception of Grand Avenue, are pinched and narrow. Grand is wider because, in the early days when it was laid out, Colonel James McGee insisted it be wide enough for him to turn his buggy around without having to drive all the way to the corner.

As you no doubt know, the state line slices through Kansas City. At least the Missouri part of town, which is a good four fifths of it, feels that Kansas City, Kansas, has less éclat, generally speaking, than Kansas City, Missouri. Traveling Kansas Citians are alleged to say only "I'm from Kansas City" if from the Kansas side, and "I'm from Kansas City, Missouri," if from that ennobled community.

Many firms, because of the state-line situation, pay taxes in both states. And back in the old days when Missouri was slave and Kansas anti-slave, John Brown used to raid across it, snatch slaves and free them. One of the principal properties that the state line divides is the stockyards.

Now the stockyards, in the first place, are nothing but a cow hotel. There is even room service—water and hay delivered to the pens. Commission men handle transactions between rancher and packer or feeder. The stockyards cover 350 brick-floored acres and, on the days when they handle fifty or sixty thousand animals, there are cattle constantly moving in one direction on the ground and loping, clattering and mooing in the other direction on overhead runways as they are bought and sold by men on horseback. Here atop the stockyards companies' office building—although in a blindfold test the bottom two floors would cause you to guess Barnum and Bailey's—is the extremely pleasant Hoof and Horn Club, where the livestock elite meet to tipple and talk and nibble a rib.

To the east of the stockyards, more in the center of town, is the Grain Exchange, which has a nice, old-fashioned feeling, with grain samples spilled on the floor, with traders in the pit yelling as if a panther had them, and those not trading at the moment leaning, chatting, on old long-legged tables that have no stools. Most of this buying and selling is not gambling, but hedging to take the gamble out of the elevator and milling and baking businesses. And the importance of grain to Kansas City's life, the changing ownership of which flows through the exchange, can hardly be overstated. One of the yearly crises in the city's existence, since the coming of the combine has reduced the harvest season from ten weeks to six, is the Niagara-like influx of the wheat crop. Though Kansas City has twelve trunk railroads and elevator capacity of 64,000,000 bushels, there are times when 7,500 cars of wheat are coming in each week and her freight yards are swamped and there is twenty-four-hour hell to pay until the grain is stored.

From the exchange, it's hardly more than the river's width to the municipal airport nestling in the bend of the Missouri, almost in the heart of the city. At the moment, the river is the subject of a dispute: Who shall cope with it, who undertake to deprive it of its notorious convulsions? The Army engineers or the Missouri Valley Authority? Kansas City knows what it wants. It wants dams built, floods controlled, electricity generated and the river level controlled for navigation—this last more as a club to use against high railroad rates than as a thing of vast importance in itself. But, by and large, Kansas City business interests want the Army engineers to handle the job of harnessing the river. They are content to let the government sell the electricity, but they are afraid of the collateral grants of power that would go to the River Authority people.

Yet though the river question is a facet of the future, it is only a facet. Kansas City has been worried about the future and wanted a panacea. It feared that when the war ended, it would have empty war plants and idle workers. That might also be true all over its realm. It figured further. Its industrial managament would not be the same old management, but injected by war experience with the magic ingredient of know-how, in terms of larger operations and in terms of change and adjustment. Moreover, its idle workers would not be merely the practical, elementary mechanics who had trooped in off the farms. They would have become skilled workers. In addition, the fighting men of the region would be bringing back with them many new skills and abilities. The problem was how to use them, this accruement of plant and skilled management and skilled labor.

Somebody hit upon the idea of industrial research. The open technological frontier. Would it be possible, with these new facilities, for the region, utilizing its own resources, to manufacture some of the things which had always been imported from the East—after the manufactured value had been added to Midwestern raw materials? Maybe this whole blurted one-word dream of research would cure the Midwest's ills of declining population due, among other things, to the mechanization of farming. In a region where industries were mostly too small to have their own research laboratories, perhaps a regional research body was the answer. If a man needed to make paint stick where it didn't want to stick, maybe the scientists could tell him how. If his cream became water-thin from pasteurization, maybe science could tell him how to make it thick again, so it would sell better. These and ten thousand other questions. Maybe science could pull the Midwest out of the hole.

That was the notion in the minds of real-estate men and merchants, newspapermen, bankers and railroad men. Abandoning the whole "show-me" policy, men like Mehornay and Nichols first sold themselves, then their neighbors over six states, and in all kittied in $500,000 to get the Midwest Research Institute started.

First they raided the Armour Institute in Chicago for some of its best talent and went to work, renting every kind of old building, including the old Westport police station, that would house test tubes and burners and mixers. The Midwest Research Institute is now a going concern. And industrialists are covering it up with projects. Since it is a non-profit organization, it pays no taxes, although it makes money on every project. That money goes not to stockholders, but for the acquisition of more equipment and brains.

The Institute is supposed to keep the Midwest's technical industrial problems solved, on the one hand, and also to create new uses and processes for the area's mineral and vegetable resources. It likes to do liaison work between the producer and user of, say, wheat—the farmer and the baker. For while the farmer tries to make wheat drought-proof and rust-proof, he may also tend to make it, to some degree, bread-proof. The Institute is supposed to umpire that game.

In any case, Kansas City is proud of its new baby and anxiously awaits its miracles. It is also proud of its orderliness and civic virtue restored. But, down in its heart, it is just as proud of its turbulent, hell-roaring and remarkably happy past. And whatever industrial adventures await Kansas City, it is probable that alchemy will continue to be its main stock in trade—turning land and light and the wheeling seasons into the bread and meat that feed America.

2 1: *Rockdale, Texas*

S INCE most Americans live not in cities but in or near small towns, it seems meet to include, in this album of cities, a single snapshot of a small town (pop. 2,000) snapped at what is probably its most interesting time: Saturday afternoon.

For it's on Saturday afternoon that rural America comes to town to buy its week's supplies, to sell its eggs, get its hair cut, see a movie and visit with its friends. It is, therefore, a time of mild, recurrent festival.

When I was a boy in Rockdale, Texas, twenty-five years ago, and my father ran one of the town's two drugstores, Saturday was a more violently exciting time. Prohibition had not yet materialized, and people got drunk and hollered and fought each other with knives on the main street. By sundown the calaboose was full. Our house was a couple of blocks away, and there was always one man who, about eleven o'clock on Saturday night after my father had closed the drugstore and gone wearily to bed, would begin yelling out the jail window: "Andrew! Come get me out!" And he would keep it up until my father, who was a kind man and who also knew that otherwise he would get no sleep, would get up, put on his blue serge suit and go back to town to bail out this erring and troublesome friend.

In those days, the farm families hitched their teams to the wagon and started to town as soon as the cows were milked on Saturday morning. The papa and one of the oldest boys rode on the spring seat and drove. Mama and the older girls, scrubbed and in their stiff starched Saturday's best, sat in cane-bottomed chairs a little farther back in the wagon amid the buckets of eggs, a half-dozen or so chickens with their feet tied together, and the week's accumulation of surplus butter. A dog or two, that had hid behind bushes for the first mile or two of the trip until it was too late to be sent home, finally came out in the open and trotted along just under the tail gate.

Every house within a block or two of the small business district had signposts along the curb which said: "Five dollar fine to hitch here." It was to these posts that the papa tied the team, after he'd first dropped the wagon tongue and draped the traces up over the collar hames.

Well before noon, the produce had been sold, but buying had not heavily begun. If you were going to buy a roast for Sunday—more frequently spoken of as "a piece of fresh meat," as opposed to the cured contents of your smokehouse—you wanted it to stay in the butcher's icebox as long as possible. Too, since cattle were then at large, one of these strolling bossies might get her front feet up in the back of the wagon and eat most of your sack of flour and strew the rest over the street. The main activity of the family during this early part of the day was to clog the sidewalks by holding confab in family groups.

If you got hungry before noon, you walked into any of the grocery stores where you traded and pulled a banana or two off the bunches hung in the middle of the store. You didn't ask for them and you weren't stealing. They were your due. And the sidewalks were heavily booby-trapped with banana skins.

Come noon, and you had yourself a good canned dinner in the back of the store. Fried chicken and ham and hot biscuits were what you had at home. These Saturday feasts of canned salmon and baloney and canned peaches and cheese and, above all, canned oysters, were exotic urban fare.

The fighting ordinarily started about three or four in the afternoon. And in the event that no impromptu conflict came into being, there was usually an outbreak or two between the members of a couple of feuding families from the south of town. By sundown the doctors would have sewed up several gladiators in the back of the drugstore, flesh that had been sundered with pocket knives, brass knucks, billiard cues or, the real favorite, new white-hickory ax handles.

The mainstay of our existence, the thing on which we bet most heavily in labor and the future, was cotton, and the corn needed to empower our mules to cultivate that cotton. In those days, if boll weevils, droughts or floods destroyed the cotton, we, as a community, were destitute. In the good years, three cotton gins roared and hummed and tooted for the next wagonload far into the night. Weighing yards were piled high with the baled cotton. The ginners walked along the lined-up wagons, handing out free meal tickets, so that the waiting farmers might pass the time more pleasantly amid the fellowship and pepper-sauce bottles of one of our local chile emporiums.

Today all that is changed. The land was gutted of its fertility by too many scores of cotton crops. Now only one gin runs a part of the time. These days most of our people are able in the spring to resist sowing the tired earth with cotton seed. The sight of thousands of acres of deep, blue-green cotton plants, blooming pink and white, is a thing of the past. No longer at cotton picking time do the housewives lose their Negro cooks, who always went to the fields at this season to labor in the August sun, to earn the money that would clear up old debts, to renew their acquaintance with the earth and their friends; for in those days all the Negroes—men, women, and children—went to the fields when the bolls broke open and the locks of cotton hung dazzling white in the sun.

At that time, the thousands of little cotton towns through the South did most of their year's business on the fall and winter Saturdays. It was at this season that the year's bills were paid, if they were paid at all. And when they were, my father always reached in the cigar counter, where a wet sponge kept the case humid, and fished out a box of Travis Club cigars, which cost a dime each, and gave the payer not one but two, and if there were kids along, they got candy. Today, our little town still does 30 per cent of the week's business on Saturday; but on Saturdays which stretch, with reasonable impartiality, throughout the year.

Where does the money come from that is spent on these year-round Saturdays? In the spring, it comes from chicken eggs. Our people bring about thirty-five hundred dollars' worth to town per week. We are a plain, unpretentious people. We do not dress extravagantly or live expensively. And that egg money is very important to us, and we get by on it very well.

Maybe that figure will drop off, along with the exuberance of the hens, in the hot summer months to about $3,000 a week. But then there is the yield of sweet potato, watermelon and garden patches to be brought to town on Saturday excursions and sold to the stores. And by now the cattle, which people the abandoned cotton fields, have begun to grow fat. Yearlings are going to market. Say half a million dollars' worth in all. Then that manna of the post-oak lands, acorns, begins to fall. And the pigs wander in dreamy glory, gorging themselves, growing fat and marketable.

In the fall, there is a dribble of cotton. Perhaps $50,000 worth for our town. Just as important is the opening of the pre-Thanksgiving turkey market.

A decade ago, turkeys were a thing that the farm woman raised on the side so that when the bank took the cotton crop, which was inevitably mortgaged, there would be a few dollars left with which to buy the children some school clothes and perhaps a trinket or two for Christmas.

Turkeys are trouble. To raise them no grand, exhilarating gestures with plow and mules are needed, just patience and doggedness, walking, walking, fighting off rapacious foxes and hawks, hungry dogs and neighbors. For turkeys walk eternally, picking up weed seeds and acorns, fattening stupendously when the grasshoppers become pestilentially thick. Endless trouble, but profitable. The wife increased her flocks and began to be the principal breadwinner.

These days the turkey crop brings our people as much as or more than cotton. Remember, we are a tiny town surrounded by impoverished land that is, like so much of the Faulknerian South, haunted by the ghost of cotton. The sale of the turkeys makes a fine pile of Saturday money, not too much of which is owed the bank. And not only is there the value of the birds themselves, but our people, who used to pick cotton, now pick turkeys at our local dressing plants, from which the plucked birds are sent out in refrigerator cars to the distributing centers in the East. To us, the turkey is truly a bird of thanksgiving, the source of whatever modest plenty with which we may be blessed in November and again at Christmas.

But on to Saturday afternoon. As far back as Tuesday or Wednesday the merchants have decided what items they plan to feature as bargain specials to attract Saturday customers. The ads had to be placed then, because the weekly paper comes out on Thursday. Friday is largely spent in getting the store in shape to do business on Saturday. The dry-goods merchants make sure that extra clerks will be on hand. Butchers cut up all their meat and arrange it in the refrigerated display counters. The restaurants buy steaks and roasts on Friday to serve on Saturday. And the butchers' meat grinders are going like sixty, milling meat for tomorrow's hamburgers and the big kettles of chile that every eating place will keep warming on the back of the stove. Also, since human nature is the same here as anywhere else, and since the stores will be crowded, the merchants try to arrange their wares so that the small and easily pocketed items will be in the best-lighted part of the store. In the darker corners the grocers will put large boxes of breakfast food or soda or soap flakes. Soap in bars, cans of sardines and the like will be brightly illuminated. At the hardware store, new saddles and bridles will be temptingly displayed on full-size horses that are made of papier-mâché.

On Friday night before a grocer goes to bed, he is very apt to step out on his front porch and look at the weather. If tomorrow's weather is bad, turning country roads into quagmires, he will lose an important part of the week's business. The value of the newspaper ad will have shrunk mightily. Business a grocer loses on Saturday when the country folks couldn't get to town is business he never gets back. In place of the roast a farm family planned to buy for Sunday dinner they will have a chicken or something from the smoke-house.

If the day dawns fair, Saturday morning will still not be a time of excitement and bustle. Since almost all farm people now have cars, they do a morning's work at home, have their midday meal, give the dishes a lick and a promise, pile in the car and head for town.

As they drive in, mama's mind is on her shopping. If any flour or stock feed is to be bought, its selection falls as much in the province of mama and the girls as in papa's. For these items are sacked in bright cotton prints, with the label stamped on in easily removable water color. Many of Saturday's most dashing dresses contained hog feed before they clothed those excited, handsome country girls. As the car bounces on toward town, papa may be planning to see who wants to buy a couple of his steers, or to arrange a fox hunt for after the stores close. The girls will be thinking about boys, the boys about girls, and the little flirtatious adventures that they all hope will, and which so often do, come about. Since these are prosperous times, the small boys usually have forty-five cents in their pockets and three objectives: an ice cream cone, a bowl of chile, and to see Saturday's inevitable shoot-'em-up movie.

But one of the most important things of all, and the reason for a part of the haste, is where the car is to be parked. Most families have a special place. Perhaps one where they used to park the wagon before cars came into use. This is a very practical arrangement. Your friends know your parking place and where to watch out for you, just as you know theirs. So you must hurry in order to get there before somebody beats you to it.

There are many necessary little chores to do once town is reached and the car is parked: have a plow point sharpened at the blacksmith shop where tethered saddle horses wait to be shod, buy a set of hinges at the hardware store, or take one of the kids down to the corner to be examined by Dr. Sessions who will be, not in his office, but hanging around on the sidewalk outside, for fear he might miss something he hasn't already seen in his eighty restless years.

Do odds and ends of business, see the movie, but mainly pass the time of day with friends and neighbors. "How many hogs did you raise this year and when do you plan to kill?"

"Are you having trouble with those dadburned foxes? Got six of my hens last week."

"Way I look at it, cow prices ought to hold up a year or two more."

"An' she said the way that woman switched around an' carried on was a scan'lous thing to see."

Farmers call on town landowners to try to rent this or that farm for the coming year, perhaps to make a final settlement on the land accounts of this expiring year. The bank is full of farmers depositing turkey receipts, perhaps drawing out funds for holiday expenses, while others wait with obviously varying degrees of confidence, to get into the vice-president's office where they will try to get credit for next year's farming operations. The place is churning with exaltation and fear and every emotion in between.

Maybe an itinerant preacher will drop his hat on the curb and start preaching to whoever will listen. His gaunt wife and seedy children will start singing *Rock of Ages*. A medicine show is apt to be more lively—the "doctor" and a black-face comedian who plays the banjo and performs on the back of a truck. A man who makes keys may park near the bank, hang out his sign, and do a thriving business for the day. The cedar post man with his truckload of red-and-brown-and-lavender posts is waiting at his regular place for buyers to appear. Willie, the old Negro hot tamale man, is dead, and his little pushcart and the aromatic tinkle of his bell is gone. But hamburgers are frying by the scores and hundreds, and the street begins to be imbued with the mingled scents of fried meat and onions, pomade and perfume. Folks are drinking soda pop—iron brew, cream soda and strawberry—out of the grocery-store coolers. The barbershops are packed, and the shine boys are today shining as many pairs of high-heeled cowboy boots as of plain shoes, being careful to shine only the foot of the boot for fear of obliterating the colored stitching on the top.

It's winter now, and blankets and long drawers, heavy socks and rubber boots are passing across the counters. Then as this Saturday afternoon, like the thousands of others that have enlivened our town, begins to wane, the heavy buying of provisions, of fifty-pound sacks of flour and every other staple, begins.

In the beer joints caps are popping. In the liquor store there is a brisk business in half-pints which are soon thereafter consumed behind the telephone poles in the paved, treeless downtown alleys. The domino hall—a nickel per game per player and the losers pay—has every table going and the place will be well anointed by the ruminant tobacco chewers.

By now the store clerks' feet are killing them, and some have put on sneakers. Christmas isn't far off, and, just as twenty-five years ago, jelly beans and gaudy ties, bright suspenders and manicure sets, a thimble for an old lady, a bottle of expensive perfume for a young one, are being wrapped in red and green holly paper.

As night falls and folks start back to the country, the old cars are cranked up and backfire with the flatulence of thunder. One more of the little weekly climaxes in our life as a town has been reached and passed. Buying and selling, visiting and dreaming, fearing the bank, an undeterrable chicken-devouring fox, a malicious neighbor, a drop in cattle prices, a season too wet or too dry, the while forgetting a strength that has stood them through a rocky, bewilderingly modulating past. Desires, frustrated or fulfilled, for a red velvet hat, a single shot .22, the brush of a hand. Yet this Saturday is but one in a long continuum. Its excitements, its pleasures, its exertions will, like the movie that today left a handsome cowboy hanging off a cliff, be continued next Saturday.

☆ ☆

22: *Washington*

WASHINGTON is a city that is maddening in detail, often cynical and uncourageous in its methods, and amusing in its society-struck monkeyshines. Yet Washington is a beautiful city, both physically and in concept. It is, in a sense, as if the great seal of the United States had been set down in granite on the banks of the Potomac as an earnest of this nation's belief in man's ability to attain, through the avenues of a free society, a place of dignity and decency on earth. This city is the outgrowth of a conception so bold, represents so complete a willingness to walk forward among the terrors of the unknown, that in it despair is obscene.

In practice, the Federal government, in whose behalf Washington toils, is a modern adaptation of feudalism in which power is exercised, not by squads of yeomen, but by blocks of ballots which, generally, are steered by coalitions of the ballot-controlling lords of various economic, racial, religious or regional realms.

The thing that makes living in Washington so exciting is that this representative government sits on the lid of a wildly dynamic coun-· try that is, and always has been, a complex system of explosive stresses that exist in a state of chronic and varying imbalance. The high tariffs that please the East put the Southerner on the warpath. The Rocky Mountain West demands inflated silver prices at the expense of every other region. There is seldom a time when one or another of the nation's tributary sections is not erupting or about to erupt: a race riot in Detroit or Houston, some weird shenanigans on the part of the New York Communists or, most shattering of all, when Old Bituminous Brows, assuming a Jove-like stance, rears back and, to the tune of his homemade thunder and lightning, lets loose one of his nation-paralyzing coal strikes.

Fortunately, these wild surges and bumps and jerks by the nation's factions have only once burst through the delicately protective membrane that holds the nation together. That one occasion was the War Between the States. Then Washington, by the grace of God and the advanced industrial condition of the Northeast, was able to cause the dismembered union to readhere.

What is the town itself like? Your first impression is of grass, trees and marble, in columns, in broad, pyramiding piles of stairs. The ear-pricking sound of foreign accents and languages. Military uniforms in infinite variety—most, seemingly, spangled with the emblems of high rank. Negroes; lots of them—more than a fourth of the population, inheritors of this emblematic city's slums and alley dwellings.

The scooting, tooting crush of Washington transportation. Bulging busses. Aromatic in the summer with humanity and carbon monoxide. Streetcars with so much moxie they can run out from under you. Hordes of incoming passengers at the Union Station being loaded like cattle, according to their destination, into cabs, while the hackies chant place names, possibly those of such famous hotels as The Mayflower, the Willard, the Shoreham, the Statler, the Wardman Park. The centrifugal wheeling of traffic at any of the great circles, as individual vehicles, like slow-motion meteors, are slung off down the avenues. Traffic rules and routes that invert themselves twice daily to adapt to the ingress and egress of the city's workers, since great numbers of them stream to and from such Washington suburban adjuncts as Arlington, Alexandria, Georgetown, Chevy Chase, Silver Spring or Bethesda.

Telephones ringing. Scores of thousands of young girls typing. Government girls lunching either amid the clatter of huge cafeterias or having a sandwich and a pint carton of milk on grassy lawns. In little manless droves at cheap tea shoppes in the evening.

Old scholars dozing in the Library of Congress. The flowering trees in Rock Creek Park. Vistas of greensward, piquant with the condiment of hopping squirrels. Former Cabinet members hearing music for the first time in the chirruping of that Washington nuisance, the starlings. The chastened yet relieved attitude of ex-Congressmen, reluctant to go home, living on as lobbyists and/or lawyers here at the scene of their prior glory. The creaking of the city's nerves as the wartime tension eases off. The spring-fever atmosphere that hovers over Congress on a routine day. The tense, tough excitement in the packed galleries when something big is coming up.

Newsmen by the hundreds, some of them the ablest in the world, beating their brains to cull out the empty verbiage of loquacious officials. Getting the news on the wire, on the air, or into Washington's own *Post, Evening Star, News,* and the sometimes fractious *Times-Herald.*

Society columns avidly reporting who dined at Evalyn Walsh McLean's last night, and speculating on what was said to whom. The crush at the enormous embassy and legation parties, when police have to be called out to handle the crowds of guests, some of whom are invited legitimately, but many of whom received their invitations by the simple stratagem of leaving calling cards at an embassy during the year.

Opening day at Griffith Stadium, when the President himself throws out the first ball to the city's less sedentary Senators. The antics at the Gridiron Club dinners, where not pigskin but fresh-honed lampoons are flung at the government hierarchy.

But there are a central handful of impressions which in caliber, and in their plangent effect on Washington living, supersede most others. Factors such as the vileness of the weather along the Potomac's miasmic banks, muggy heat and damp cold; pressure eternal, exerted through every artifice, but most often by sheer din and clamor; mimeographed sheets coming from everywhere, going everywhere, seeming to litter the very air like the detonation of a hand grenade in a featherbed; Washington hostesses' meticulous observance of protocol, or who gets first grab at the turkey; talk, most often of intrabureau politics—and birds of a bureau flock together with a constancy and durability that is utterly amazing; the brutal, merciless scourge of visitors, who, as far back as George Washington's time, deprived him of a single dinner alone with his family for twenty years; and finally, trundle out the shaker and spread up the hors d'oeuvres: COCKTAILS—Martinis, Manhattans, Daiquiris—temporarily annealing tattered nerve-ends, drowning olives and cherries by the barrel, making the frayed badinage of the *fonctionnaire* bearable, making social obligations a little cheaper to pay off, and, it follows, making lots of folks drunk as goats.

Then there are the picture-post-card sights with which every American is so familiar and which, when actually seen in three dimensions, make him feel at home. The Capitol, just as he has always seen it pictured, and, farther down Pennsylvania Avenue, the White House. The huge government buildings. The great monuments to our patriots and statesmen. The obelisk that commemorates George Washington. The Parthenon-like memorial where "as in the hearts of the people for whom he saved the Union the memory of Abraham Lincoln is enshrined forever." The memorial to the great Thomas Jefferson which, alas, strikes some observers as being egg-headed to a degree that deprives the eye of pleasure.

The beautiful Tidal Basin, along whose banks in the spring bloom those shameless and insatiable old publicity hounds, the cherry blossoms. The Washington Cathedral, churches, universities busily giving night courses to government workers. The great museums and galleries such as the Smithsonian, the Corcoran and the National, containing such famous collections as the Mellon. Riches of this kind too numerous to be named, yet each offering a deep and prideful experience for every American. The whopping big zoo, which goes by the official name of the National Zoological Park, and which frying-size Washingtonians like best of all.

The War Department's famously huge Pentagon Building is on the Virginia side of the Potomac. Not far away, overlooked by the mansion of General Robert E. Lee, lies Arlington National Cemetery, the hallowed resting place of the nation's honored dead. And by following the Mount Vernon Memorial Highway a few miles, you'll come to General Washington's reasonably stupendous plantation. When you get there, your first emotion at finding it costs a quarter to see this national shrine will probably be a hot flash of fury. But after you have paid it, entered the estate and seen the magnificent job of restoration and preservation achieved by the Mount Vernon Ladies' Association, you may be prompted to see if they will not accept another quarter as you leave.

The view this house commands, of the Potomac on the one hand and of the plantation on the other, seems almost too wonderful to be real. The whole general scheme on which subsidiary structures were built and gardens planted bespeaks the magnitude of General Washington's mind. And if the house resists your eagerness to sense warmth in it, it seems only decent to attribute that lack to the cooling hand of the years and the fact that this nation, which greedily devoured and thrived on George Washington's strength and fruitfulness, left him little time to indulge the whimsicalities that sometimes make lesser mortals seem warm and alive and lovable.

As a direct outgrowth of his extraordinary ability, General Washington inherited, among other national problems, that of building a national seat of government. He might have been spared this had not a group of unpaid American soldiers caught the Continental Congress in Philadelphia and made this otherwise satisfactory seat of government a little too hot for sitting. Once the Congress was on the move, the location of its permanent home became a point of fierce political contention between the North and the South, and the present location was the result of a hard-fought compromise.

A grant of land that formed a ten-mile square on the Potomac was made by Virginia and Maryland, though Virginia later turned out to be an Indian giver and took her part back. Meanwhile, President Washington was able to get such land from his manorial neighbors as would be needed for government buildings and streets without cost to the government; this after giving the landowners a pep talk on what the government's presence would mean in terms of increase in the value of such lands as the original owners retained.

But the landowners did not sense the scope of vision of the French military engineer, Pierre L'Enfant, who, having lent a hand with the Revolution, persuaded Washington to let him lay out the Federal city. When the land grantors learned that by "street" L'Enfant did not mean a place where two oxcarts, if handled with caution, could pass, but instead, meant avenues that were from a hundred and ten to a hundred and sixty feet broad, they yelled bloody murder. Washington, who had a professed weakness for huge, bold enterprises, let them yell. He gave L'Enfant his head until this zealous architect, to preserve the openness of a vista where the largest landowner of the Federal Region, Daniel Carroll, was building a mansion, simply pulled down the house and hauled it off. This was too much even for Washington. He dismissed L'Enfant, who subsequently died in poverty and frustration, but who has, in later years, been disinterred and, with the best wishes of a grateful nation, re-interred in Arlington Cemetery.

Though L'Enfant's plan has ultimately found fulfillment, Washington was for a long time pretty much of a joke. You could look about you and see—as did George Washington's second Secretary of the Treasury, Wolcott—nothing except brick kilns and temporary huts for laborers. During the administration of John Adams, Mrs. Adams complained that the President's House had no fence "or other convenience without" and that she was hanging out her washing in the large unfinished reception room, which later was to be known as the East Room. Yet the Adamses were much more socially inclined than Jefferson who, as far as possible, left the social duties to Dolly Madison, wife of his Secretary of State. When her husband acceded to the presidency in 1809, she became the empress of Washington society.

Meanwhile Washington's existence as "the Federal City" had become imperiled. There was a movement afoot simply to give it back to Maryland and Virginia, abandon what to many appeared this overambitious enterprise, and move the capital to some established city. As it was, except when Congress was in session, Washington was a graveyard. Yet the British helped make it something of a hallowed spot when they captured it and burned most of its public buildings in the War of 1812.

During the subsequent and more or less silk-stocking administrations of Monroe and John Quincy Adams, the city pulled itself together, as well it might have, since in 1828 tough old Andy Jackson would be elected president.

This event put Washington in a gloomy tizzy. For until now, with the exception of Jefferson's somewhat pastoral conception of the due of the plain citizen, the country had been run largely according to the views of General Washington's aide, Alexander Hamilton. And Hamilton had felt that government, to retain power and stability, must enlist the backing of the substantial, propertied classes by acting, at least to a limited degree, as their agent in the affairs of the nation. Now Andrew Jackson was coming to town as the rough-and-rowdy agent of the great unwashed, who'd put him in office.

But he was not content simply to revolutionize the city's concept of government. He completely disrupted its social life with *l'affaire* Eaton. Pretty Peggy O'Neale Eaton, who was not only the daughter of an innkeeper but was reputed to have been around, was now married to Jackson's Secretary of War. In the eyes of such highly placed Washingtonians as the inflexible Mrs. Calhoun, wife of the Vice-President, Peggy was not fit to be received on their own social level. Thereafter, Jackson, who kept newspapermen in his Kitchen Cabinet along with the nutmeg, rambunctiously ran the country with his right hand and, with his left, the Eaton affair. The latter not only kept social Washington in a complete dither, but, according to some interpretations, caused Calhoun to withdraw from the Democratic party, with the result that Van Buren, who'd been loyally pro-Peggy, got the vice-presidency in 1832 and, four years later, the presidency.

The Washington scene had also been enlivened mightily by such oratorical wizards as Henry Clay, Daniel Webster and such homespun hotshots as Davy Crockett who, when he failed to be re-elected to Congress, told his constituents that he was going to Texas and they could go to hell. But the city of Washington was nevertheless having much difficulty in growing to fit the great clothes L'Enfant had tailored for it. As late as 1842, Charles Dickens reported that the city was a system of "spacious avenues that begin in nothing and lead nowhere; streets a mile long that only want houses, roads and inhabitants; public buildings that need but a public to be complete. . . . One might fancy the season over, and most of the houses gone out of town with their masters." What's more, he thought it would stay that way. At the time Washington contained less than 50,000 people, but by 1860 it had jumped to 75,000 and was already highly aware of the stresses that would shortly pull the nation bodily in two.

During this war of brother against brother, Washington was full of misery, as drums beat all day, as the bonnie boys in blue singing "The Girl I Left Behind Me" as they marched, headed south past the northward-bound ambulance-wagons. Finally the war ended. Lincoln was assassinated and a venomous Congress officiated at the rape of the prostrate South.

In the period that General Grant occupied the White House Washington was a gay and growing place, full of excitement, lavish social functions, scandals and, as a result of the mighty zeal of Alexander Shepherd, last of its territorial governors, Washington was now fast coming of age.

Garfield was shot in 1881. Chester Arthur played his brief role. Benjamin Harrison was sandwiched in between Cleveland's two terms, in the second of which Cleveland quelled Coxey's Army. After an assassin's bullet felled McKinley in 1901, there was a blinding flash of king-sized bicuspids, and Teddy Roosevelt charged onto the scene, to be followed, more circumspectly, by Ohio's William Howard Taft. Just as President Wilson inherited World War I, President Hoover, after the boom times presided over by Harding and Coolidge, later inherited the great depression of the 'Thirties.

But the city of Washington, despite its previous passages through the wringer, hadn't really seen anything yet. On March 4, 1933, Franklin Delano Roosevelt took office, and began to lay about him. The alphabetical agencies, among them a relief program on a scale heretofore unimagined, began to come into being. Organized labor got such a break as it had never dreamed of. The great wild rivers were caught and harnessed to the dynamos that spark the South and West. As an incidental phenomenon, in his four precedent-breaking terms, he boomed Washington, D. C. to bursting, as, also incidentally, he yanked, with high irreverence, the tails both of big business and the Supreme Court. In a somewhat more head-on way, he rode out the depression and marshaled the war effort which played such a dominant part in flattening Germany, Italy and Japan.

In Washington, the echoes of Franklin Roosevelt's dynamism still ring like a kicked gong, and Washington, as to a certain extent is the nation, is still largely run by his appointees. As a matter of fact, the titular head of Washington's city government, J. Russell Young, a former White House correspondent, is one of them.

Washington's somewhat extraordinary city government is run by a triumvirate of commissioners, appointed by the Chief Executive and, generally speaking, with the 531 members of Congress as its city council. Though the city is mainly financed by taxes levied upon its residents, they are denied the right to vote on the affairs of their city government, which is as directly operated by the Federal government as is your own post office.

It's been costing something like $65,000,000 a year to run the city. The Federal government, whose vast holdings in land and property are tax free and which, moreover, get full city service such as fire protection and water without cost, kicks in only $6,000,000, while a recent survey indicates that twice that figure is what the Federal government should pay. Once the city government has made out its budget, Congress, with a persnicketiness that it seldom exercises on those who can get its tag at election time, directs how the money is to be spent and even sets the city's speed limits. This is taxation without representation and, according to some of its less reconciled citizens, is the reason why the city and/or District government is "such a mess."

For years Washingtonians have struggled to gain the ballot, but no bill that would give it to them has ever got out of committee. At the moment, one proposed by Senator Carl Hatch of New Mexico would give them national representation through the election of presidential electors and a member of the House of Representatives. But this bill is in the habitual roosting place of all the others, which is to say, in committee. If it ever gets out and is passed, it will give Washingtonians a voice, however indirect, small and squeaky, in their government and at least a vestige of a weapon to aim at the man who appoints their government and for whom they work.

Yet Congress is understandably hesitant to turn over the seat of national government to its local residents, since Washington, in a sense, belongs almost as much to the people of Montana or Georgia as it does to the citizens of the District of Columbia. Again, the Federal government wishes to control, for the good of all the people, such matters as adherence to the city's plan for maintaining its dignity and beauty and for guiding its future building program.

There are models in the offices of the National Capital Park and

Planning Commission, headed by Major General Ulysses S. Grant III, that are of interest to every American. They show that only about half of the capital's planned development has been carried out. At present most of the great public buildings stretch from the Capitol westward to the Potomac. In the future there'll be almost as much again in the way of public edifices stretching toward the Potomac's Eastern Branch, the Anacostia River. Quite near it will be a great recreation center, designed to handle such affairs as the Olympic Games.

Though legislation already exists for the replacement of its slums, Washington's hospital facilities, according to a recent medical survey, are fearful. As this is written, a social survey is afoot which will certainly take into account such facts as that the Washington jail is a municipal sieve which makes every prisoner his own Houdini, and in which every can opener, bobby pin and nut pick attains the efficacy of an acetylene torch.

Yet these things are not merely the result of the schizoid process by which Washington is governed. These, along with such plagues as her housing shortage, the granddaddy of them all, and her overtaxed transportation system, are in a large part due to the fact that Washington is a boom town. Between 1920 and 1940, Washington's population, beside which the green bay tree seems stunted and puny, soared 36 per cent, with an over-all increase in its metropolitan area of 43 per cent.

Washington expected a decrease of population at the end of the war. Instead, its inhabitants are still growing more numerous. Though there will in all likelihood be decreases in the government payrolls over the nation as a whole and some in Washington, many a government agency that has been crowded into exile will get the longed-for chance to move back to every U. S. bureaucrat's home, sweet home.

With 200,000 government workers and 400,000 privately employed, out of the 1,200,000 people in its metropolitan area, Washington is a very fat cat indeed. The sum of its 1945 pay rolls was $1,800,000,000. Its effective buying income per capita in 1944 was $1,899—$733 above the national average. As a place to do business for anybody with something to sell, Washington has been and is pickin's that are real.

But not everybody in this metropolitan area is engaged in selling time to the Government or goods and services to the Federal folk and to the 200,000 out-of-towners who annually make their way to Washington. For example, eleven persons are engaged in coal mining, and an equal number in the production of crude petroleum; 22,238 work at manufacturing; the largest group of these, some 9,000, are busily printing up the torrents of words that pour from Washington mouths and pens. Six thousand and ninety-nine are making iron and steel products. However, it is pleasant to report that in this area of beautiful trees, only three persons are engaged in logging.

But to the nation, to the world, and to its own people, Washington means one thing: government. And government, like another dangerous business, rodeo work, involves, among other things, the problem of staying in the saddle. Yet no wild-horse rider ever had a harder seat to keep than Washington has today. With the country still in the violent throes of its labor revolution, threatened by momentary inflation and long-run depression, and with a red-hot atomic bomb to handle, Washington must reconcile the attitude expressed in that deep-reaching slogan, "One world or none" with that expressed in the at-least-as-realistic slogan, "no world if necessary."

Washington has never had a president, including Lincoln and Roosevelt, who was called upon to face more tedious problems, had to face them with such complete aloneness, or has had implicit in them so explicit an outcome, than President Truman.

To realize completely Washington's governmental mechanism, it is necessary to be conscious of the pulsations of Pittsburgh, the curious old ways of Boston, the re-emergence of the South, and the whooping expansion of the West, as are so many Washington people who commute from those parts of the country, in the same way that many others commute from the riddles of Palestine, China, India or the ruins of gutted Europe. It is like watching the complicated works of a gun's firing-data computer as, in the midst of battle, it compensates the aim of the batteries of your own fast-moving ship on an equally fast-moving target.

But Washington isn't that simple. It is a Laocoön group caught in the toils of the serpentine red tape and a shifting public support. It is pierced by the thorn of every American or foreign conflict, and yet burdened with the remorseless responsibility to America and mankind to find a way out, whether one exists or not.

To see Washington in terms of any one crisis or set of inter-related crises is to lack historical perspective, and to lose sight of the organism it is supposed to control. To sense fully this nation's deep-rooted ebullience and strength is ammoniac and stimulating to the point of shock. And it's Washington's urgent job to tend the trellis on which this Jack's beanstalk does, however restively, burgeon.

Living in contemporary Washington, caught literally and physically in L'Enfant's dream, and encountering on every hand the brave mementoes of Washington, Jefferson, Jackson, Lincoln and Roosevelt, is to live as close as possible to both the source and climax of one of the major sequences of the human story.

Bibliography

THE AGE OF JACKSON, Arthur M. Schlesinger, Jr., Little, Brown & Company, 1946
THE ALLEGHENY, Rivers of America Series, Frederick Way, Jr., Farrar & Rinehart, Inc., 1942
ALLURING SAN ANTONIO, Lillie May Hagner, The Caylor Company, 1940
THE AMERICAN CHARACTER, D. W. Brogan, Alfred A. Knopf, Inc., 1944
ANYBODY'S GOLD: The Story of California's Mining Towns, Joseph Henry Jackson, D. Appleton-Century Company, Inc., 1941
BALTIMORE, A NOT TOO SERIOUS HISTORY, Letitia Stockett, Norman, Remington Company, 1928
BALTIMORE YESTERDAYS, Meredith Janvier, H. G. Roebuck and Son, 1937
THE BARBARY COAST, Herbert Asbury, Alfred A. Knopf, Inc., 1933
THE BIG FOUR, Oscar Lewis, Alfred A. Knopf, Inc., 1938
CABLE CAR DAYS, Edgar M. Kahn, Stanford University Press, 1940
CHICAGO: Crossroads of American Enterprise, Dorsha B. Hayes, Julian Messner, Inc., 1944
CINCINNATI: A Guide to the Queen City and Its Neighbors, American Guide Series, The Wiesen-Hart Press, 1943
CINCINNATI SYMPHONY ORCHESTRA YEARBOOK, Cincinnati Symphony Orchestra, 1942-1943
CITY DEVELOPMENT, Lewis Mumford, Harcourt, Brace and Company, 1945
CITY MANAGEMENT: The Cincinnati Experiment, Charles P. Taft, Farrar & Rinehart, Inc., 1933
COLORADO: A Guide to the Highest State, American Guide Series, Hastings House, 1941
COLORADO YEARBOOK, 1943-1944, Colorado State Planning Commission
COMBUSTION ON WHEELS: An Informal History of the Automobile Age, David L. Cohn, Houghton Mifflin Company, 1944
CONTINENT'S END: A Collection of California Writing, edited by Joseph Henry Jackson, Whittlesey House (McGraw-Hill Book Company, Inc.), 1944
CROWN OF GLORY, O. W. Riegel, Yale University Press, 1935
DESERT SAINTS, Nels Anderson, University of Chicago Press, 1942
DETROIT: Dynamic City, Arthur Pound, D. Appleton-Century Company, Inc., 1940
DETROIT IS MY OWN HOME TOWN, Malcolm Wallace Bingay, The Bobbs-Merrill Company, 1946
FABULOUS NEW ORLEANS, Lyle Saxon, D. Appleton-Century Company, Inc., 1928
FARTHEST REACH, Nancy Wilson Ross, Alfred A. Knopf, Inc., 1944
FESTIVALS IN SAN FRANCISCO, James Ladd Delkin, Grabhorn Press, 1939
FLAVOR OF SAN FRANCISCO, James Ladd Delkin, Recorder-Sunset Press, 1945

THE FLOWERING OF NEW ENGLAND, Van Wyck Brooks, E. P. Dutton & Company, Inc., 1937

GEORGIA: Unfinished State, Hal Steed, Alfred A. Knopf, Inc., 1942

GIANTS GONE: Men Who Made Chicago, Ernest Poole, Whittlesey House (McGraw-Hill Book Company, Inc.), 1943

GONE WITH THE WIND, Margaret Mitchell, Macmillan Company, 1936

THE GREAT LAKES, Harlan Hatcher, Oxford University Press, 1944

GUMBO YA-YA, Lyle Saxon, Robert Tallant, and Edward Dreyer, Houghton Mifflin Company, 1945

HAPPY DAYS, H. L. Mencken, Alfred A. Knopf, Inc., 1940

HEATHEN DAYS, H. L. Mencken, Alfred A. Knopf, Inc., 1943

HISTORY OF PITTSBURGH, Sarah H. Killikelly, B. C. & Gordon Montgomery Company, 1906

LIFE ON THE MISSISSIPPI, Mark Twain, Bantam Books, 1945

THE LIFE STORY OF BRIGHAM YOUNG, Susa Young Gates and Leah D. Widtsoe, The Macmillan Company, 1931

LOS ANGELES, American Guide Series, Hastings House, 1941

LOUISIANA: A Guide to the State, American Guide Series, Hastings House, 1941

LOUISIANA HAYRIDE, Harnett T. Kane, William Morrow and Company, Inc., 1941

MACHINE POLITICS IN LOUISIANA 1897-1926, George M. Reynolds, Columbia University Press, 1936

MAINE: A Guide "Down East," American Guide Series, Houghton Mifflin Company, 1937

MARYLAND: A Guide to the Old Line State, American Guide Series, Oxford University Press, 1941

McTEAGUE: A Story of San Francisco, Frank Norris, The Colt Press, 1941

MISSOURI, American Guide Series, Duell, Sloan & Pearce, Inc., 1941

THE MISSOURI, Rivers of America Series, Stanley Vestal, Farrar & Rinehart, Inc., 1945

NEW ENGLAND: INDIAN SUMMER, Van Wyck Brooks, E. P. Dutton & Company, Inc., 1940

NEW ORLEANS CITY GUIDE, American Guide Series, Houghton Mifflin Company, 1938

NEW YORK: A Guide to the Empire State, American Guide Series, Oxford University Press, 1940

NEWSPAPER DAYS, H. L. Mencken, Alfred A. Knopf, Inc., 1941

NO MEAN CITY, Simeon Strunsky, E. P. Dutton & Company, Inc., 1944

NORTHWEST GATEWAY, Archie Binns, Doubleday, Doran & Company, 1945

PATHWAY OF PROGRESS: A Short History of Ohio, David W. Bowman, American Book Company, 1943

PENNSYLVANIA: A Guide to the Keystone State, American Guide Series, Oxford University Press, 1940

PHILADELPHIA: Holy Experiment, Struthers Burt, Doubleday, Doran & Company, 1945

PHILADELPHIA FOLKS, Cornelius Weygandt, D. Appleton-Century Company, Inc., 1938

PINE, STREAM AND PRAIRIE, James Gray, Alfred A. Knopf, Inc., 1945

PORTLAND CITY GUIDE, American Guide Series, The Forest City Printing Company, 1940

SAN ANTONIO, American Guide Series, The Clegg Company, 1941

SAN ANTONIO: City in the Sun, Green Peyton, Whittlesey House (McGraw-Hill Book Company, Inc.), 1946

SAN FRANCISCO'S LITERARY FRONTIER, Franklin Walker, Alfred A. Knopf, Inc., 1939

THE STORY OF AMERICA, Hendrik Willem Van Loon, Boni & Liveright, 1927

TEXAS: Guide to the Lone-Star State, American Guide Series, Hastings House, 1945

TRENDING INTO MAINE, Kenneth Roberts, Doubleday, Doran & Company, 1945

WASHINGTON, D. C.: A Guide to the Nation's Capital, American Guide Series, Hastings House, 1942

A WAY OF LIFE, Sir William Osler, The Remington-Putnam Book Company, 1932

WHERE THESE ROCKY BLUFFS MEET: The Story of the Kansas City Ten-year Plan, Kansas City Chamber of Commerce, 1938

WISCONSIN: A Story of Progress, William F. Raney, Prentice-Hall, Inc., 1940

THE WORLD ALMANAC, 1945

THE WORLD ALMANAC, 1946

Index